# Islamic Spirituality

## ALSO AVAILABLE FROM BLOOMSBURY

*The Bloomsbury Companion to Islamic Studies* edited by Clinton Bennett,
*Contemporary Muslim Christian Encounters*, edited by Paul Hedges
*Towards Building a British Islam*, Haifaa A. Jawad

# Islamic Spirituality

## Theology and Practice for the Modern World

*Zeki Saritoprak*

Bloomsbury Academic
An imprint of Bloomsbury Publishing Plc

BLOOMSBURY
LONDON · OXFORD · NEW YORK · NEW DELHI · SYDNEY

**Bloomsbury Academic**

An imprint of Bloomsbury Publishing Plc

50 Bedford Square                                    1385 Broadway
London                                               New York
WC1B 3DP                                             NY 10018
UK                                                   USA

**www.bloomsbury.com**

**BLOOMSBURY and the Diana logo are trademarks of Bloomsbury Publishing Plc**

First published 2018

© Zeki Saritoprak, 2018

**British Library Cataloguing-in-Publication Data**

A catalogue record for this book is available from the British Library.

ISBN: HB: 978-1-4725-7204-2
PB: 978-1-4725-7205-9
ePDF: 978-1-4725-7206-6
ePub: 978-1-4725-7207-3

**Library of Congress Cataloging-in-Publication Data**
Names: Sar̟toprak, Zeki, author.
Title: Islamic spirituality : theology and practice for the modern world / Zeki Saritoprak.
Description: New York, New York : Bloomsbury Academic, 2017. |
Includes bibliographical references and index.
Identifiers: LCCN 2017036068 | ISBN 9781472572042 (hardback) | ISBN 9781472572059 (paperback)
Subjects: LCSH: Islam. | Sufism. | BISAC: RELIGION / Islam /Theology. | RELIGION / Islam / Sufi. |
RELIGION / Islam / Rituals & Practice. | RELIGION / Islam / Koran & Sacred Writings.
Classification: LCC BP161.3 .S374 2017 | DDC 297.5/7–dc23 LC record available at
https://lccn.loc.gov/2017036068

Cover design by Dani Leigh
Cover image © Granefelt, Lena / gettyimages.co.uk

Typeset by Deanta Global Publishing Services, Chennai, India
Printed and bound in Great Britain

To find out more about our authors and books visit http://www.bloomsbury.com.
Here you will find extracts, author interviews, details of forthcoming events and the
option to sign up for our http://www.bloomsbury.com/newsletter newsletters.

*To my parents who are now in the Realm of Eternity*

# CONTENTS

# ACKNOWLEDGMENTS

I would like to thank my friends and colleagues at John Carroll University, particularly the members of the Theology and Religious Studies Department for their unwavering support during this project and beyond. My graduate assistants, Matthew Michels, Pam Cheney, Deborah Zawislan, and Raul Botha, all helped with the research on the project. I would also like to thank my assistant, Patrick Laughlin, for his invaluable ideas and way with words. Additionally, the students who have taken my course on Islamic Spirituality over the years have provided me with many thought-provoking questions and comments, which helped shape the way I present the information herein. As a professor with a substantial teaching load, I am especially grateful for having received the Grauel Fellowship from John Carroll University in 2015. The fellowship allowed me to spend one semester concentrating on research, and without it I could not have completed this project in the time that I did.

It is also imperative to thank everyone at Bloomsbury—especially Lalle Pursglove and Lucy Carroll—who not only saw the value in my idea for the book, but were patient when I had to reschedule the due date for the manuscript. I have to emphasize that all errors and inaccuracies are mine, and I would appreciate any comments that readers have.

I would like to thank my wife, Ozlem; my children; and now grandchild for their support and understanding during my work on the project.

Most important, I would like to thank God for giving me health and the ability to produce this work.

# NOTE ON TRANSLITERATION

In order to make this work more accessible, I have avoided the specialized language of academia as much as possible. I have limited the use of diacritics, with a few exceptions. When necessary, for meaning, pronounciation, or clarity, I have retained the 'ayn and the hamza. The hamza is represented in the text by an apostrophe ('), the 'ayn by a single opening quotation mark ('). Underdots and other diacritics have been removed. Instead of having a separate glossary, Arabic words have been italicized and explained within the text.

Though "the Prophet" is standard, I have used "the Prophet," "the Prophet of Islam," and Muhammad interchangeably in this book. It is recommended that when one mentions the name of the Prophet, one should always follow by saying "peace and blessings be upon him." This is true for all other prophets as well. As I note in the introduction, I take the liberty to say this once and have it carry through the entire book. The word "Hadith," which are the sayings of the Prophet, has been used for both plural and singular forms. Hadith is capitalized when the corpus of the Hadith is meant and lowercased when referring to individual hadith. Note citations are given in full when they are first cited, then in short form. Some authors have been cited by their most commonly known names. For example, Abu Dawud al-Sijistani is cited as "Abu Dawud" instead of "al-Sijistani."

Unless otherwise expressed, all Qur'anic verses, sayings of the Prophet, and renderings from Arabic and Turkish sources used herein are my own translations. However, especially for the Qur'an, I do consult others' translations, particularly those of A. J. Arberry, Mohammad Pickthall, and Muhammad Asad for guidance. For quotations for the Bible I have used the New Revised Standard Version. As for the citations of Hadith references, I preferred to use, with slight changes, A. J. Wensinck's method, which he employed in his famous concordance to the Hadith, *Concordance et Indices de la Tradition Musulmane*. Thus, the hadith collections are cited with the name of the author, followed by the name of the work in italics, followed by the name of the book/chapter in quotes, ending with the number of the section in the chapter.

As this book is designed to be used as a guide, rather than a full academic bibliography that repeats all of the sources mentioned in the book, the bibliography contains works that are especially useful to English language readers who wish to delve more deeply into the topic. All of the bibliographic information for the works cited in the book is given in the footnotes where that work is first cited.

# Introduction

## Spirituality

Spirituality is related to the world of spirit. "Spirit" in Islamic parlance is related to the word *ruh*. In the Qur'an, *ruh* is mentioned on several occasions, and for me the most important aspect of spirit from the Qur'an is how little knowledge human beings have of it. "And they ask you [O Muhamad] about the spirit, say: 'The spirit is from the command of my Lord. Of it you know but a little'" (17:85).[1] Muslims have always been fascinated by the concept of *ruh*. Many have written books on the subject, and it is widely considered that reaching the level of spirit and heart is ideal for humanity. Significantly, in many cases *ruh* is viewed as the opposite of body; if the body is the house, *ruh* is the dweller. As mystics would say, if the body is a cage, *ruh* is the bird in it. Because of the importance of *ruh* in Islamic mysticism, my use of "spirituality" means anything that relates to the spirit. Therefore, I define spirituality as efforts to free oneself from worldly attachments and imperfections and reach the level of spirit. The level of spirit is not one stage, so even approaching that level is a great gain in this effort. Ideally, this level is manifested in model human beings known by Muslim mystics as perfected human beings. My definition of spirituality derives from the Islamic mystical approach to the spirit. Body is important, but it is the spirit that constitutes the essence of human beings. Furthermore, the reason I choose the term "spirituality" over "mysticism" or "Sufism" is that it has a larger connotation and is more inclusive. It does not limit itself to a specific group of people, but is the concern of everyone. Further, I would argue that spirituality is more Qur'anic than the word Sufi. In actuality, I will at times use "Sufism" and "spirituality" interchangeably, but this is done to break up the monotony of "spirituality this" and "spirituality that." Theologically speaking, "spirituality" is preferable, as everything has a spiritual dimension. In other words, everything has two dimensions. One is *mulk,* the corporal dimension. The other is *malakut,* the spiritual dimension. Everything that exists in the corporal dimension, from a fly to an elephant, from an atom to a mountain to a planet, also exists in this spiritual dimension.

Despite the prevalence of spirituality within the Islamic tradition, it is not well known in the Western world. Islamic spirituality consists of a variety of practices, some of which—such as preformed prayer—are highly visible within the tradition, while others—such as contemplation and supplication—remain private, and even many Muslims do not understand their full significance. There have been some works in English on the subject of Islamic spirituality, but most of these have been related to historical aspects of spirituality or to specific Sufi masters and their practices. This present work's distinctive contribution is its focus on both theological dimensions of Islamic spirituality as well as its practical aspects. In this work, the author's goal is to shed light on this poorly understood aspect of Islam. One can argue that the daily life of a Muslim revolves around spirituality, even though we may not call it spirituality per se. All religious obligations of Muslims, from the prescribed five daily prayers to the ritual prayers on various occasions, such as traveling, riding or driving, eating, drinking, and sleeping, and fasting during the month of Ramadan have something to do with the spiritual life. For this reason, as I try to argue in this book, in Islam every aspect of life, even those thought of in the modern world as mundane—eating, drinking, etc.—if performed with good intention can become spiritually rewarding.

## Life, death, and spirituality

Spirituality, both theologically and practically, has been a part of the lives of Muslims since the time of the Prophet. The Prophet's meditation in the cave of Hira, prior to his first experience of revelation, was in fact a practical aspect of his spiritual life. It can be argued that this experience prepared the Prophet for the coming of Divine revelation. Following the path of the Prophet, some early Muslims spent a period of their lives in caves to meditate and contemplate on the presence of the Divine. But as times change, perhaps the ways of spirituality also change. In our modern world, we do not have many people who live in caves to obtain spiritual perfection. However, the present work argues that it is possible to live in the modern world and still be spiritually strong; as such, there is no intrinsic contradiction between spiritual life and modern life. In other words, spirituality and modernity are not at odds with one another.

Still, this begs the question: Do we need spirituality in the modern world? Does humanity need spiritual satisfaction in an age of tremendous technological development? I hope the reader will agree that the answer is yes. Yes, today we have new technologies which enable us to lead very different lives from one generation to the next. However, certain aspects of the human condition have not changed since the beginning of life on earth. Most notable is the reality of death. There is an innate human anxiety about death. Perhaps our technologies and biomedical innovations have even increased our anxiety about death. Human beings try to escape it, but there is no way to ignore it. On an average day, more than 150,000 people die. As an Islamic scholar standing over a large graveyard said, "this graveyard that has buried this entire city time and time again has some important questions for the living."[2] Perennial spiritual questions have always been asked: Who am I? What is the purpose of my life? Where have I come from and where am I going? Islamic spirituality responds to these questions eloquently. In order to overcome the weakness of human beings with regard to their worldly lives, Muslim mystics follow the tradition of remembering death. Generally, they meditate on the eventuality of their dying and being put in the grave. They contemplate death so that they will not be deceived by worldly pleasures and by the deceptive human imagination telling them they will live on earth forever. This practice of Muslim mystics comes from the famous saying of the Prophet: "Frequently remember the destroyer of pleasures [death]."[3]

Since death has not been overcome, human beings need a spiritual life that deals with this reality and what lies beyond. The Islamic understanding of the spiritual life is not limited to this worldly existence. It is a way that makes both life and the afterlife fruitful. It is a way that can turn five minutes of life into not five hours, but into eternity. "God has purchased from the believers their selves and their possessions in return for the gift of Paradise. . ." (9:111). A spiritual commentary of this verse suggests that the world is the marketplace of the spiritual life. People are encouraged to use their reason, their eyes, their tongues, etc., according to the will of their Creator. In this way, the value of these organs will be multiplied; the reward for it is Paradise. Examples of this are as simple as the Islamic phrase as *Alhamdulillah* or "All praises be to God." This phrase is repeated twenty-one times in the Qur'an as the prayer of the Prophet of Islam and many prophets before him. If said with sincerity and faith, in exchange for saying this phrase, one receives a gift in Paradise, or this turns into a fruit of Paradise in the afterlife. Yet, even that gift or fruit should not be the goal of spiritual actions; the real goal is the pleasing of God. Speaking this and similar phrases, as well as the beautiful Names of God, is a means for human beings to connect with and pray to God.

As the Qur'an is in part a book of prayer, one can argue that prayer constitutes the most important aspect of Islamic spirituality. There are many forms of prayer in the Qur'an, and many Muslims take their prayers from the Qur'anic narratives. The following is a powerful example of the Qur'anic way of addressing God.

> Those who remember God while standing or sitting or lying on their sides and give thought to the creation of the heavens and the earth, saying, Our Lord, You did not create this aimlessly; exalted are You above everything; protect us from the punishment of the Fire. Our Lord, indeed whoever You admit to the Fire—You have disgraced them, and for wrongdoers there are no helpers. Our Lord, indeed we have heard a caller calling to faith, saying, "Believe in your Lord," and we have believed. Our Lord, forgive us our sins and remove from us our misdeeds and cause us to die

among the righteous. Our Lord, grant us what You promised us through Your messengers and do not disgrace us on the Day of Resurrection. Indeed, You do not break Your promise. (3:191-194)

One-fourth of the Qur'an is about God and His[4] Divine names, and one saying of the Prophet suggests that God has ninety-nine names which are called *al-Asma al-Husna* or the Beautiful Names of God. The Qur'an encourages people to address God with these beautiful Divine names. The very first chapter of the Qur'an starts with three Names of God: Allah [the God], *al-Rahman* [the Most-Merciful], and *al-Rahim* [the Most-Compassionate]. This factual reality of the Qur'an shows two things: the importance of the Divine names and that believers should turn to God for help. Many Qur'anic verses ask believers to call upon God by His beautiful names: "God has the most beautiful names, call on Him by them" (7:180). Another Qur'anic verse specifically speaks of two Divine names—Allah and *al-Rahman*—and encourages believers to call God with one of these names as they prefer. The verse says "call on Allah or *al-Rahman* by whatever name you call on Him, His are the most beautiful names. Pray neither with too loud voice nor in silence but between these extremes seek a middle course" (17:110). At the end of chapter 59, there is a unique set of verses which gives many Divine names in a row. This passage teaches how one should address God with His Divine names. It states that God is: the Knower of visible and invisible worlds; the Most-Merciful; the Most-Compassionate; the Sovereign Lord; the Holy One; the Giver of Peace; the Keeper of Faith; the Guardian; the Mighty One; the All-Powerful; the Most-High; the Creator; the Originator; and the Modeler. The verse ends with the following: "His are the most beautiful names. All that is in the heavens and in the earth gives glory to Him. He is the Mighty and the Wise One" (59:22-24).

In the mystical tradition of Islam, Divine names are frequently repeated. And it is believed that repeating and chanting Divine names strengthens the spiritual lives of believers. Historically, Muslims would use this counting and chanting of Divine names as a way of measuring time. Early Muslims, as part of their spiritual duty, would use a rosary for counting and chanting the ninety-nine Names of God. Modern-day Muslims can use a rosary but can also use smartphone apps for that counting and chanting. The change is only technological, while the spirit is the same. While some might feel the use of technology in praying is improper, in fact technology gives more accuracy if used correctly. Therefore, one can say blessed is the technology that serves the human spirit. A modern Islamic scholar rightly called the radio, through which one can hear the Qur'an recited millions of times, a heavenly *hafiz* [someone who recites the Qur'an by heart].[5] This heavenly *hafiz*, as a reciter of the Qur'an, does not lessen the importance of human beings' memorization of the Qur'an, but enhances it.

In this work I will refer to major Islamic sources, particularly the Qur'an and the sayings of the Prophet. If the Qur'an is the word of God as described in Islamic theology, and God is eternal and addresses all times, then the Qur'an should have something to say to the people of our time. My research in the Qur'an has shown me that the Holy Book of Islam does, in fact, have a lot to say to the twenty-first century. Despite the changes in the human lifestyle, the fact that human beings are made of body and soul remains inherent. Therefore, even though we might be highly advanced with regard to technological developments, the necessity of feeding our spirit and soul is still essential. Today, perhaps more than ever, the attractiveness of the material life can be deceptive. This deception causes human beings to forget the purpose of their lives. According to Islamic spirituality, the body dies but the spirit remains forever. Therefore, the feeding of the spirit is essential in Islamic teachings and is at least as important as feeding the body.

One should not make bodily pleasures the primary goal of human life. This is why Muslim mystics concentrate on death. Contemplation on death reduces the desire for deceptive pleasures. In fact, the real pleasure is the spiritual one. Muslim mystics give the analogy of cage and bird: the physical body is like a cage while the spirit is like the bird in it. This analogy has frequently been understood as degrading the importance of the body. However, in Islamic spirituality the body is also important. The physical body is valuable, and Muslim mystics would argue that it can become eternal if used properly and led in the right direction. Every limb of the physical body of the human being has a purpose, and if used properly that limb will receive eternity in the afterlife. To illustrate this idea of using elements of the human body properly, we can use the example of the eye. Sight is one of the human senses. It is a window for the spirit to see this world. If one does not use it properly but rather employs it for selfish purposes, it will sink to the level of being a servant to lust or bodily desires. If one uses it in the way that God commands, then it will rise to the rank of a great reader of the book of the universe, a remarkable witness to the miracles of God in nature, and will rise again to the rank of a blessed bee of the flowers of the Divine Mercy in this garden of the earth.[6]

# Major elements of Islam and Islamic spirituality

Before delving into the details of Islamic spirituality, it might be useful to give a basic primer on the background principles of Islam: the Five Pillars and the Articles of Faith. When speaking about Islam, it is impossible not to mention the Five Pillars, which are considered to be the practical aspect of the religion. The first Pillar is the *shahadah*, or the testimony of faith. This is to testify that there is only one God and Muhammad is His messenger. This is considered the main gate of Islam. Anyone who believes this, whether speaking it or keeping it in his or her heart, is considered a Muslim in the sight of God. Belief in God is easy, but also it is difficult. It is easy because it is just a few words, but it is difficult when one considers the different levels of faith; as we shall discuss, the light of one's faith can be that of firefly to the light of the sun.

The second pillar is *salat*. This is to pray five times a day. The times of these prayers are morning, noon, afternoon, sunset, and evening. Because these times are related to the movement of the cosmos, they change according to the seasons, becoming longer or shorter each day. Technology has made the calculation of prayer times easier and more accessible. The purpose of prayer is to leave the business of daily life and make connections with the Divine. The details of these prayers can be found in many sources of Islamic jurisprudence. One might wonder how long these five prayers might take to be fulfilled. This depends on an individual's choice. If a person wishes to recite more verses of the Qur'an it will take longer, and it will take shorter if fewer verses are recited. I will discuss this more in Chapter 7, but in general each prayer is 10–15 minutes. Prayer is so important that every Muslim after the age of puberty is required to perform *salat*. Prior to puberty, prayer is recommended, but not required. Travelers can also combine, according to their convenient times, the noon and afternoon prayers as well as the sunset and evening prayers.

The third pillar is giving charity, *zakat*. It is a compulsory duty for any Muslim with sufficient wealth to give 2.5 percent of their wealth to the needy. There is also *sadaqa*, which is charity that one can volunteer to give: 10, 20, even 50 percent can be given. This kind of generosity is highly praised, but not required. *Zakat* is actually a part of *sadaqa*. *Sadaqa* is a larger element of charity. This is perhaps one of the most attractive aspects of the Islamic tradition that is highly admired by others—especially People of the Book, that is, Christians and Jews—as it is given to worthwhile causes for the betterment of society. Originally *zakat* was collected by the government, but for centuries it has been done individually as a personal aspect of worshipping God. In Turkish there is a phrase which roughly translates as "Serving people is serving God."

The fourth pillar is *sawm*. This is fasting in the month of Ramadan. This fasting is required for any Muslim who has reached the age of puberty. For the entire month, each day from dawn to sunset all Muslims are required to fast. The length of this month is determined by the lunar calendar, so at times this fast can take longer. The Qur'an speaks of fasting as a tradition that was inscribed upon the societies before Islam, indicating the People of the Book. The process of fasting in Islam includes abstaining from eating, drinking, smoking, and sex. Even gossiping, anger, and other negative behaviors are all to be avoided because Ramadan is a month of piety, reciting the Qur'an, mercy toward others, and charity. The dinner breaking the fast of Ramadan is called *Iftar*. Many people often come together for a communal meal at this time. *Iftar* dinners have also become an occasion of interfaith cooperation and communion. The breakfast that is considered the start of the fasting is called *Sahoor*. *Sahoor* is generally served about one hour to forty-five minutes before dawn. People are expected to eat less, speak less, and sleep less during the month of Ramadan so that the month will be an occasion of spirituality for them.

The fifth pillar is called Hajj, which literally means travel or pilgrimage. The Hajj is a pilgrimage to the holy shrine of Islam, the Ka'ba in Mecca in Saudi Arabia. Muslims who are financially and physically able are required to perform the Hajj at least once in their lives. Annually, about four million Muslims gather on this occasion. Major media outlets have called it the largest religious gathering on the planet. Male Muslims are required before starting the pilgrimage to remove their clothes and cover themselves with two large pieces of cloth with no stitching to indicate that one day they will die and be in the presence of their Lord with no worldly clothes. Also, removing the possessions that clothes represent demonstrates the equality of all, as everyone is dressed in the same way. Female Muslims generally wear white outer garments, but have their regular clothes on beneath.

There are certain rituals during pilgrimage. One circumambulates the Holy Shrine seven times, praying to God and indicating their response to the call of God; indicating the oneness of God; reaffirming that praise belongs to God, that all bounties belong to God, that all sovereignty belongs to God, and that God has no associates. The remarkable voices of millions together all strive to eradicate worldly attachments to position and possessions. In other words, it is God who owns everything and people can only distribute the bounties of God to their fellow human beings in peace. In this place and during this occasion, even uprooting a plant or killing a fly is a crime. If such a crime is committed, you have to expiate the crime by giving charity to those in need or by fasting.

There is also the ritual of symbolically stoning Satan. This ritual connects Muslims to the forefather of Christians, Jews, and Muslims: Abraham. In this ritual, pilgrims throw pebbles at a column which symbolizes the presence of Satan. This is done several times, and is detailed in the books of Islamic jurisprudence. The ritual is a commemoration of Abraham and his son Ishmael in the Islamic tradition—although some commentators have said it is Isaac, as the Qur'an does not specify the name of the son—unlike the Hebrew tradition, which says it is his younger son, Isaac. According to the narrative, when God commands Abraham to slaughter his son, Satan tells the son to disobey his father. The son of Abraham throws a stone at Satan, rejecting temptation and obeying his father. The Qur'an describes this part of the story, "And the son said, 'Father do what you are commanded and God willing you will find me among those who are patient'" (37:102).

As for the Six Articles of Faith, the first is to believe in God. It is almost an axiom in Islam that the purpose of creation is to believe in God and to increase our knowledge of God. Therefore, the ninety-nine Names of God are significant aspects of the faith in that understanding them will lead to knowledge of God and stronger faith in God. Chapter 112 in the Qur'an clearly defines this article of faith, which is comparable to Deut. 6:4, "Hear, O Israel: The Lord our God, the Lord is one." Chapter 112 in the Qur'an says "Say, 'God is One. God is the Refuge. God does not beget and is not begotten and there is no one like God.'" Ideally Muslims are expected to increase their knowledge of God until the end of their lives and even the one who had the most knowledge of God, the Prophet of Islam, would say "Lord we have not known You as You deserve."

The second article of faith is belief in the angels of God. In Islamic theology and spirituality, angels are real creatures. They are innumerable. They constantly pray to God. They are created from light. They cannot disobey God and are always obedient to God. The greatest of them are: Jabrail (Gabriel), Azrail (Azrael), Israfil (Seraphiel), and Mikail (Michael). Angels are not the helpers of God; they are creatures of God. They are commanded by God and they fulfill the Divine commands. There are many categories of angels, including: guardian angels, angels who record peoples' actions, angels who question people after they die, angels who are in charge of Paradise, angels who are in charge of Hell, angels who carry the throne of God, etc.

The third article of faith is to believe in God's scriptures. In Islamic theology, God speaks. Since God speaks, there must be communication between God and human beings. This communication happens through revelation. God reveals His message to a group of people who are chosen by God to declare God's message to human beings. These scriptures have been compiled and put in the form of books. Therefore, when Muslims speak of the books of God, they speak of four great books. In fact, this is so profound in Islam that it is taught to very young children in the beginning of their education. These four great books are: the Torah (Tawrah), the message of God revealed to Moses; the Psalms (Zabur), the message of God revealed to David; the Gospel (Injil), the message of God revealed to Jesus; and the Qur'an, the message of God revealed to Muhammad. Muslims also believe that there were also 100 scrolls that contained the Divine revelation to other prophets, including Abraham and Seth. Most importantly, Muslims believe that the Qur'an is the final revelation of God. It is believed that the Qur'an confirms and completes the pre-Islamic revelations. With 114 chapters, it speaks extensively about the major themes of Islam, which are the Five Pillars and the Six Articles of Faith. But because it is the final revelation, it dedicates one-third to death, the end of human history, and the afterlife, that is, eschatology.

The fourth article of faith is to believe in the prophets of God. A hadith speaks of 124,000 prophets before Muhammad. Some of these prophets are mentioned by name in the Qur'an and are also mentioned in the Bible: Adam, Seth, Noah, Abraham, Ishmael, Isaac, Jacob, Moses, David, Solomon, and Jesus. Others, such as Hud and Salih, are only mentioned in the Qur'an. In addition to the named prophets, there are many whose names are not known. Muslims must believe in all prophets of God and not make any distinction between the messengers of God. Among all of the prophets of God, five are known as "the Possessors of Steadfastness." These are: Noah, Abraham, Moses, Jesus, and Muhammad. Because these names are frequently mentioned in the Qur'an, many Muslims name their children after these messengers of God. Also, when one mentions the name of one of the prophets, one is to ask God to give peace and blessings to him. This is why you will often see or hear, written after the name of Muhammad, "Peace and blessings be upon him (PBUH)."

The fifth article of faith is to believe in the Day of Judgment. Muslims believe that there is a life after this life. People will be questioned about their actions in this world, and they will go to an eternal place, either Paradise or Hell. It is believed that this life is transient and the afterlife is the eternal one. This worldly life is no bigger than a station from where one travels to eternity. The Prophet of Islam himself says that in this world he is like a traveler resting under a tree, and then he will continue his journey to the afterlife. Knowledge of the afterlife in Islam comes from Qur'anic descriptions. In fact, those descriptions of Paradise have inspired Muslims throughout history in regard to architecture, painting, design, etc.

The sixth article of faith is to believe in the encompassing Divine plan, or *Qadar*, measuring out. Accordingly, the Divine plan allows for human beings having free will, but that free will is within the encompassing plan of God. They exercise their free will, and that is why they are accountable for their actions. But at the same time, this exercise occurs within the limit that the Divine plan has designed for human beings. Muslims have produced a tremendous literature on the idea of human beings' will versus God's will. Many theological groups have had extensive debates, some supporting that human beings have free will and that God does not have anything to do with their free will, while others have argued that human beings have no free will and the only will is that of God. Both of these approaches are understood as extreme. The mainstream view would be that of major Islamic theologians, who argue that human beings have free will, and God's will is involved but does not interfere with humans' free will so that human beings have accountability. Mystics, unlike theologians, avoid focusing on this debate. They focus more on what to do to be closer to the Divine. They relate all power to God and all will to God. Not because they wish to avoid accountability, but because of their utmost trust in God's will and God's power.

All of these Articles of Faith are understood fully through the experience of the development of Islamic spirituality. On one occasion, Hanzala, a companion of the Prophet, came to him and told him, O Messenger of God, Hanzala has become a hypocrite because he feels more when he is in your presence and when he leaves he feels less of the Prophetic message.[7] The Prophet responded that if he managed to continue in his state when he was with him, angels would come and shake his hand. In other words, Islamic spirituality strengthens human beings to reach the level of spirit in order to have not only knowledge-based faith in these principles of Islam, but also experience-based faith. Faith is to be made experiential. For this, various dimensions of Islamic spirituality can be practiced.

Three major elements of Islamic spirituality are purification, remembrance, and prayer. The first is purification of the soul. The second is the remembrance of God. The third is prayer to God. It can be argued that these three elements complement each other. That is to say, if one has purified his or her soul, he or she will definitely have the remembrance of God. The remembrance of God is directly related to the purification of the soul. And if these two elements are fulfilled, the result will be a sincere prayer to God. There are many Qur'anic verses that communicate the essence of Islamic spirituality: "And by the soul and what made it perfected and inspired its evilness and piety. Surely the one who has purified it [his or her soul] is successful. And surely the one who has corrupted it, has failed" (91:7-10). This illustrates two aspects of the soul that are highly discussed among Muslim mystics. One aspect is about the purification of soul, which has connection to human free will, and that is the positive aspect. The Qur'an praises the purification of the soul, giving good news to those who have purified their soul and describing them as the successful ones. It uses a language of losses and gains: those who have purified their souls are winners, while those who have failed to purify their souls are losers, deceived by Satan. Elsewhere, the Qur'an speaks of the purification of souls and immediately mentions a group of people who remember the Divine names and pray to God accordingly. "Surely, those who have become successful are those who rectified their soul and remembered the Name of their Lord and prayed" (87: 14-15).

The best way of praying to God is described in one of the sayings of the Prophet, known as the Hadith of Gabriel. According to the tradition, when the Prophet was in Medina several years before his death, the angel Gabriel visited him and asked him several questions. Among these, the angel asked, "What is *ihsan*?" And the Prophet replied, "It is to pray to God as if you see Him even if you do not see Him, He sees you."[8] The word *ihsan* comes from the word *husn*, which means beauty. Literally, *ihsan* is to make something beautiful or to do what is beautiful. This is the essence of Islamic spirituality as found in the Hadith literature. The Prophet's description of it is more terminological than literal. The term that the Prophet used for prayer in this hadith is generic, and it includes all forms of worshiping God. These can be vocalized or bodily gestures, and can be prescribed or voluntary prayers. The style or type of prayer may change but, as the hadith describes, the essence of all prayer is to have the feeling of the presence of God while praying. The first chapter of the Qur'an, which is repeated in every prescribed and voluntary prayer, has a verse that alludes to this aspect of prayer. The verse says, "You alone we worship and to You alone we turn for help" (1:4). Grammatically speaking, the Arabic personal accusative singular pronoun *iyyaka* that is translated as "You" is used only for those who are present. Addressing God with this pronoun illustrates that God is present when one worships God. Perhaps the Prophet was alluding to this verse when he said that one has to worship God as if one sees God.

The Qur'an uses the term *ihsan* twelve times.[9] One verse says, "Indeed, God orders justice and *ihsan* and giving to relatives; and forbids immorality and bad conduct and rebellion. He advises you so that perhaps you will remember" (16:90). The Qur'an also uses the derivatives of this term. The most frequently used of these are the active participle *muhsin,* which means one who acts beautifully and is charitable, as well as its plural form *muhsinun.* The Qur'an speaks of the support of God for the *muhsinun* and that God is with them and that God loves them. Interestingly, one Qur'anic verse uses this term along with a derivative of the word jihad. "But those who struggle [make jihad] in Our cause, certainly We shall guide them in Our ways; and God is surely with the *muhsinun* [those who are doing what is beautiful]" (29:69).[10]

While the above verses are considered essential to the practice of spirituality, the Holy Book of Islam frequently refers to historical events and groups of people as a way of emphasizing the importance of spiritual practices. In the following verse, the reference is to the Children of Israel and how God would be with them as long as they remained faithful and practiced spiritual principles. The verse specifically refers to the Divine covenant with the children of Israel that God will be with them as long as they observe these five practices: devoutly preforming prayer, giving charity, believing in the messengers of God, supporting them, and giving beautiful loan (i.e., helping the poor) for the sake of God. The verse goes as follows:

> And God had already made a covenant with the Children of Israel, and We delegated from among them twelve leaders. And God said, "I am with you. If you establish prayer and give charity and believe in My messengers and support them and you loan to God a beautiful [the word here is also related to *ihsan*] loan, I will surely forgive your sins and admit you to Gardens beneath which rivers flow [i.e. Paradise]. But whoever of you disbelieves after that has certainly strayed from the straight path. (5:12)

It is evident, as this verse states, that when one achieves a positive spirituality and commits to spiritual practices, there is a remarkable reward, and that is Paradise. This Qur'anic verse gives the Children of Israel as an example for Muslims to imitate. In other words, it addresses Muslims, telling them that if they fulfill these five principles they will also receive God's support and rewards; the Children of Israel illustrate for human beings the Divine's covenant with humanity.

Both the Qur'an and the Prophetic Hadith give paramount importance to a devout connection to the Divine. In the preceding verse, it was prayer that made this connection. Broadly in the spiritual tradition, this connection is called *taqwa* which can be translated as respect for God, the state of being in awe of God, or simply piety. This state has a strong connection with heart, *qalb*. Verses about heart, as will later be mentioned in detail, are considered the backbone of Islamic spirituality in the Qur'an. Of course, what is meant by the heart in Islamic spirituality is not the physical heart that pumps blood to the body. Rather, it is the spiritual heart, which is related to the spirit of human beings. The Qur'an speaks of some hearts as sick. Therefore, an individual may be physically very healthy, but still might have a spiritual sickness in his or her heart.

A good example of this are the hypocrites who outwardly believe but inwardly do not believe. While there is a chapter of the Qur'an, chapter 63, that is named after the hypocrites, in the beginning of the second chapter of the Qur'an, there are several verses which speak of their behaviors. The Holy Book describes them as those who have sickness in their hearts; evidently, this is a sickness that is not physical but spiritual. One verse says, "In their hearts is disease, so God has increased their disease; and for them is a painful punishment because they [habitually] used to lie" (2:10). In other words, a heart can be sick for the lack of faith in it, or it can be sick for a lack of *taqwa*. This is by no means to degrade the importance of the physical curing of the heart. In fact, the physical curing of the heart is a reflection of the Divine name *al-Shafi*, the Healer, though this is not the point of discussion here. This invisible sickness cannot be detected by physical means of diagnosis, and the individual may not be aware of it. The Qur'an presents Divine revelation as a cure for sick hearts. As stated in the Qur'anic verse, "O People! There has come to you guidance from your Lord and a healing for that which is in the hearts, and for those who believe, a guidance and a mercy" (10:57).

Similar ideas are found in the Hadith. On one occasion the Prophet pointed to his chest and said three times "*taqwa* is here."[11] On another occasion, the Prophet draws attention to this dimension of heart, saying, "Beware! There is a piece of flesh in the body; if it becomes good [rectified] the whole body becomes good but if it gets spoiled the whole body gets spoiled and that is the heart."[12] This hadith can have two dimensions. One is spiritual and the other one is physical. It is possible the Prophet meant both, because arguably the heart is the center for both physical and spiritual health.

The Qur'an indicates that the tradition of piety and fear of God is not limited to Muslims, as it can also be found in God's communication with pre-Islamic societies. The Qur'an refers to others, especially the People of the Book, saying that they are also expected to have *taqwa*. After referring to the heavens and earth as God's belongings, the verse says, "Verily We have instructed the People of the Book [Christians and Jews] before you, and you [O Muslims] to have *taqwa* [be pious]" (4:131). Therefore, it can be deduced from various Qur'anic verses that *taqwa* is a key term in Islamic spirituality. The concept of *taqwa* can be practiced by diverse people. While the Qur'an describes it as necessary for Muslims' salvation, it also makes it accessible for the salvation of the People of the Book; indicating the inclusive nature of Islamic spirituality.

My goal in this book is to shed light on one of the important elements of Islam that has been there all along but has gone unnoticed: Islam's spiritual dimension. The book has nine chapters that lay out the important elements of Islamic spirituality. Chapter 1 takes a deeper look at the concept of spirituality in Islam and its connection to Sufism. Chapter 2 explores Islamic spirituality as presented in the Qur'an. As part of this, the chapter examines pre-Islamic prophets as presented in the Holy Book of Islam to find some connection between Muslims and earlier traditions, particularly those of Judaism and Christianity. Chapter 3 discusses Islamic spirituality as presented in the Hadith, or the collected sayings of the Prophet. After this, in Chapter 4, there is a detailed discussion of some of the important concepts found in Islamic spirituality that have been employed and practiced by Muslim mystics throughout Islamic history. The next three chapters explore the ideas of important historical and contemporary figures in Islamic spirituality, al-Ghazali, Bediuzzaman Said Nursi, and Fethullah Gulen. These three figures were chosen because they are both theologians and mystics. Al-Ghazali is one of the most well-known mystics in the history of Islam. Nursi likewise has been called the Ghazali of our time. Gulen is important because of his presence in the contemporary world. Given the importance of the living tradition of Islamic spirituality to the present work, including one of the foremost living mystical scholars seems of utmost importance. Chapter 8 then explores prayer and asceticism in the Islamic spiritual tradition while Chapter 9 discusses the relationship between Islamic spirituality and ecology. After the conclusion, there is also a series of appendices which give translations of a selection of important spiritual documents, sample prayers from the Qur'an, and prayers of selected mystics.

# PART ONE

# Theological foundations

# 1

# Islamic spirituality, Sufism, and sainthood

Before delving into the details of spirit in Islam, it is important to give some etymological background. The Islamic term that is used for the spirit is the word *ruh*. The plural of this word is *arwah*, the root of which is r-w-h,[1] similar to the Hebrew word *ruach* or *ruah*. Most words in Arabic that have something to do with wind, scent, energy, breath, and power all come from this same root. Another word that comes from the same root, *rawh*, has the connotation of resting, mercy, and grace. Occasionally, the plural form *arwah* is also used to describe a group of spirits, such as *al-arwah al-tayyiba*, "the good spirits," and *al-arwah al-khabitha*, "the bad spirits." Here, Islamic spirituality is used to indicate anything that is related to the realm of spirit. The word *ruh* is mentioned in the Qur'an on at least twelve occasions. For instance, "And they ask you [O Muhammad] about the spirit [al-ruh], say: 'The spirit is from the command of my Lord. Of it you know but a little'" (17:85). Despite the Qur'anic verse, Muslim theologians have made efforts to explain the concept in their theological discourses. One modern theologian described the spirit as "a conscious law and living principle that comes from the realm of Divine command. The Divine power envelopes it with an external existence."[2] To a certain extent, it is similar to the law of gravity. One can imagine that if the law of gravity had a consciousness and occupied a subtle body, that law would be the spirit of that body. Al-Jurjani (d. 1078) defines the human spirit as "a cognitive and discerning subtlety in human beings built on the animistic spirit coming from the realm of Divine command about the essence of which reason is unable to comprehend. This human spirit can be free and sometimes can be enveloped by a body."[3] Perhaps this idea of *ruh* as a conscious entity can best be seen in the creation of Adam. The Qur'an says: "I [God] have shaped him [Adam] and breathed My spirit into him" (15:29).[4] In the Qur'an, *ruh* is occasionally used in connection with the word "holy" to describe the Holy Spirit or Ruh al-Qudus, which in Hebrew is Ruach ha-Kodesh. For Muslim theologians, this Holy Spirit is understood as the Divine presence. The Qur'an speaks of the angel Gabriel as the Holy Spirit who brings revelation of the Qur'an to the Prophet. When his people accused the Prophet of being a forger, the Qur'an responds: "Say: The Holy Spirit has brought it from your Lord with the truth, that to make steadfast those who believe and as a guidance and good news for *muslims* [lit. those who submit to the will of God]" (16:102). In another verse, the angel Gabriel is presented as the "trustworthy spirit" (26:193) who brought down the Qur'an to the heart of the Prophet. Elsewhere, the Qur'an says Jesus was given clear evidence and supported with the Holy Spirit (2:87), and on another occasion Jesus himself is said to be a spirit from God (4:171). There is also an occasion (40:15) in the Qur'an where *ruh* is used as a name for the Divine revelation: "Exalted above all ranks, Owner of the Throne, He sends the *ruh* of His command to whomever He wills of His servants that they will know the Day of Judgement." An important early commentator on this verse says, "By *ruh*, revelation and prophethood are meant. The reason why these are called *ruh* is because human beings receive life through them since *ruh* connotes life as well. That is to say people revive from the death of disbelief by the spirit of Divine revelation that guides to the rightness."[5] Another commentator describes it as "a true purity put in the body through a Divine principle or law that God creates or makes life as long as it is in the body."[6]

Two other related words are *rih*, scent, and *rawh*, mercy or resting, and they should be mentioned briefly. Interestingly, the Qur'anic chapter on the story of Joseph uses the word *rih* to mean the smell of Joseph. Jacob, who was longing for his son Joseph, perceives the smell of Joseph in a passing caravan and says, "Surely I have found Joseph's scent, unless you think I am doting" (12:94). *Rih* is also used to mean a destructive wind or energy (e.g., 14:18, 17:69, 22:31, and 51:41), and sometimes to mean a more constructive force (e.g., 21:81, 34:12, 38:36, and 42:33). Regarding *rawh*, as in 12:87, it is presented as the mercy of God, suggesting that believers should not be hopeless of the mercy of God; only disbelievers become hopeless. It is also presented to mean rest [in Paradise] in 56:89.

Therefore, when we speak of Islamic spirituality, we have to remember that its concern is the development of the human spirit; it intends to go beyond the limitations of the physical body. If one develops to the level of prominent Muslim mystics, such as Abd al-Qadir al-Jilani (d. 1166), Muhammad Baha al-Din al-Naqshabandi (d. 1389), or Ahmad Sirhindi (d. 1624), one can use celestial bodies, such as the sun and moon, as beads of one's rosary while praising God and chanting the Divine names. The realm of physicality becomes minute in relation to the realm of the spirit, and the result is happiness in both worlds, here and in the afterlife.

The major goal of Islamic spirituality is to take human beings one step higher into the realm of the life of spirit, *ruh*, and heart, *qalb*. As we shall discuss later, heart and spirit are closely connected in the Islamic mystical understanding. There is a brief mention in the Qur'an of an instance, known as *bazm-i alast*, at the beginning of humanity when God brought all human beings' spirits together and asked them, "'Am I not your Lord?' And they said, 'Yes. We witness that You are our Lord.' And you [the souls] should not say on the Day of Resurrection, 'We were unaware of this [the distinction between the right path and the wrong path]'" (7:172). Muslim mystics have developed this idea, that all human beings initially agreed to follow the right path, but since then some of them changed or broke their promise. Returning to the spiritual life is like a homecoming for the spirit. Because every human being was given this potential at his or her creation, all people are encouraged to elevate themselves and reach the level of spirit.

Islamic spirituality has become a large discipline with a variety of terms and concepts associated with it. In fact, some have argued that there are over a hundred definitions for the concept of spirituality within Islam. It is not worth reciting all these, but it is worth mentioning the one most commonly known in the West, Sufism.

# Sufism

A contemporary scholar of Sufism described Sufism as:

> mystical Islamic belief and practice in which Muslims seek to find the truth of divine love and knowledge through direct personal experience of God. It consists of a variety of mystical paths that are designed to ascertain the nature of humanity and of God and to facilitate the experience of the presence of divine love and wisdom in the world.[7]

While this quote is somewhat problematic in that Sufis themselves would generally not describe what they are doing as attempting to understand the nature of God, which is not recommended in Islam (rather, they are attempting to understand the arts of God through which, along with other spiritual practices, one can become more knowledgeable about God), this definition helps grasp the immense totality of Sufi practice.

Grammatically, "sufi" is related to the Arabic term for Islamic spiritual practice, *tasawwuf*, which can briefly be defined as "purification of heart from worldliness and the abandonment of base behavior."[8] The followers of this path are called Sufis and are known as the people of truth (*ahl al-haqiqa*). Sufism seems to be more formalized via mystical orders, while spirituality is a more open term and gives more space to various practices that people might use to receive knowledge of God. Hence, in the text I will use "Islamic spirituality" to describe "Sufism," because I find it to be broader and more generally applicable than Sufism. I personally have an affinity for Islamic spirituality because all Muslims, whether or not they identify themselves as Sufis, are in some respects practicing Islamic spirituality, and to signify that one does not have to identify oneself as a Sufi to add elements of the Islamic spiritual tradition to one's own life.

The path of Islamic spirituality is the path that is described in the first chapter of the Qur'an, "the path of those whom You have favored" (1:7). Muslims, in their daily prayers, ask God at least seventeen times to guide them to this path. But what is the path of those God has favored, and who are those who have received God's favor? Almost all commentators of the Qur'an say that those who have received His favor are the prophets and other righteous people. Al-Qushayri (d. 1074), a mystic and commentator of the Qur'an, says,

> The path [tariq] of those whom You [i.e. God] have favored with guidance to the straight path and these are the friends [awliya'] and purified ones [asfiya']. And also it is said that this is the path of those whom You have annihilated from themselves and raised up through You for You so that they do not stop along the path and the hidden tricks [makr] do not keep them away from You. It is also said this is the path of those whom You have favored with upholding Your rights [huquq] without being moved towards the seeking of their worldly desires [huzuz].[9]

More concise definitions of this path are found in other Islamic sources. It is "abandoning your freewill and trusting in God" and "making every effort to have intimacy with God" all the while "avoiding complaints." It is "the purity of relationship with God" and it is "patience" with regard to the Divine commands and prohibitions or "[self-]annihilation [of one's ego] in the presence of God." Perhaps one of the shortest and most encompassing definitions of the path would be the following: "To be attributed with the Divine attributes."[10] The path of Islamic spirituality requires people to follow the principles of Islamic law internally so that they will see the wisdom in it in the inner self, and also to follow its principles externally so that they can see the wisdom in it in the outer self. By this, a mystic will reach perfections because they abide by law. Along these same lines, it can be described as:

> the purification of heart from the created world and abandoning natural attributes, extinguishing human weaknesses, getting rid of egoistic claims, reaching spiritual attributes, and holding to the real knowledge [the knowledge of God]. Also, using what is more important to internal life and advising the entire community and fulfilling their promise to God in a real sense and following His Messenger in the principles that he brought.[11]

Finally regarding the path, an encompassing contemporary definition is: "Sufism is the path followed by an individual who, having been able to free himself or herself from human vices and weaknesses in order to acquire angelic qualities and conduct pleasing to God, lives in accordance with the requirements of God's knowledge and love, and in the resulting spiritual delight that ensues."[12]

Practitioners of an Islamic spiritual life have historically been called Sufis. Etymologically, there are three not mutually exclusive possibilities as to why they took this name. The first is that the word comes from the root s-f-w, specifically the word *al-safwa*, which means purity. For this reason, in the parlance of the mystics, the path aims at the purification of the heart from the love of anything other than God and from indulgence in "the decorations of the worldly life."[13] This is accomplished by engaging in the religious practices of following the Divine commands and abandoning what God prohibits by following the path of the prophets. It is this group of people who are described as the People of Righteousness.

Among the various ways of categorizing Muslim mystics, one is to describe "seven classes of Muslim mystics: the seekers, the pupils, the workers, the runners, the flyers, and those who have reached. The seventh of them is known as *al-Qutb* [which literally means the pole], whose heart is directly connected to the heart of the Prophet. Among the people he [or she] is the inheritor of Divine knowledge through the Prophet."[14] All such categorizations of mystics are subjective, and it is the mystics themselves who have developed them. Moreover, categorizations are not an entirely useful way of distinguishing individuals, since mystics of a high spiritual level are prone to hiding their spiritual accomplishments and their mystical connections with God and the Prophet. They prefer to be seen as ordinary people, and for this reason only those who are at a similar level can discern them. These people have annihilated their egoism in the presence of God. Perhaps the first examples of People of Righteousness in Islam would be the companions of the Prophet, who were the purest of the community. Contemporaries of the companions, or *tabi'un*, also played an important role in development of Islamic spiritual life, and both are known as ascetics (*zuhhad*) and worshippers (*ubbad*), who have dedicated themselves to an ascetic life and constant prayer.

The second possible meaning behind "Sufism" is that the word derives from the root s-w-f, specifically the word *al-suf*, "wool." Early mystics would wear garments made of wool to demonstrate their abandonment of the pleasures of worldly life. Mystics were known for such a way of life. Third, although it is not mentioned by scholars who have attempted to find a meaningful origin for the word Sufism, it seems to me that there is some relationship between "Sufi" and those who in the Islamic tradition are called Ashab al-Suffa. The word *al-suffa* refers to the lodge adjacent to the mosque of the Prophet, in which some companions of the Prophet were taught and educated and later sent to different places as teachers. It is believed that about 120 companions of the Prophet attended this lodge. These companions were pupils of the Prophet who received a special teaching. Although linguistically the two words do not come from the same root, there is a meaningful similarity between the terms, and they both have a connection related to the meaningful function of "Sufi."

# The realm of spirit

Islamic spirituality is the way of purity and clarity that is praised in every society and every language. It is the opposite of ugliness and impurity. Both in the Qur'an and in the sayings of the Prophet, purity is counterposed to ugliness to indicate the importance of good characteristics. A human being's spirit plays a crucial role in attaining these characteristics.

The realm of the spirit is one of the most unique aspects of Islamic spirituality. It is a different world, beyond this physical world. According to Islamic theology and mysticism, spirits are eternal; they are created, but they will exist eternally and will not die with the death of the body. They reside in the realm of spirits (*alam al-arwah*) prior to the creation of their physical bodies, and when a body dies the spirit housed in it does not die, but returns to the realm of spirits. In this realm, spirits are grouped together with spirits that have similar characteristics. So spirits with good characteristics reside near others with good characteristics, while those with bad characteristics reside near those who also have bad characteristics. The Prophet is narrated to have said that if someone sends him blessings from God, he receives them immediately and knows the sender. Also, one way employed by Islamic spirituality to make a connection with the Divine, in addition to the purification of heart and spirit, is the tradition of *rabita*, an awakening of the heart. It is a method of psychological concentration where there is a deep focus on the spiritual connection with the Prophet, and eventually with God. Through this, one can attain closeness with the Divine, and it should be done frequently. Perhaps this is what is called finding the truth, *haqiqa*.

# Shari'a, tariqa, and haqiqa

Despite the historical importance of spirituality to the Islamic tradition, there has and continues to be a tension between mystics and scholars of Islamic jurisprudence. This tension is most notable with regard to certain practices and rituals. Scholars of Islamic jurisprudence, or *shari'a*, claim that Islamic spirituality does not give enough importance to the practical dimension of Islam, that it emphasizes only internal qualities rather than external rituals; they consider this a deficit in spiritual practices. Sufis and other mystics would counter that these same scholars give undue importance to the external practice of religion and de-emphasize the importance of the inner dimension. This debate centers around three terms which are essential in the understanding of Islamic spirituality: *shari'a*, *haqiqa*, and *tariqa*. *Shari'a* is the law. *Tariqa* is the way to reach the truth. *Haqiqa* is the truth. This tension should not be understood as pitting all legal scholars against all mystics; indeed, many legal scholars have also been mystics. For example, one of the greatest scholars of Islamic law, as well as an important commentator on the Qur'an and scholar of Hadith, was the medieval Egyptian scholar Abd al-Rahman al-Suyuti (d. 1505). Al-Suyuti belonged to one of the main Sufi orders, known as al-Shadhaliyya. For this reason, there is a consensus among the majority of mystics and jurists that *shari'a* and *tariqa* are complementary and not in opposition. Importantly, al-Suyuti defines *shari'a* as following the practice of prayers externally, while *haqiqa* is to experience the Lordship of the Divine.[15]

Furthermore, the five daily prayers can be used as an example of this. If we consider the ritual of the five daily prayers as the essence of *shari'a*, Sufis would say that sincerity and feeling the presence of God during prayer, haqiqa, is the essence of the prayer itself. This is the means by which one attains the path of Islamic spiritual life, *tariqa*. Therefore, while performing rituals is important, without sincerity, that performance is not worthy of reward. Conversely, a mere sincerity with no performance of ritual also is not complete. For example, in a famous hadith, the Prophet describes prostration as the closest state to God.[16] If someone prostrates before God in his or her daily prayer, mystics would suggest that the performer has to be sincere and purify his or her heart to feel the presence of God. Muslim mystics argue that the rituals and practices of the Islamic tradition must be empowered with spiritual feelings and experiences, and that is the meaning of *haqiqa*. That is to say, in this way individuals will find the truth of religion. Hence, *haqiqa* is the goal, *tariqa* is the way to reach the goal, while *shari'a* is the body of principles and frames that should be practiced while working toward reaching the goal. Both inner and outer dimensions are necessary.

A good example of this is the recitation of the first chapter of the Qur'an. The recitation is outward, but contemplation on its meaning and what is said in it resides in the inner dimension. One of the sayings of the Prophet refers to the importance of this first chapter of the Qur'an in prayer and its recitation. This suggests a serious contemplation on its meaning. The importance of the first chapter of the Qur'an comes from the fact that it is recited by Muslims in every unit of prayer. A Muslim who performs the five daily prayers repeats this at least seventeen times a day. It is composed of seven verses, and it is argued that folded within it is the whole of the meaning of the Qur'an.[17] A version of this hadith is found in many collections of the sayings of the Prophet. According to one narration, God says:

I have divided the prayer between Me and My servants into two halves. Half of it is for Me and the other half is for My servants, and My servants gets what they ask for." Thus, when they say, "Praise be to God, Lord of the Worlds," God, Exalted is He, says, "My servants have praised and thanked Me." When they say, "the Most-Merciful, the Most-Compassionate," [God says], "My servants have extolled Me." And when they say, "Owner of the Day of Judgement," [God says], "My servants have glorified Me. These verses are for Me and for My servants is what they ask for [in the verses that come]." When they say, "You [alone] we worship, and You [alone] do we ask for help. Guide us to the straight path, the path of those upon whom You have given Your blessings and not the path of those who have been condemned [by You], or [the path] of those who have gone astray," God says: "These are for My servants and My servants shall receive what they ask for."[18]

As a mystic would not degrade the importance of the five daily prayers, a jurist would also not degrade the importance of sincerity and feelings of the Divine presence during prayer. This is true for other Pillars of Islam such as charity, fasting, and pilgrimage. The Prophet encourages no animosity among people, and mystics willingly avoid animosity. The strong opposition by Wahhabis and other literalist groups to the spiritual tradition of Islam, and specifically the Sufi tradition, has no foundation in the Qur'an or in the Hadith, and hence their animosity is misguided. Today, the Islamic world and Muslims in general suffer from the misconceptions of which focuses on the apparent dimensions of law while ignoring the essence of it. While Islamic spirituality provides a solution for many problems of literalism, those who oppose Sufism and Islam's spiritual dimension fail to provide any solution for modern-day problems of the human soul. Followers of the Islamic spiritual tradition have opened their hearts to all Muslims and people of other faiths by following the path of the Prophet, which strongly encourages brotherhood and peace among people. Following the path of the Prophet, one should not respond to evil with evil, and instead should respond to it with good. The Prophet makes it clear that one should not abandon speaking with his or her brothers and sisters for more than three days, and the best is the one who starts conversations with the greetings of peace.[19] All of this suggests that one has to be vigilant about his or her spiritual life. Sometimes a small thing may become important in the sight of God; therefore, one should not ignore small good deeds or belittle small bad deeds. Each has great potential to become a ladder for or a hindrance to spiritual development.

Attaining a spiritual level or state does not mean it is unchangeable. This is one of the important mysteries of spiritual life. People can develop and increase their spiritual level, but can also contribute to the decrease of their spiritual level. Human spiritual development is like a graph. One day it can be up and the next day down, or it can always be trending up. It depends on each person's use and misuse of his or her capacities. Many examples from the history of Islam can be given for this phenomenon. The story of Hanzala bin al-Rabi (d. 665), one of the companions of the Prophet and one of his scribes, is a good example of how people can change frequently. Hanzala's concerns show that one's spiritual level can increase and decrease. Hanzala narrates:

Abu Bakr met with me and said, "How are you?" and I said, "Hanzala has become a hypocrite." Abu Bakr said, "What are you really saying?" I said, "We are in the presence of the Prophet and he reminds us of Hell and Paradise as if we see them with our naked eyes. When we are not in the presence of the Prophet, we are involved with family, children, and property and we forget a lot." Abu Bakr said, "I swear to God I am also like you." Abu Bakr and I went to the Prophet. We entered his presence and I said, "O Messenger of God, Hanzala has become a hypocrite." And the Prophet said, "Why is that?" I said, "O Messenger of God, when we are with you, you remind us of Hell and Paradise as if we see them with our naked eyes. When we leave your presence and become involved with family, children, and our property, we forget a lot [of what you have told us]" The Prophet said, "In whose hand my soul is, if you could continue on the state when you are with me and on remembrance, angels would shake your hands on your beds and in your ways. But, O Hanzala, a moment and a moment" The Prophet repeated this three times.[20]

This hadith is a great example of human spiritual conditions. By repeating "a moment and a moment," the Prophet suggests that human beings are not like angels. They have free will, and because of their free will they may rise and fall spiritually. Therefore, it requires major efforts for people to keep their spiritual level as if they are in the presence of the Prophet. This is why some Muslim mystics would ask God to elevate them to the stage of *ihsan*, which is described by the Prophet as "to worship God as if you see God. Even if you do not see God, He sees you."[21] The Prophet also gives some clues for a belief that at a certain spiritual level, people can meet with angels and shake their hands. Because of the rollercoaster ride that is the level of spirit, the Prophet says, "'Renew your faith.' They asked, 'O Messenger of God, how can we renew our faith?' The Prophet said, 'Say often the phrase of *la ilaha illa Allah* [there is no deity but God].'"[22]

There is an important spiritual understanding of this hadith from Said Nursi which says that since human beings and the world in which they live are being continuously renewed, they need constantly to renew their faith. For in reality, each individual human being consists of many individuals. They may be considered a different individual for every year of their life, or every day or even every hour. Since single individuals are subject to time, they are like a model, and each passing day dresses them in the form of another individual. Furthermore, just as there is within each person this plurality and renewal, the world in which they live is also in motion. It goes and is replaced by another. It varies constantly. Every day the door of another world is opened. As for faith, it is both the light of the life of each individual in that person, and it is the light of the world in which they live. And the phrase "There is no deity but God" is a key with which to turn on the light. Then the evil-commanding souls—desires, doubts, and Satan—exercise great influence over human beings. Frequently, they damage one's faith by taking advantage of a person's heedlessness or by tricking that person, and thus with suspicions and delusions they cover up the faith. Also, human beings are prone to act and speak in such a way that seems to oppose the Shari'a, and which some religious authorities may consider to be unbelief. Therefore, there is a need to renew belief all the time, every hour, every day.[23]

# Saints

The remaining question is: Who are the followers of the path, those who renew their faith and keep their level of spirituality high? The Prophet is a human being and a model to be imitated. In fact, Muslim mystics trace their spiritual lineage to the Prophet as the one who started the path, and the history of Islam has witnessed many model Muslim mystics since his time. The four rightly guided caliphs—Abu Bakr, Umar, Uthman, and Ali—who learned directly from the Prophet and are known for their piety and spiritual life come next, followed by the grandsons of the Prophet, Hasan and Husayn. Many Islamic mystical orders trace their lineage to either Abu Bakr, the first caliph and the closest friend of the Prophet, or to Ali, the cousin of the Prophet and the fourth caliph who is known in Islamic mysticism as the Sultan of Saints. It seems that the Prophet speaks of the pious of the Islamic community as those who hold the essence of the religion. The Prophet speaks very highly of them, saying, "The earth will never become empty of forty people who are as kind as Abraham, the friend of God, in their generosity and in their hearts. It is because of them God sends you water and His help. When one of them dies, God replaces him or her with another one." The narrator says, "We have no doubt that Hasan [the grandson of the Prophet] was one of them."[24] In another hadith the Prophet describes the qualities of these people, saying, "They have not reached that level of spirituality through their prayer, fasting and charity . . . . [They reached it] through their generosity and counsel."[25] These people are the saints who are known in the mystical tradition of Islam as the *Abdal*, which has a connotation of replacement, since when one dies another one replaces him or her.

Although there are only forty Abdal, there can be an unlimited number of saints alive at any given time. Saints walk among us and are often seen as regular people. It is important to note that, unlike in Catholicism, sainthood is not achieved through recognition or appointment by a religious authority. In fact, saints are careful not to reveal their spiritual dimension, because it is a form of a covenant between the saint and the Divine; make their sainthood is known only to God. Occasionally, even saints do not know that they are saints. They will only become aware of it in the afterlife. Saints are not at the level of the prophets. Prophethood is a much higher rank in the realm of spirituality. In other words, every prophet is a saint, but not every saint is a prophet. Yet, like prophets of God, saints are also gifted by God with the ability to perform extraordinary miracles. Prophets such as Muhammad, Jesus, Moses, Abraham, Isaac, Jacob, etc. (peace and blessings be upon them all), challenge people and perform miracles through the power of God to show they are messengers of God. One of the major differences between the extraordinary events that they preform is that what the prophets preform is called *mu'jiza* which means "the one that makes people fail to imitate it" and the extraordinary power of saints is called *karama*. This is a Divine gift that may be given and may not be given. Therefore, while prophets may challenge others to prove their prophethood, saints cannot challenge others to prove their sainthood, as this is not their mission. As a matter of fact, saints do not want to have their extraordinary spiritual power revealed, because this life is a test and there must be certain level of ambiguity in order for people to exercise their free will. The presence of mystery and Divine wisdom must remain so that people will believe or not believe through their own choice and free will. We see a similar Divine wisdom in the secrecy of several occasions. For example, the Night of Honor, or Night of Power, after which Chapter 97 of the Qur'an is named, is hidden in the year. It is a single night that is better than one thousand months. If one is able to catch it, it will be as if one has spent around eighty years of his or her life in prayer. The Prophet gave some clues suggesting that this night is within the month of Ramadan. More specifically, he suggests that people should look for it in the final ten days of Ramadan, although this is not necessarily the case. Still, since the Prophet mentioned these ten nights, Muslims generally spend these nights in prayer to try to catch the Night of Honor. Similarly, there is an unknown moment every Friday where if one is praying in that moment, God accepts whatever prayer one asks for.

These are certain principles in Islamic piety that people must always be alert to, such as constantly searching and doing good things on the off chance that it might occur within such hidden nights and moments. Therefore, unlike what we are familiar with in the West, it is a truism among Muslims that one has to consider every stranger a saint. Thinking positively about every person we do not know increases solidarity in the community. In the same mode of thinking, one has to treat every night as the Night of Honor, and every moment on Fridays as a special moment.

While some saints become known after they die, during their lifetimes, for the most part, they are known as good people but not saints, per se. Sainthood in Islamic spirituality is not by formal appointment. They are accepted by overall public recognition despite their will. As the Qur'an says of saints and other pious people, "The Friends of God will certainly have nothing to fear, and they will not grieve. Those who believe and are pious towards God, for them is good news both in this life and in the afterlife. The words of God do not change. This is the supreme triumph" (10:62-64). The title used here, *Awliya Allah* (the Friends of God) or simply *Awliya*, is used for prominent Muslim saints. If one were to give a list of some *Awliya*, the following names perhaps would be the most well-known ones. The famous mystic and biographer Abu Nu'aym al-Isfahani (d. 1038) dedicated his remarkable book, *Hilyat al-Awliya* or *The Ornament of the Saints*,[26] to the stories and the sayings of 650 monumental figures in Islamic spirituality.

Still today, each of these remarkable individuals deserves a separate study. Working from al-Isfahani and other writers,[27] this list is chronologically ordered by date of death.

- Fatima bint Muhammad (d. 632), the daughter of the Prophet and wife of Ali.
- Abu Bakr (d. 634), the first caliph who is considered a model for devotion. His poems and his prayers are well known in the Islamic spiritual tradition. As an example, in one of his poems addressing God he says:

  > My Lord, bestow generously upon me Your grace, I who have little provisions.
  > I the bankrupt of truthfulness am coming to Your door. O the Almighty!
  > My sins are so great. You forgive the great sins of mine.
  > I am a stranger and sinner and Your humble servant.
  > From me is disobedience, forgetfulness, and mistake after mistake.
  > From You is kindness, bounties, and abundant gift after gift.[28]

- Umar bin al-Khattab (d. 644), the second caliph and model for spiritual life.[29]
- Uthman bin Affan (d. 656), known for his recitation of the Qur'an and for his love for the Qur'an.[30]
- Ali bin Abi Talib (d. 661), known for his piety and his title as the Sultan of all saints. Many Sufis trace their lineage to Ali.[31]
- Hasan bin Ali (d. 670), the grandson of the Prophet, known for his piety as well as peace-making and conflict resolution.
- Abu al-Darda (d. 652), who was one of the Ashab al-Suffa. He was one of the early Muslim ascetics.
- Abu Dharr al-Ghifari (d. 653), known also for his ascetic life and devotion, as well as abandonment of the worldly pleasures.
- Uwais al-Qarani (d. 657), who lived in the time of the Prophet but could not meet with the Prophet because of his mother who needed care. He is considered a companion of the Prophet in absentia.
- Husayn bin Ali (d. 680), the grandson of the Prophet and son of Ali.
- Ali bin Husayn or Zayn al-Abidin (d. 713), a prominent master of Islamic spirituality. He prayed 1000 units of prayer in one day and that is why he received the title of the Adornment of the Worshippers.[32]
- Hasan al-Basri (d. 728), a mystic, theologian, ascetic, and critic of some leaders' wasteful, boastful behaviors.
- Ja'far al-Sadiq (d. 765), a major figure of Shi'ite Islam, well known for his mystical experiences and prayers.[33]

- Umar bin Abd al-Aziz (d. 770), a model of piety as a ruler who avoided worldliness.
- Ibrahim bin Adham (d. 777), an ascetic mystic.
- Rabia al-Adawiyye (d. 801), a female ascetic mystic who never married, dedicating her life to God.
- Shaqiq al-Balkhi (d. 810), a mystic who emphasized the importance of trust in God.
- Ma'ruf al-Karkhy (d. 815), a prominent mystic of Baghdad.
- Bishr al-Hafi (d. 841), a famous ascetic Muslim known for his title "the Barefoot."
- Fatima of Nishapur (d. 849), a female mystic.
- Harith al-Muhasibi or al-Harith al-Muhasibi (d. 857), a well-known mystic and the founder of moral psychology in Islam.
- al-Sarri al-Saqati (d. 867), a mystic of Baghdad.
- Abu Yazid Tayfur bin Isa al-Bistami (d. 875), known for his unruly statements.
- Ibrahim al-Khawwas (d. 904), a mystic from Baghdad who was known for his trust in God.
- Abu al-Husayn al-Nuri (d. 907), the author of the book called *The Stations of Hearts*.
- al-Junaid al-Baghdadi (d. 910), a mystic, ascetic, and jurist.
- Abu Bakr al-Shibli (d. 945), a mystic from Bagdad, originally a high government official.
- Abu Nasr al-Sarraj (d. 988), a mystic and theorist in the Sufi tradition.
- Abu Bakr Muhammad al-Kalabadhi (d. 990), a historian, mystic, and well-known author in the mystical tradition.
- Abu Talib al-Makki (d. 996), known for his book *Qut al-Qulub* (*The Food of Hearts*).
- Abu al-Hasan Ali al-Kharaqani (d. 1033), was known by some mystics as the king of Sufi masters.
- Abu al-Qasim Abd al-Karim al-Qushayri (d. 1074), known for his book *Al-Risala* (*The Message*).
- Abu Hamid al-Ghazali (d. 1111), theologian, jurist, and polymath who took up the spiritual path after a spiritual crisis.
- Abd al-Qadir al-Jilani (d. 1166), the founder of the eponymous Qadiri Sufi order who came from the lineage of the Prophet.
- Abu al-Najib Abd al-Qahir al-Suhrawardi (d. 1168), known for his writing of the rules for behavior of Sufis.
- Ahmad al-Rufai (d. 1182), the founder of the Rufaiyya Sufi order.

- Ruzbihan Bakli (d. 1209), a mystic and the author of *Kashf al-Asrar* (*The Unveiling of Secrets*).
- Abd al-Khaliq Ghijduwani (d. 1220), known as Khwajagan (the Master) of the Naqshbandi Sufi order.
- Farid al-Din Attar (d. 1221), a poet mystic, who is known for his work, *The Conference of the Birds*.
- Ahmad Yasawi (d. 1225), the founder of the Yasawiyya Sufi order in central Asia.
- Mu'in al-Din Chisty (d. 1236), the major figure of the Chistiyya Sufi order in India.
- Muhyi al-Din bin al-Arabi (Ibn al-Arabi) (d. 1240), an Iberian scholar-mystic and the author of *Al-Futuhat al-Makkiyya* (*Meccan Revelations*).
- Abu al-Hasan al-Shadhali (d. 1258), the founder of the Shadhaliyya Sufi order.
- Haji Baktash Wali (d. 1270), a Sufi from Khorasan, eponym of the Baktashiyya Sufi order.
- Jalaluddin Mawlana Rumi (d. 1273), a poet, Sufi, and mystic, eponym of the Mawlawiyya Sufi order and author of the *Mathnawi*.
- Muhammad Baha al-Din al-Naqshabandi (d.1389), known as Shah Naqshaband, founder of Naqshabandiyya Sufi order.
- Ahmad al-Faruqi al-Sirhindi (d. 1624), is known as the renewer of the second millennium of Islam and remarkable Sufi master from India.
- Mawlana Khalid al-Baghdadi (d. 1827), a Kurdish Sufi master who founded a branch of the Naqshabandi Sufi order known as Khalidiyya.
- Bediuzzaman Said Nursi (d. 1960), the author of the *Risale-i Nur* (*Treatises of Light*). He was not attached to any Sufi order, although he had a strong connection to the Qadiriyya Sufi order.

# 2

# The Qur'anic roots of Islamic spirituality

The Qur'an is considered the first source for all Islamic knowledge, which includes the realm of Islamic spirituality. One has to remember that one-fourth of the Qur'an is about spirituality and prayer alongside Divinity, prophethood, and afterlife. In fact, a close examination will show that spirituality is the essence of the Qur'an and can be found within the three other major themes of the Qur'an. Also, it should be noted that these Qur'anic themes appear throughout the Qur'an and can be found in any one of the 114 chapters. On almost every page of the Qur'an one can find information related to spirituality. This chapter is focused on Qur'anic verses which relate directly or indirectly to Islamic spirituality. While some of the verses discussed have a firm foundation in the literature on Islamic spirituality, others are the ones I have discovered through my own reading of the Holy Book through the lens of Islamic spiritual life. This is not to say I have exhausted the Qur'anic roots of Islamic spirituality; there are numerous elements which I will not discuss and perhaps others which have yet to be discovered. I will only focus here on a few of those elements which I see as most important.

## The Qur'an

Before delving into the details of Qur'anic verses on Islamic spirituality, it is important to say something about the Qur'an. A standard definition of the Qur'an is that it is a revelation from God to Muhammad (peace and blessings be upon him)[1] through the angel Gabriel. The Qur'an is considered the word of God verbatim and not the words of Muhammad, which are referred to as the Hadith.[2] It is known as a book of prayer, a book of worship, a book of wisdom, a book of invocation, and a book of contemplative prayer reflecting the Divine names in the heavens and earth. References are given to the Torah, Psalms, and Gospel. It is unique in its eloquence and its beauty of recitation. Arab poets would prostrate before its beauty and eloquence. The Qur'an is memorized by thousands of young Muslims. Its first chapter, comprised of seven verses is recited in every unit of daily prayer and is comparable to the "Our Father" prayer in Christianity. The Qur'an challenged Arab poets to produce a written work like it, but they were unable to fight against the Qur'an with words. As the famous writer al-Jahiz (d. 868/9) said, "because Arabs were unable to fight [it] with words, they fought [it] with swords."[3]

There are also contextual definitions of the Qur'an. For example, the Qur'an can be described as the "translation of the book of the universe." That is to say, God has two books: the Holy Qur'an and the book of the universe, that is, nature, the earth, the cosmos, etc. The former explains the latter. The Qur'an is also described as the book of law, because it contains many laws related to social and economic life (e.g., the Qur'an details the proper distribution of inheritance to one's heirs). It is also considered a book of prayers because it includes many examples of prayers and supplications, some of which will be mentioned in this section. The Qur'an is further a book of worship, a book of wisdom, a book of invocation, as well as a book of contemplation.[4] The Qur'an contains 114 chapters and over 6,000 verses of varying length. While the first chapter is among the shortest, the remaining chapters are organized more or less by decreasing length. For this reason, some English translators of the Qur'an suggest that beginners read the Qur'an from the end, because the end chapters are shorter and generally easier to understand. An important aspect of spiritual life for many Muslim mystics is to read the Qur'an daily as an act of worship. The Prophet encourages all Muslims to read the Qur'an, and for each letter of the Qur'an read there are ten rewards and ten expiations. He clarifies that when he says, "By each letter I mean: *alif* is ten, *lam* is ten, and *mim* is ten."[5] A method of reading the Qur'an is based on monthly cycles, in which there are 30 parts known as *juz'*. Each part is 20 pages. If one reads 20 pages daily, he or she will finish the entire Qur'an in a month. The Prophet himself told his followers to "read the Qur'an every month."[6]

As indicated in the last chapter, there are several words which can be used to describe Islamic spirituality, with *tasawwuf* perhaps being the most common. Qur'anic spirituality is also related to pre-Islamic messengers of God, such as Noah, Abraham, Isaac, Jacob, and the family of Imran, which is also the house of the father of Mary. Although the word *tasawwuf*, per se, is not found in the Qur'an, there are many verses that contain a derivative of the word and can be considered a reference from the Qur'an to the etymology of the word *tasawwuf*. The following Qur'anic verses all have to do with both being chosen and purified.[7] The first verse tells us that there are human beings and angels who are chosen or purified by God, including prophets and saints. "God chooses/purifies [*yastafi*] messengers from the angels and human beings; surely God is All-Hearing, All-Seeing" (22:75). Similarly a Qur'anic verse uses *istafa*, which also shares the same meaning of purity to show that Abraham was chosen and purified by God. "And Abraham advised his sons with this and Jacob likewise: 'My sons, God has chosen/purified [*istafa*] for you the religion; So do not die unless you are *muslims* [have submitted yourselves to the will of God]'" (2:132). Another verse again describes Abraham, Isaac, and Jacob as purified and chosen by God. "[Muhammad], recall Our servants Abraham, Isaac, and Jacob, all of whom possessed virtuous hands and clear visions. Surely We purified them with a pure quality: the remembrance of the Abode [afterlife]. In Our eyes they were of the chosen, virtuous people" (38:45-7). The same word is used to describe the purification of Adam, the Family of Abraham and the Family of Imran. "God chose Adam and Noah and the House of Abraham and the House of Imran above all the worlds" (3:33).

Another verse that uses the same word for purification is related to the unidentified servants of God, making it even more encompassing and inclusive. The Prophet is asked to say blessings for them. "Say: 'Praise belongs to God, and peace be on His servants whom He has chosen'" (27:59). The Qur'an uses the same word when it speaks of the angels' conversation with Mary who was purified by God. "'Behold,' the angels told Mary, 'God had chosen you, cleansed you, and given you distinction over all women of the worlds'" (3:42). Here, I have chosen the meaning of *al-safa*, which is also narrated by al-Kalabadhi.[8] Muslim mystics are called Sufi for their inner purity. Therefore, a Sufi is one who has purified his or her heart. Reynold Nicholson also prefers this term that originally has the connotation of purification, rather than the wearing of wool garments. "In most Sufis, flying in the face of etymology, have derived it from an Arabic root which conveys the notion of purity. This would make Sufi mean one who is pure in heart or one of the elect."[9]

# Reflection on the first chapter of the Qur'an

According to most mystics, all basic principles of spirituality can be derived from the Qur'an. Key elements of Islamic spirituality are found in the first chapter of the Qur'an. The first element includes the Divine names. The first chapter starts with three names of God: Allah,[10] *al-Rahman*, and *al-Rahim*. The Divine names are one of the most important components of Islamic mysticism. In this chapter, in addition to these three names, two other Divine names are given: *Rabb al-Alamin* (The Lord of the Worlds) and *Malik Yawm al-Din* (Owner of the Day of Judgment).

Another element of mystical tradition of Islam mentioned in this chapter is the concept of praising God. Mystics repeatedly praise God with specific formulas and words. The first phrase of the first chapter of the Qur'an is "*al-Hamdu Li Allah*," literally "praise belongs to Allah," and is usually rendered in English as Alhamdulillah. This is a phrase repeated by mystics time and time again. In fact, all Muslims are asked to repeat this phrase thirty-three times after each prayer, as the Prophet practiced and suggested that Muslims practice as well. The Prophet has spoken often about the importance of this phrase. In one of his sayings, he describes this phrase as something easy on the tongue and heavy on the scale in the afterlife.[11]

A third element is the concept of worshipping God sincerely. In this chapter, this principle is indicated by the phrase, "You alone we worship." This phrase has two aspects. One aspect includes sincerity. The other aspect includes all forms of prayer, and not only the five daily prayers—morning, noon, afternoon, sunset, and evening—that all Muslims who reach the age of puberty are required to perform. Mystics typically do significantly more than the five daily prayers. They perform many voluntary night prayers as well as voluntary prayers during the day. A hadith Qudsi, which is an extra-Qur'anic divine text, says that while the prescribed prayers bring human beings close to God, "My servants come even closer to Me with voluntary prayer to the extent that I become the ear through which they hear, the eyes through which they see, the hand through which they act, and the feet on which they walk."[12] These are some reflections on the first chapter of the Qur'an that show that one can find elements of Islamic spirituality in many Qur'anic chapters and verses. While reading the Qur'an through a spiritual lens, it is remarkable to see how Qur'anic verses reflect the mystical tradition of Islam.

# Terminology

The verses that follow, at least some of them, are not typically found in mainstream sources of Islamic mysticism. In this regard, this chapter takes a unique approach toward the connection of Islamic spirituality to the Qur'an.

In the Qur'an there are many terms such as *birr*, *taqwa*, *khawf*, *ihsan*, *salah*, *ikhlas*, and *dhikr* which are used in relation to positive spiritual qualities. Likewise, there are terms, including *nifaq* and *riya*, which indicate the destruction of a human's spiritual life. Al-Ghazali calls these *muhlikat*, or the qualities that cause the spiritual destruction of human beings. The first term to discuss is *birr*. *Birr* can encompass the overall spiritual life. It can be translated as righteousness or piety. The following verse is perhaps the most encompassing verse on the subject.

> It is not piety [*birr*], that you turn your faces to the East and to the West. Instead, the pious one [*barr*; lit. the one who is pious] is the one who believes in God, and the Last Day, the angels, the Book, and the prophets, and who gives of one's substance, however cherished, to one's relatives

and orphans and the needy and travelers and beggars and to free the slave and to pray and to give charity. And those who fulfill their covenant when they have engaged in a covenant, and endure with fortitude misfortune, hardship and peril, these are those who are true in their faith, these are the truly righteous. (2:177)

Commenting on this verse, al-Baydawi (d. 1280) says, "The verse, as you see, is encompassing all ideal principles of perfection for human beings, either directly or indirectly. All these perfections with the variety of their branches are combined in the three major themes: the soundness of belief, good behaviors with regard to others, and rectification of the soul." [13] In other words, these are principles that Muslim mystics seek out and look for in striving to reach the level of the perfected human being, or *al-Insan al-Kamil*. Al-Baydawi also refers to a saying of the Prophet on this specific verse: "Anyone who acts according to the meaning of this verse surely has a perfected faith." [14] Another hadith, which discusses the perfection of faith again, suggests that one has to get rid of one's egoism, be selfless, and act for the sake of God only, without expecting any benefit or reward in return for one's actions: "Those who love for God, anger for God, give for God, avoid for God, surely have perfected their faith." [15] Among the most significant spiritual terms found in the Qur'an is *dhikr*. It is this that we now examine.

## *Dhikr* (remembrance of God)

The first place in the Qur'an that people are asked to remember God in a direct connection to pre-Islamic prophets is in the case of Zachariah. This is meant to remind Muslims of his story, and also to guide them toward his long path of spirituality. Here Zachariah is addressed by the Divine saying: "[Zachariah] remember your Lord often and glorify Him in the evenings and in the mornings" (3:41). This is a supplication that has connection to Qur'an 2:186, which indicates that God is close to you. Similarly, there are at least four verses that directly ask the Prophet, and by extension all people, to remember God. They are: "Remember your Lord in your soul humbly and fearfully, without a loud voice, in the mornings and evenings. And do not be among the heedless" (7:205); "Remember your Lord when you forget and say, 'Perhaps my Lord will guide me to what is nearest to the right conduct'" (18:24); "Remember the name of your Lord and devote yourself to Him with devotion" (73:8); and "Remember the name of your Lord in the morning and in the evening" (76:25). It seems that here the remembrance of God is emphasized in the daily prescribed morning, noon, and afternoon prayers. Verses 8:2-4 in the Qur'an also describe believers as those whose hearts soften when they hear of God, and thus themselves remember God. These verses suggest that *dhikr* is not simply a passive action. Believers perform actions that are directly related to their *dhikr*: giving charity, doing good deeds, etc. This is what *dhikr* looks like:

> Surely the believers are those who, when God is remembered, their hearts become soft with fear and when His verses are recited to them their faith is increased and in their Lord they trust; those who are praying and give from what We have given them, those truly are the believers and there are high positions from their Lord for them and forgiveness and a generous sustenance. (8:2-4)

The Qur'an has many additional references to the Sufi concept of *dhikr*. *Dhikr* literally means remembrance of God. Some mystics define *dhikr* as forgetting everything other than God. Al-Qushayri defines *dhikr* as "the total immersion of the one who makes *dhikr* in the presence of the One who is remembered. And his annihilation in the existence of the One who is remembered to the extent that nothing is left of the one who makes dhikr to be remembered. It would be said once upon a time there was such a person."[16] One of the most repeated Qur'anic verses for most Sufis is one that refers to the remembrance of God: "Those who believe, their hearts are at rest in God's remembrance. Surely in God's remembrance only hearts rest" (13:28). A similar verse says, "Their skins and their hearts soften to the remembrance of God" (39:23). The Qur'an defines this as a quality of the pious, that their hearts soften to the remembrance of God and their bodies follow what is in their hearts by sharing this calmness and rest. Yet achieving this through the remembrance of God requires tremendous effort, as there will always be obstacles and beguilers.

One of the greatest obstacles is no doubt Satan. A Qur'anic verse states that Satan puts animosity and hatred among people and draws them away from the remembrance of God (5:91). There is another verse which says, "Satan has overcome them and made them forget the remembrance of God" (58:19). These and similar verses from the Qur'an show that one of Satan's tasks is to prevent human beings from remembering God, and that is why the Qur'an insistently reminds people that they have to frequently remember God. Relatedly, the Qur'an reminds that there might be some obstacles to the remembrance of God, such as people's business and family life. Although these are positive things, they can be considered a test at the same time. "O believers, let neither your possessions nor your children divert you from God's remembrance; whoever does that, they are the losers" (63:9). In contrast to this, the Qur'an praises a group of people whose lives and livelihoods are not obstacles for them: "There are houses that God permitted to have His name raised and remembered in and people are exalting God day and night. There are human beings whose buying and trading do not deviate them from the remembrance of God and from praying and from giving charity. They are in awe of a day when hearts and eyes are trembled" (24:36-37). It seems that because of the importance of the remembrance of God, the Qur'anic expectation for believers is that when they hear the revelation of God their hearts should be softened to the remembrance of God. As the verse says, "Is it not the time that the hearts of those who believe should be humbled to the remembrance of God and the Truth which He has sent down?" (57:16).

Mystics following this Qur'anic instruction have made the remembrance of God a central part of their rituals and chanting. Perhaps because of this Qur'anic command, some mystics assigned their students the task of reciting many of the ninety-nine names of God after morning and afternoon prayers. This is known as "the translation of the greatest name of God." Although the Qur'an does not limit the remembrance of God to certain mystical rituals, it can be argued that mystics' emphasis on the remembrance of God through chanting and repeating Divine names and other mystical practices is helpful and compatible with this Qur'anic understanding. The importance of the Divine names has led to the great popularity of chanting the names of God. Today, social media have become popular venues for chanting the Beautiful Names of God. My internet search for *al-Asma al-Husna* brought nearly 200,000 YouTube results, which shows how popular the chanting of the Divine names is. Furthermore, the most popular of these videos have been viewed millions of times.

Because the Divine revelations such as the Torah, the Psalms, the Gospel, and the Qur'an are venues for remembering God, they are referred to as *dhikr* in and of themselves. For example, in reference to the Torah, a Qur'anic verse says, "Surely, We gave Moses and Aaron the Salvation and a Radiance, and a Remembrance for the God-fearing" (21:48). In reference to the Qur'an as a remembrance another verse says, "So We relate to you stories of what has gone before, and We have given you [Muhammad], a Remembrance from Us" (20:99).

A Qur'anic verse refers to those who believe and do good deeds as people who are guided to the beautiful words. Despite the connotation of this verse, specifically the term "beautiful words," some commentators of the Qur'an mention that "beautiful words" refers to Sufis' chanting of *dhikr*. These are: "There is no deity but God," or, "*La ilaha illa Allah;*" "God is the most exalted," or, "*Subhan Allah;*" and "God is greater than everything," or "*Allahu Akbar.*" The Prophet refers to the first of these as the best of *dhikr.*[17] It is well-known that these phrases are also highly emphasized in the sayings of the Prophet, and are very much repeated in the mystical tradition of *dhikr*. Although there are literalist groups who claim that there is no reference in the Qur'an to the practices of Muslim mystics, this Qur'anic verse can be viewed as a reference from the Holy Book of Islam to the spiritual tradition of remembrance of God: "And they had been guided [in worldly life] to beautiful words, and they were guided to the path of the praiseworthy" (22:24).

The first chapter of the Qur'an starts, after the formula of *Bismillah*, with praising God by saying, "All praises belong to God" (1:2). This illustrates the importance of *dhikr* in the Qur'an as the praising of God. In the Islamic tradition, when one begins anything honorable and good, such as eating, drinking, praying, walking, driving, by saying, "In the name of God the Most Compassionate and the Most Merciful," one will receive blessings and help from God through three divine names, Allah, *al-Rahman, al-Rahim*. Besides this verse, there are others which emphasize this importance. One says, "All praises belong to Him in this world and in the afterlife" (28:70). In sum, this phrase is mentioned twenty-one times in the Qur'an. It is a short phrase, but it is very significant in the mystical tradition of *dhikr*. It is recommended to repeat this frequently, because on the Day of Judgment when good and evil deeds are weighed on the scales, this phrase is one of the heaviest phrases on the side of good. The phrase indicates that God is the source of all bounties that occur through conscious and unconscious causes. Because God is the Cause of causes, all praises go to God automatically, even if people are not aware of it. For example, if someone takes you to a municipal park and you praise the person who takes you to the park, your praise also goes to the municipality itself because they are the cause of the park. Thus, ultimately your praise goes to God because it is God who creates all green things, all beauties of the park: trees, grass, and flowers. Thus, whether there is awareness of it or not, all praises go to God.

The Holy Book of Islam connects God's remembrance by His servants with God Himself. "Remember Me, and I will remember you. And be thankful to Me and do not be ungrateful to Me" (2:152). Commentators of the Qur'an have greatly elaborated on this verse by referring to a remarkable story from ancient Israel and Judah. It is believed that Moses asked God, "How should I thank you, my Lord?" And God said, "Remember Me and do not forget Me. When you Remember Me, you will thank Me. When you forget Me you will deny Me." A Qur'anic verse states, "O Believers, be pious towards God as God truly deserves" (3:102). Some Islamic scholars interpret this to mean that God must be obeyed and one must not sin against God. Also, God should be remembered and not forgotten, and God should be thanked and not denied. Hasan al-Basri in his interpretation of this verse says, "God asks people to remember Him by doing what God has commanded them to do and God will remember them about what He promised for them."

Another mystic interprets the verse as if people remember God through their prayers and obedience, "God will remember them through His rewards, bounties, and by showering them with all good things."[18] There is one narration from the Prophet that says, "God says those who remember Me in their hearts, I will remember them too. Those who remember Me in the presence of people, I will remember them in the presence of groups that are better than them."[19] Another version of this hadith includes, "If you remember Me in a group of people, I will remember you in a group of Angels."[20] Mahmud al-Alusi (d. 1854), an Iraqi Islamic scholar and a prominent commentator of the Qur'an, after mentioning that *dhikr* encompasses the ear, tongue, and other organs, divides *dhikr* into three categories. The first one is *dhikr* by tongue, and that is to praise God through verbal statements, to exalt God, and recite the Qur'an, the Word of God.

The second one is *dhikr* by heart. This is contemplation of the evidence on the responsibilities of human beings with regard to the Divine commands and warnings. Also, it is to contemplate the attributes and the mysteries of the Divine Lordship, *Rububiyyah*. The third one is *dhikr* by actions, and that is to act according to what God has commanded, and avoid what God prohibited. Since the daily prescribed prayers encompass various bodily actions of *dhikr*, they have been called *dhikr* in the Qur'an.[21]

A well-known mystic, al-Qushayri in his famous commentary called *Lata'if al-Isharat* (The Subtleties of Allusions), has important points on the interpretation of this verse, especially on the statement "Remember Me." According to him, the people who look at the external meaning of the verse will understand this as following the Divine commands. A group of people who understand the inner meaning of the verse will understand this as remembering God is to abandon every desire other than God. He goes further and makes comments on these two Qur'anic statements by saying,

> Remember Me with your humbleness, I will remember you with my bounties. Remember Me with a broken heart, I will remember you with goodness. Remember Me with your tongue, I will remember you with the heart. Remember Me with your hearts, I will remember you by fulfilling your requests. Remember Me at the door with your service, I will remember you with My response of fulfilling all My bounties on the carpet of closeness to Me. Remember Me by rectifying your inner life, I will remember you with My full kindness. Remember Me with your efforts and struggle, I will remember you with My generosity and gifts. Remember Me with My attribute of peace, I will remember you on the Day of Judgment when repentance is no longer valid. Remember Me with awe; I will remember you with fulfilling of your requests.[22]

One of the most important aspects of remembering is to remember the names of God. As the Qur'an says, "Remember the name of your Lord" (73:8 and 76:25). In the following section I will introduce the Divine names, specifically what is understood by some mystics as "the greatest name of God" or "*al-Ism al-A'zam*." Also, I will discuss some Sufi concepts such the concept of heart and what can be called the actions of heart. The heart is the central theme of Islamic spirituality, without which everything is nothing but shell. I will also elaborate on prayers of the prophets. It is fascinating to see so many prayers of the prophets, which I think are considerably understudied.

# Divine names

> He is God, than Whom there is no other God, the Knower of the invisible and the visible. He is the Most-Compassionate, the Most-Meciful. He is God, than Whom there is no other God, the Sovereign [Lord], the

Holy One, the Peace, the Keeper of Faith, the Guardian, the Majestic, the Compeller, the Superb. Glorified be God from all that they ascribe as partner [unto Him]. He is God, the Creator, the Shaper out of naught, the Fashioner. His are the most beautiful names. All that is in the heavens and the earth glorify Him, and He is the Mighty, the Wise. (59:22-4)

Many early Muslims wrote extensively on the Beautiful Names of God. Ibn Jarir al-Tabari (d. 923), al-Bayhaqi (d. 1066), al-Ghazali (d. 1111), Fakhr al-Din al-Razi (d. 1210), al-Tamimi (d. 1363), and more recently Nursi (d. 1960) are among the most prominent figures who have dedicated some of their works to the understanding of the Divine names.

Muslim mystics use various names of God in their supplications and prayers. The hadith that refers to the ninety-nine names of God indicates the multiplicity of Divine names rather than to limit them to ninety-nine. The Prophet says that "there are 99 names of God; 100 except one. Anyone who memorizes them enters Paradise. God is One [odd number] and loves odd numbers."[23] Hadith commentators have elaborated on this. Al-'Ayni (d. 1451), a commentator on al-Bukhari, says some have said God's beautiful names number ninety-nine only, while others have said that because God's praises and merits are unlimited, this hadith is not meant to limit the names of God, but to speak of the entrance of Paradise. He also gives examples of odd numbers, such as praying five times a day, circumambulating the Ka'ba seven times in pilgrimage, washing hands and feet three times during ablution as other instances of how God loves odd numbers.[24]

Two well-known Divine names are *al-Aziz,* which means the Almighty, and *al-Rahim,* which means the Most-Merciful. These names are the most frequently mentioned in the Quran in connection to the prayers of the prophets. Thirteen times these Divine names are mentioned together with regard to how God supported His prophets Moses, Abraham, Noah, Hud, Salih, Lot, Jethro, and Muhammad. The verses end with this formula: "Surely your Lord is the Almighty and the Most-Merciful."[25] These two Divine names have connotations of mercy but also justice. Through *al-Rahim,* God sends His mercy to His messengers, and through His Divine name *al-Aziz,* God applies justice to oppressors by punishing them for their oppression and wrongdoing. Thus when his people rejected him the Prophet of Islam was commanded to say that Divine names are mentioned as a support for him, as they were mentioned in the case of other prophets, and the Prophet was commanded to put his trust in these two Divine names. The Qur'anic verse says: "And if they disobey you, then say, 'Indeed, I am disassociated from what you are doing. Put your trust in the Almighty, the Most-Merciful'" (26:216-17). Divine names are directly connected to the mystical tradition, and therefore mystics when they supplicate to God use both names that are related to His compassion and mercy, but also to the Divine names that are related to His justice and might.

As far the as the number of the Divine names is concerned, there are various opinions. Some have said they are unlimited because the Divine qualities of goodness are unlimited. Some have said there are 1,001 names of God. These Divine names are most prominently recorded in Zayn al-Abidin's (d. 713) *Al-Sahifa al-Sajjadiyya* or *Al-Jawshan al-Kabir* which, while only recently more prominent in the Sunni tradition, has been very well known in the Shi'ite tradition.[26] Ibn Manda (d. 1004) in his book *Al-Tawhid* lists 148 Divine names, while al-Bayhaqi in his book *al-Asma wa al-Sifat* records 154 Divine names.

There are hadith that mention "The Greatest Name of God" (*al-Ism al-A'zam*), though it is believed that only a few people know to which name this term refers. A hadith mentions, "God has a name. Anyone who calls upon God with that name will receive his or her request." Some have said that this name is Allah, others have said it is *al-Rahman*, while others believe that this name is hidden and only known through spiritual advancement in one's knowledge of God. The Greatest Name of God has been a point of debate and discussion among Sufis. Al-Jilani says the greatest name of God is Allah. Some say it is the Divine names *al-Hayy* and *al-Qayyum*, which are mentioned together in verses 2:255 and 3:2 of the Qur'an. Another view is that it is contained in 2:163, which says, "Your God is One. There is no god but He. He is the Most-Merciful, Most-Compassionate."[27] Others say God has hidden it among His names as the Night of Honor is hidden within the year. During prayer, if one asks God as follows, "My Lord, I am asking You with Your Beautiful Names and Your most-high attributes," this will include the Greatest Name of God. All told, there are about forty views as to what the Greatest Name of God is, and I will discuss this more in Chapter 6.

Nursi's understanding seems to combine the hadith on this regard, and it is different than the traditional mystical understanding. He sees it as a combination of six divine names: *al-Hayy* (the Most-Living), *al-Qayyum* (the Sustainer), *al-Hakam* (the Final Judge), *al-Adl* (the Most-Just), and *al-Quddus* (the Most-Holy). Nursi related a prayer called *sakina*—which has a connection to the Hebrew word *shekhinah*, which has the connotation of settling and dwelling of the Divine presence—in his well-known short treatise, which could be translated as "The Book of Prayer." The word *sakina* is mentioned twice in the Qur'an. In one place, *sakina* is sent by God to the hearts of believers (48:4), and the other verse states that God bestows *sakina* upon the believers (48:18). The prayer starts with the phrase *Allahu Akbar*, "God is greater than everything," repeated ten times. Following this, the six names of God are recited, and various verses of the Qur'an containing Divine names are mentioned. The prayer ends with the words: "You alone we worship. And from You alone we ask for help. All praises belong to God, the Lord of the Worlds." This prayer is generally repeated nineteen times.[28] It is believed that this is a prayer that brings the feeling of the Divine presence, spiritual harmony, and calmness. As a principle, this prayer should be recited just for God, and not for the possible spiritual or material benefits. The spiritual benefits may happen or they may not. What is important is that to attain spiritual harmony and peace one should take refuge in God's greatest names, the six Divine names mentioned above. It should be noted that since hadith suggest that many Divine names are considered His great names, one has to consider all Divine names important. In fact, each name has greatness within itself.

In the Islamic spiritual tradition, in order to understand the Divine names and their relationship to God, the analogy of a ruler is given. A ruler has the attributes of justice, so he is called the just ruler. At the same time, he has the attributes of knowledge, so he is called the knowledgeable ruler. In the realm of military power he is called the commander in chief. In a similar way, God has many names and attributes, which, though God is too highly exalted to be like human beings, make God closer to human minds. Though, even with such names, God's essence is beyond human capacity to understand, with the names, one is able to grasp certain elements of God's infiniteness. Each name has a superiority of reflection in each of God's creations. When one name is superior in a certain creation, other names are reflected, but in a secondary way.

To broaden our horizon of contemplation in the realm of nature and its connection to the Divine names, the following example should serve well. One of the Divine names is *al-Hayy*, or the Most-Living. That is to say, the source of life is God. The reflection of the Divine name can be witnessed in all living creatures, from the greatest to the smallest. Therefore, a small bird in the sky, or a small fish in the sea, or even a fly has a direct connection to the Divine name, *al-Hayy*. Every creature may reflect more than one Divine name. For example, when God's name, *al-Khaliq*, the Creator, reflects in a thing, a creature comes into existence. After the creation, another name of God, *al-Musawwir*, the Fashioner, reflects in order to give form to this creature in the best possible way. It has to be noted that this is not theophany. It is more related to the analogy of the sun and its reflection in mirror-like objects, such as glass or water. Considering the Divine names in the realm of creation, there are two types of reflection. One is called *al-Wahidiyya* and the other is called *al-Ahadiyya*. The first is uniting everything under the umbrella of a Divine name and the latter is the reflection of the Divine names individually in every creature. A conscientious human being should see these two types of Divine reflection in themselves and in the realm of creation. When the Qur'anic verse says, "Didn't We make two eyes for him and a tongue and two lips?" (90:8-9), it indicates the Divine name *al-Basir*, the All-Seeing, and *al-Mutakallim*, the All-Speaking. This verse indicates two reflections. The first is individual. This allows every human being to thank God for being given eyes and tongue and lips. At the same time, through uniting one's understanding of the Divine names, one can see all the eyes of all human beings and all the eyes of all living creatures. All of these can at once be seen as a reflection of the Divine name *al-Basir*. This is true for all other reflections of the Divine names. If in a living creature the name *al-Hayy* reflects, then the name *al-Razzaq*, the Provider of Sustenance, will reflect in order to fulfill all the needs of that living creature. Then the Divine name *al-Rabb*, the Lord, reflects to give that creature proper training for the conditions of life in the environment. A fish living in the sea must know how to swim; a bird must know how to fly. All of these are the reflection of *al-Rabb*.

The Qur'an invites human beings to contemplate on themselves and on the realm of creation; to discover the treasures of the Divine names. Perhaps when a hadith Qudsi says, "I was a hidden treasure and loved to be known. I created the world of creation so that I will be known,"[29] it is referring to this understanding of the reflection of the Divine names. This opens a remarkable horizon for all people who are studying and trying to understand the realm of nature. Through this understanding, human beings will become much more aware of themselves, the realm of nature, and the Divine, who says in the Qur'an, "He is closer to you than your jugular vein" (50:16).

In the mystical tradition of Islam, one can spiritually develop by contemplating the reflection of a certain name of God. When a human being reflects on a certain Divine name, he or she develops in the direction of that Divine name. For example, reflecting on the Divine name *al-Rahim*, or the Most-Merciful, one becomes more merciful toward creation. Perhaps this is the reason the Prophet says: "become attributed with the attributes of God."[30] That is, be kind to creation as God is kind to creation; be merciful to human beings as God is merciful. Some prophets mentioned in the Qur'an are known among mystics as reflections of certain Divine names. For example, among Sufis, Jesus is known as the reflection of many Divine names, more specifically the Divine name *al-Qadir*, or the Most-Powerful. It was because of the reflection of this Divine name that Jesus was able to perform miracles and raise the dead to life. Some are the reflection of the Divine name *al-Hakim*, the All-Wise. Some are known as the reflection of the Divine name *al-Alim*, the Most-Knowledgeable, or *al-Rahim*, the Most-Compassionate or *al-Wadud*, the Most-Loving. Because the tradition of Islamic spirituality is known as the path of love, it is believed that the entire path of the Islamic spiritual tradition is a reflection of the Divine name *al-Wadud*. Some mystics will make their supplications through various Divine names.

The master of such supplications is the Prophet of Islam who is believed to have opened his heart to God and supplicated with 1,001 names of God. We have a reference to this supplication through Ali bin Husayn (d. 713), the fourth imam of the Shi'ite tradition, in *Al-Sahifa al-Sajjadiyya/Al-Jawshan al-Kabir*. The supplication consists of 100 units and each unit has ten Divine names, and with the name Allah they add up to 1,001. One unit of the prayer recounts ten Divine names, then repeats the following: "You are exalted. O the One there is no deity but You, [we ask for Your] help, [we ask for Your] help, protect us from the Fire [Hell]."

As an example of the reflection of the Divine name *al-Quddus*, the Most-Holy, one can see the purity and cleanliness in the universe and on the earth. In fact, the whole universe can be compared to a factory. If it is not cleaned up carefully, it will not be possible for human beings to live in it. What is witnessed on the planet is that if not polluted by human beings, every place is clean, and that shows the reflection of *al-Quddus*. Every creature has a share in this reflection. A fly by cleansing its small face, a bird by cleaning its wings, or a vulture or an ant that eat dead animals are all reflecting the name *al-Quddus* by making the planet clean and free of ugliness. Here we see a remarkable connection between spiritual and physical cleanliness. Matter matters when it becomes a reflection of the Divine name. Human beings as observers and practitioners will conclude from what they see, and they will become thankful to and knowledgeable of God as a result of this. In the same way, with such an intent and reflection, human beings' acts of cleanliness become acts of worship. Therefore, when an individual washes, knowingly or unknowingly, he or she reflects the Divine name *al-Quddus*.[31] This is why the Qur'an says, "God loves those who repent [doing spiritual cleansing] and those who keep themselves clean [physical cleanliness]" (2:222), and the Prophet said, "Cleanliness is half of faith."[32]

When the Qur'an speaks of spiritual cleansing, it refers to the purification of the heart. It is well known in the Islamic tradition that sins leave stains on the heart, and the way to cleanse the heart is through repentance. As one can clean one's physical dirtiness with water, repentance is a way of cleaning the dirtiness of the heart. If there are spiritual stains on the heart, repentance is a way of cleaning them (see 66:8). Because of the importance of the heart, the Qur'an refers to the heart in many verses, and much of Islamic spirituality centers on the concept of the heart.

# Prayer

As we have mentioned, one of the actions of heart is remembrance of God. This remembrance is often accomplished through *dua,* or prayer. Prayer is one of the most important elements of Islamic spirituality, and many prophetic prayers are given in the Qur'an, serving as a source for mystics in their own supplications to God. Mystics follow the path of the prophets in their supplications, and the Qur'an provides this path. In fact, the Qur'anic verse states that God cares for people because of their prayers: "Say [O Muhammad] My Lord would not care for you were it not for your prayer" (25:77). In other words, the importance of human beings is centered around their prayers to God. Since the prophets mentioned in the Qur'an are models of prayer, I will focus on their prayers as presented in the Qur'an. Before delving into the details of those prayers, however, it is important to elaborate briefly on the significance of prayer for Muslim mystics.

In the Islamic spiritual tradition, prayer is considered the most significant and mysterious means of relationship between humans and the Creator. Prayer is the spirit of servanthood to God. The Qur'an states that all creatures in their own tongues pray to God, both consciously and unconsciously.

Humans, angels, and the *jinn* (invisible creatures that are parallel to humans) all pray to God consciously.[33] Since these are conscious creatures, their prayers are conscious. However, there are also unconscious creatures that also pray to God. Animals, birds, and even the celestial bodies all pray to God in obedience to the Divine command. Human beings' prayers are the most important, because they are the masters in the realm of creation.

The Qur'an states that God hears every prayer, and every prayer is answered. "And your Lord said: 'Call upon Me and I will answer your call'" (40:60). Again, the Qur'an says, "Who is the One who answers the desperate, when he calls unto Him . . . . Is there a god with God?" (27:62). Therefore, no one returns empty-handed from His court, because from an Islamic perspective, when people pray, they ask the One who can meet all of their needs, just as they would complain to a doctor who can heal all illnesses. When people pray to God, their mind, intelligence, and senses must be in a receptive state, so that they know surely that their prayer is heard. The etiquette of prayer is to glorify God first, as it is presented in the first chapter of the Qur'an, "Praise be to the Lord of the Universe." The prophetic and Qur'anic examples of prayer are the best forms of prayer. They are considered model because it was the greatest of experts who used them to address God. Prayer formulas such as, "Our Lord, grant us good in this world and good in the hereafter," (2:201) are considered in accordance with the Qur'anic format of prayer. Similar are prayers such as "Our Lord, do not let our hearts deviate after You have guided us. Grant us mercy from Your presence, for You are the granter of bounties [without measure]" (3:8), and "Our Lord, surely we have heard a cry calling unto faith. 'Believe in your Lord.' So we believed. Our Lord, therefore, forgive our sins. Remove all our evil deeds, and make us die with the righteous" (3:193).

# Prayers of the prophets

Broadly, Islamic spirituality is the path of those who are favored by God (1:7), mainly messengers of God, including pre-Islamic prophets, as well as pious and righteous people, both pre-Islamic and those who have lived in the Islamic era. Since the Qur'an is the most important source of Islamic spirituality, which refers to early messengers of God and sets them and their prayers as examples of piety to be imitated, it is important to focus on the prayers of the prophets in the Qur'an.

The Qur'an refers to many prophets of God with at least twenty-five prophets mentioned by name. These include many prophets in the Jewish and Christian traditions, as well as some who were unknown before. God always responds to the prayers of those in need of help. A Qur'anic verse, 27:62, says it is God who responds to the prayer of the desperate. The prayers of the prophets as presented in the Qur'an have been repeated by Muslims on a daily basis since the beginning of Islam. For example, the

Qur'an refers to Adam, a prophet and the first father of humanity, and his disobedience of God. He received some words from God and he fullfilled them. He and his wife were both forgiven through their prayers. This is their prayer: "Our Lord, we have wronged ourselves. If You do not forgive us and do not have mercy on us, surely we are of the lost" (7:23). Similarly, the prayers of Noah, who is also known in the Islamic tradition as the second father of humanity, are considered exemplary prayers in the Qur'an. In one verse Noah asks for help from God: "My Lord, help me because they accuse me of lying" (23:26). Noah has another prayer that God commands him to say after he is rescued from the flood, in which Noah thanks God and praises God. "And when you [Noah] have boarded the ark you and those with you say: 'Praise be to God, Who has saved us from the people who do wrong.' And say: 'My Lord, cause me to land at a blessed landing-place, for You are Best of those who help disembarking'" (23:28-9). The last part of Noah's prayer was repeated by the Prophet of Islam when he migrated from Mecca to Medina. The Prophet asked God to make Medina a blessed place for his dwelling. Even today, the prayer is so important among Muslims that when they move from one place to another, they still ask God that both the old and the new places be blessed. In another Qur'anic verse, Noah speaks of the stubbornness of his people and asks God to rescue him and other believers. "Therefore judge between us [with your] judgment, and save me and those believers who are with me" (26:118). And the Qur'an gives good news about the acceptance of the prayers of Noah, saying that God rescued Noah and those who believed in his prophethood from the calamity that occurred.

The prayer of Hud, another prophet of God in the Qur'an, is related to trust in God. After his people betrayed him, Hud prays, "Surely I trust in God, my Lord and your Lord. There is no animal but He holds it by its forehead. Surely my Lord is on the straight path" (11:56).

Likewise, one of the prayers of Abraham is narrated in one of the key sources of Islamic spirituality, namely Abu Nu'aym al-Isfahani's *Hilyat al-Awliya*. According to this source, this prayer was frequently repeated by Abraham: "O God, take me from the humiliation of sin against You to the honor of worshipping You."[34] In one instance, Abraham acknowledges the Divine bounties that were given to him, such as guidance, eating and drinking, and the forgiveness of his mistakes, after which he prays to God: "My Lord, grant me authority and join me with the righteous and appoint me a tongue of truthfulness among those who come later and make me one of the inheritors of the Garden of Bliss" (26:83-5). Some commentators on the Qur'an refer to a Prophetic saying which has some connection to this Abrahamic prayer. When Abraham asks God to have a tongue of righteousness after his death, it is believed that Abraham's prayer was accepted. As a result of his prayer, Muhammad came and spoke the truth as one of his offspring. It is narrated that the Prophet used to say, "I am the prayer of my father Abraham and good tiding of my brother Jesus."[35] Furthermore, the Prophet said that if someone dies but leaves something that continues to speak the truth after his or her death, their actions of prayer will continue. Or, as the hadith says, "When human beings die, their good deeds come to an end except for those that leave three things behind: continuing charity, knowledge that is benefitted from, or a wholesome child that prays for them."[36] And that is why there is a phrase among Muslim mystics saying that "some people die but they are still alive among the people," which indicates that they have a "tongue of truthfulness" that they left behind. The Qur'an also narrates that when Abraham was childless in his old age, he prayed that God would grant him offspring that would pray for him, and then praised God for granting him progeny: "Praise be to God, who has given me in my old age Ishmael and Isaac. Surely my Lord hears the prayer. My Lord, make me a perfecter of the prayer, and [likewise] my offspring. Our Lord and accept my prayer" (14:39-40).

In chapter 28 of the Qur'an, we find three prayers of Moses. One prayer is about interrogation of himself, as the Prophet of Islam frequently would do. Moses also asks God for forgiveness; clearly he wants to be a reflection of the Divine names, the Most-Forgiving and the Most-Merciful. "He said, 'My Lord, I have wronged myself. Forgive me!' So God forgave him, for He is the All-Forgiving, the All-Merciful" (28:16). In the same chapter, we have another prayer of Moses which indicates the frustration of his struggle against the Pharaoh, who would like to eliminate Moses and Moses's people. The Qur'an narrates his prayer as he is leaving Egypt for Midian as follows: "So he departed therefrom, fearful and vigilant; he said, 'My Lord, deliver me from the people of the evildoers'" (28:21).

We have a third prayer of Moses from when he became tired and unable to find food. Some narratives suggest he was unable to find food for a week. He did not beg, but he asked God for help. He said, "O my Lord, surely I have need of whatever good You will have sent down upon me" (28:24). Other prayers of Moses are also very significant. In one, he prays for himself and for his brother: "My Lord, forgive me and my brother and enter us into Your mercy. You are the Most-Merciful of the merciful" (7:151). Also, the Qur'an narrates the prayer of Moses before going to Pharaoh, where he asks God to open his heart and make his speech powerful. This prayer is often repeated by Muslims before speaking. "My Lord, open my heart and ease my task for me. And untie the knot from my tongue that they might understand my words" (20:25-8).

One of the most repeated prayers by Muslims found in the Qur'an is the prayer of the prophet Job, who is known as a hero of patience in Islamic spirituality. Although Job was a prophet of God, he suffered through various diseases. When the diseases harmed his tongue and his heart, he finally asked God for a cure, because the diseases were preventing him from praying to and worshipping God. He was at such a level of spirituality that he asked God for the ability to continue his praying, not for his own respite. There is nothing wrong with latter, but Job possessed a prophetic level of sincerity that rejected even the smallest amount of selfishness. In reference to Job, the Qur'an says, "And remember when Job prayed to his Lord, 'Indeed, harm has touched me, and You are the Most-Merciful of the merciful.' So We answered him, and removed the affliction that was upon him, and We gave him back his family and more and more of them as a mercy from Us, and a Remembrance for the worshippers" (21:83-4). Islamic scholars have expanded on this prayer of Job by saying this prayer is to be done or performed not only for physical but for spiritual diseases as well. This prayer of Job is frequently recited by Muslims in general and Muslim mystics in particular. It shows a great trust in God combined with utmost sincerity and purity of heart. And perhaps because of this aspect, God immediately accepted his prayer and cured him. A Muslim theologian and mystic comparing spiritual diseases and physical diseases asserted that spiritual diseases are more dangerous because they threaten peoples' eternal lives: "The diseases of Job were threatening his limited worldly life while our spiritual diseases threaten our eternal life. Therefore, we need the prayer of Job 1,000 times more than him"[37.]

Another prophetic prayer in the Qur'an is the prayer of Jonah. As is briefly narrated in the Qur'an, Jonah conveyed God's message to the people of Nineveh. However, the people of Nineveh rejected Jonah and the message of God. According to the Qur'anic narrative, Jonah saw a dark cloud approaching the city. He understood that God would punish his people so he left the city and got into a ship. The Qur'an does not give full details of what happened, but the Islamic understanding is basically in line with the Biblical understanding: he was swallowed by a whale. Under such a difficult situation, Jonah prayed to God, calling out within the various layers of darkness, saying, "'There is no deity except You. Exalted are You. Indeed, I have been of the wrongdoers.' So We responded to him and saved him from the distress. And thus do We save the believers" (21:87-8). In the mystical tradition of Islam, the evil-commanding soul is the most dangerous predator aimed at destroying individuals' spiritual lives. It is comparable to the whale that swallowed Jonah. The evil-commanding soul is more dangerous than the whale because the whale was threatening his worldly life, while the evil-commanding soul threatens human beings' eternal lives. Therefore, Muslim mystics repeatedly say this prayer of Jonah from the Qur'an to shield themselves against the evil-commanding soul. Some Muslim mystics use these prayers of Job and Jonah as part of their daily routine prayers, especially between the sunset and evening prayers. Like the Prophetic words that are repeated after prescribed prayer thirty-three times, it is some mystics recommend that one repeat these two prayers thirty-three times between the sunset and evening prayers.

Another example that can be given from the pre-Islamic prophets is the prayer of Zachariah. In this prayer, one can see Zachariah's request to have a son who will carry his message of prophethood. "My Lord, leave me not without offspring, for You are the Best of inheritors" (21:89). The Qur'an says that God responds to Zachariah's prayer by giving him Yahya, the Qur'anic name for John the Baptist. This prayer is a model prayer for Muslims, but one can question whether it is proper for people who do not have children to use this prayer as a request to ask God to grant them children. It is clear that recitation of any verse from the Qur'an is reward-worthy. However, at the same time, one must not make worldly things the main object of their prayers. In the following verse, the qualities of John, Zachariah, and his wife and how they put their trust in God are made clear. In the beginning of chapter 19, "Mary," Zachariah is described as someone who constantly prays, but has become old and is in need of someone to replace him in inviting people to the way of God.

> My Lord, surely my bones are weakened and my head filled with grey hair. And my Lord, I have never been disobedient in my prayer to You. And surely I am fearful for my kin after me and my wife is barren so give me, from Yourself, an heir who shall be my inheritor and the inheritor of the Family of Jacob. And my Lord make him pleasing [to You]. (19:4-6)

Similarly, in chapter 21, Zachariah, his wife, and Yahya are described in this way: "Surely they have vied with one another for good deeds and constantly prayed with great hope and awe. And also they are submissive to Us [God]." (21:90)

Additionally, the Qur'an contains prayers of many other prophets: Lot (29:30), Jacob (12:86), Joseph (12:101), Jethro (7:89), and Jesus (5:114). There are also prayers of other figures, such as the wife of Pharaoh (66:11), the mother of Mary (3:35-7) the People of the Cave or the Seven Sleepers (18:10), the Ribbiyun (3:147), the Israelites (2:250, 10:85-6), and the disciples of Jesus (3:53). There is also a prayer of angels (40:7-9). The Qur'an also refers to the general prayer of all believers in verses: 2:201, 2:286, 3:8-9, 3:16, 3:191-4, 23:109, 25:65-6, and 25:74. There is also the prayer of King Talut, that is, Saul, from when his army was struggling against Jalut, that is, Goliath. They said, "Lord, bestow patience upon us and make firm our feet, and give us aid against the people of the unbelievers" (2:250). The Qur'an narrates that they defeated Goliath and his army. David killed Goliath, and then God gave him the kingdom of Israel, wisdom, and the knowledge of what He wants (2:251) While the prophets have different types of prayers, they all have a common theme, and that is to testify that there is only one God. The Qur'anic verse says, "Worship only God. You have no deity other than God" (23:32). It is believed that because of the importance of this testimony of faith, Muhammad said that "the best of what I have said and what the prophets before me said is the phrase 'La ilaha illa Allah,' 'There is no deity but God.'"[38]

The Qur'an also speaks of the prayer of David and Solomon, who were chosen by God. As seen from the following verse, David and Solomon praise God and thank God for what God had given them. It is interesting to see that the Qur'anic terminology of the prayer of David and Solomon is exactly the terminology that is used today among mystics. It is compatible with the overall teaching of the Qur'an because David and Solomon were those who submitted themselves to the will of God, that is, *muslims*. David and Solomon are both significant figures in the Islamic chain of prophethood. The prayer of David and Solomon is also very well known. According the Qur'an, both David and Solomon are prominent messengers of God. In fact, Solomon, who is presented in Western literature as a person of indulgence, is not compatible with the Qur'anic presentation of Solomon. And this is true for David as well. The Qur'an says that God has given them knowledge as a gift and in response to this both David and Solomon are praising God by saying, "Praise belongs to God who has preferred us over many of His believing servants" (27:15). The Qur'an speaks of Solomon as a person of justice, stating that animals, birds, and even insects were working for him because of a Divine gift, which was his ability to communicate with them. Chapter 27, "The Ants," speaks of the story of an ant who calls the other ants into their dwellings so that Solomon and his soldiers will not step on them unknowingly. According to the Qur'an, Solomon heard the call of this ant and was pleased that God had given him this gift of understanding and prophethood. According to the Qur'an, Solomon prayed to God and said, "My Lord, enable me to be grateful for Your favor which You have bestowed upon me and upon my parents and to do righteousness of which You approve. And admit me by Your mercy into [the ranks of] Your righteous servants" (27:19).[39] There is no doubt among mystics that David and Solomon were experiencing *ihsan*, that is, feeling God at the utmost level. Their prayers and worship were all within this experience of the Divine.

The Qur'an refers to several messengers of God, including Noah, Abraham, Moses, and Aaron, as those who are at the level of *ihsan*, that is, they worship God as if they see God. Specifically, they are all called *muhsinun*, the active participle of the word *ihsan*. In other words, they do what is beautiful. In these verses, it is well understood that the highest position of spiritual life is to be fully a servant of God and to have the utmost level of worship to God. In chapter 17, the Prophet is referred to as God's servant (17:1). Servanthood is directly related to prayer, and prayer is related to the concept of worshipping God as if one sees God. One of the best ways of finding this way of spirituality is contemplation, or what is called contemplative prayer. In Islamic spirituality, contemplation is among the spiritual activities that are referred to in the Qur'an. The Qur'an encourages people to contemplate, and in the following section I will examine some Qur'anic verses on the subject.

# *Tafakkur* or contemplation

Surely, in the creation of the heavens and the earth, and the alternating of night and day, and the ships which run upon the sea with that which is of use to human beings, and the water which God sends down from the sky, thereby reviving the earth after its death, and dispersing all kinds of beasts therein, and in the ordinance of the winds, and the clouds obedient between heaven and earth are signs for people who are mindful. (2:164)

*Tafakkur*, which can be translated as either contemplation or reflection, is an important principle of Islamic spirituality, and it is among the best activities of heart and mind. Through contemplation, one can reach the highest level of understanding the arts of God in the realm of the universe. In fact, it is well known among mystics that one moment of contemplation can be more fruitful than a night-long voluntary prayer.[40] That is to say, sometimes a moment of contemplation becomes a remarkable step toward the understanding of God and can make a big change in the lives of individuals. A verse in chapter 3 of the Qur'an on contemplation says,

Surely in the heavens and earth and in the alternation of night and day there are signs for those who are mindful and those who remember God, standing and sitting and on their sides, and contemplate upon the creation of the heavens and the earth [saying]: "Our Lord, You have not created this for vanity. Glory be to You. Guard us against the chastisement of the Fire." (3: 190-191)

There are many other verses that contain the word *tafakkur* or a derivative of it, which connotes reflection and contemplation.

The Qur'an in many verses encourages human beings to contemplate. For instance, "God subjugated for you what is in the heavens and the earth, all are from Him. In this surely there are signs for those who contemplate" (45:13). The Qur'an frequently says, "Why don't you contemplate?" or "Do they not reflect on themselves?" and strongly suggests that human beings should contemplate on their lives, both physical and spiritual. Again, the invitation to contemplation is very clear: "Tell them the story so they may reflect" (7:176), or, "This way we are explaining to those who reflect and contemplate" (10:24). Another verse makes a connection between the Qur'an and contemplation on the Qur'an. "And we have sent down to you the Remembrance [the Qur'an] that you may explain to human beings what was sent down to them so hopefully they will reflect" (16:44). This is a powerful invitation from the Qur'an to all human beings who have reason and mind to contemplate on the Divine arts in nature, in human beings, and in the universe.

The Qur'an asks its readers to observe and reflect on how all elements of the universe, including the earth and human beings, are interconnected. Of special importance is how earth, and what is on it, and celestial bodies are subjugated to human beings. In many verses the Qur'an asks for reflection on the creation of the heavens and the earth, the sun and the moon, stars, mountains, trees, and animals. According to the Qur'anic verse, all these are themes to be contemplated upon. They are not created by chance and are not acting on their own behalf, but are subjugated by God to the service of human beings (22:18).

In the sight of God, human beings are the most important creatures, and as such it is important to elaborate further on this element of contemplation. Contemplation on the creation of human beings leads to spiritual elevation. First, the Qur'an speaks of the creation of human beings as a family and the beginning of the creation of humanity, and then it draws readers' attention to the creation of every individual human being, how they develop from a sperm into a full human being, and invites people to contemplate this creation. Listing the stages in the creation of human beings, the Qur'anic verse says,

> We have created human beings from an extraction of clay, then We set them, a drop, in a secure receptacle, then We created of the drop a clot then We created of the clot a tissue then We created of the tissue bones then We covered the bones in flesh; thereafter We produced them as another creature. So blessed be God, the Most-Beautiful of creators. And then after that you will die then on the Day of Resurrection you will be resurrected. (23:12-16)

All of these bounties, which are the subject of contemplation, should not be taken for granted. All of these activities are not done in vain. The creation of them is for contemplation. The Qur'an asks readers to deepen their contemplation and then be thankful. The Holy Book of Islam says:

> Say, "Have you considered if God should make for you the night continuous until the Day of Resurrection, what deity other than God could bring you light? Then will you not hear?" Say, "Have you considered if God should make for you the day continuous until the Day of Resurrection, what deity other than God could bring you a night in which you may rest? Then will you not see? And out of His mercy He made for you the night and the day that you may rest therein and seek from His bounty and perhaps you will be grateful?" (28:71-73)

Such contemplation must lead to the understanding of Divine mercy, since the cycle of day and night is the result of the mercy of God. In other words, it is the work of God's mercy, and therefore the Qur'an indicates that such an event is not random. Through contemplation, one will see the mercy of God in it. As one understands from this Qur'anic verse, the eyes of thought or heart will open to the mercy of God through contemplation. Such an important reflection on the works of God will lead to thankfulness.

Therefore, the end of the verse suggests that if human beings hear and see the art of God in the cycles of day and night, they will become more thankful.

The Qur'an as the most important source of Islamic spirituality, refers to the Prophet of Islam as a beautiful example for believers: "The Messenger of God is certainly a beautiful example for those of you who have hope in God and in the afterlife and who remember God often" (33:21). Therefore, in the following chapter I will elaborate on spirituality in the life, the actions, and the sayings of the Prophet.

# 3

# The spirituality of the Prophet of Islam

Before examining the Prophet of Islam, it is important to briefly discuss the place of prophets and prophethood in the Qur'an. From the first prophet, Adam, to the last, Muhammad, all prophets came with the message from God to humanity. While the specifics of the messages may have differed slightly based on the circumstances of each prophet, the individual messages contain no contradictions from one prophet to the next. More importantly for present purposes, each prophet is considered an exemplary individual who should be emulated. Hence, the Qur'an says of Abraham, "Surely in Abraham and those with him, there is an excellent example for you" (60:4). While the prophets' prayers and deeds are the most generally regarded prophetic elements to be emulated, their miracles also present important models of emulation for human beings. While most human beings may not be able to perform miracles, per se, within the Islamic tradition, miracles can be seen as examples of future technological and scientific advances. Prophetic stories show how spirituality and modern technological advances can be combined; they are not separate, distinct entities. Both the Qur'an and the Hadith present these figures with their stories. Looking at these stories from such a spiritual perspective is significant and also relevant to the understanding of our time, as inundated with and obsessed, rightly or wrongly, as we are with technology. Therefore, according to this aspect of Islamic spirituality, in order to have spiritual development, you do not need to abandon technology and a modern lifestyle. In fact, from this perspective, Islamic spirituality encourages technology that helps with easing the life conditions of people. While this perspective is present and theologically viable, at the same time one must not forget that spirituality is ultimately about the needs of the soul, and bodily happiness cannot satisfy the soul. The happiness of the soul has to be spiritual; a person whose body is in Paradise and whose soul is in Hell cannot be considered happy. Therefore, the Prophet of Islam has presented a paradigm for spirituality. He was in the world, with the world, but also at the utmost level of spirituality. He married, raised children, He was not a wealthy person, but was grateful for what he had. He was a thankful person and asked his community to follow him.

In sum, one can argue that the Qur'anic stories of the prophets should be understood in a way that encourages human beings to develop their spiritual as well as earthly lives through science and technology. Readers of the Qur'an should not read its stories merely as histories but as lessons for both spiritual and technological developments. This seems to have been the way the early Muslims read the text. We can deduce from this that there is no contradiction between science, technology, and spirituality. On the contrary, the Qur'an encourages the study of the sciences in order to use them for the benefit of humanity. More broadly, in Islam there is no contradiction between science and religion. That is because one searches for the created book of God, nature, and the other searches for the revealed book of God, the Qur'an. It is clear from the Qur'anic perspective, therefore, that material development must coincide with spiritual development. These are like two wings by which humans can achieve the felicity of this life and the afterlife. In other words, the Qur'an encourages humanity to imitate the prophets in their art and in their heart, in the science they pioneered and in their spirit.

In what follows, I will briefly examine the stories of a few of the most well-known prophets for what they can tell us about the relationship between spirituality and technology.

# Abraham: A pioneer of fire-proof equipment

The story of Abraham is extensive and well-documented in the Qur'an. In one portion of his story as narrated in the Qur'an, Abraham broke the idols of his people, and as a result, they wanted to punish him by throwing him into the fire. When the Assyrian King, Nimrod, ordered him thrown into the fire, he was not burned. On this, the Qur'an says as follows: "We [God] said: 'O Fire, be of coolness and peace for Abraham'" (21:69). The verse implies that there are two kinds of protective clothes against fire: spiritual and physical. The spiritual kind, which protects against the fire of Hell, is faith in God, while the physical protective cloth consists of the equipment someone wears that disables the fire from burning them physically. According to spiritual commentators, the verse adeptly encourages obtainment of both spiritual and physical protections, as God has preserved for humans such elements to protect them against fire. Through this verse, human beings are asked to search for, find, and wear the appropriate protections, and indeed modern fire-retardant suits are a reflection of this Qur'anic verse.

# Moses: Pioneer of technical equipment for finding water

Moses, as one of the greatest prophets in Islam, is mentioned in the Qur'an in various contexts. The story of his miracle that concerns us here deals with geology and technical equipment, describing how the earth can be excavated to bring out water and other natural resources, such as petroleum and natural gas, for the benefit of humankind. This verse encourages humanity to find resources within the earth, so as to prevent future wars over, for example, limited sources of water, thus bringing peace to humankind. With regard to the miracle of Moses in this context, the Qur'anic verse reads: "And when Moses asked for water for his people, We said: 'Strike the rock with your staff' and there gushed out twelve springs" (2:60). The verse suggests that even with very simple equipment, the extraction of water and other substances can be managed. A commentary on the verse says that it is as if God says,

> O Human Kind: I gave one of My servants, Moses, who trusted in Me, such a staff, by means of which he could find the water wherever he wanted. If you also rely on the laws of My mercy, you will be able to find such equipment to bring out the most essential element of life, water, wherever you want. Go ahead and find it.[1]

Following the spirituality of Moses is not just to follow his trust in God or his prayers, but it is to follow his work for justice and his efforts at finding technologies that will benefit human beings.

# Solomon: Pioneer of air transportation and modern communications technologies

In the Qur'an, Solomon is regarded not only as a king, but also as a prophet and a messenger of God. God granted him His permission to perform miracles in order that Solomon might prove that he spoke on behalf of God. The most famous Qur'anic verse about the miracles of Solomon has to do with Solomon's traveling a long distance by means of the wind. As the story unfolds in the Qur'an, Solomon was able to ride the wind and travel throughout his kingdom and among his people to listen to and do justice for them. He also possessed an ability to give a variety of shapes to melted copper and was able to subjugate the *jinn*, unseen creatures parallel to humans, and through knowledge from God was able to employ the *jinn* in the construction of buildings and bringing things from far distances. "We have subjugated the wind to Solomon, so that he may go a two-month distance in one day and We caused the fount of copper to gush forth for him and We gave him certain of the *jinn* who worked for him by permission of his Lord" (34:12). The first part of the verse hints at the importance of discovering a means of flying over long distances; that is, it portends the invention of the airplane. The Qur'an, as indicated in this verse, has been calling upon humanity to discover an aerodynamic system for almost fifteen hundred years, and there is evidence to suggest that early Muslims sought such technology.

There is another technology found in the story of Solomon and the Queen of Sheba. The Queen was a sun-worshipper and Solomon wanted to invite her to believe in God, an invitation that she eventually accepted. The Qur'anic verse explains how Solomon asked his assistants to bring her throne to him miraculously: "Said the one who had a sort of knowledge of the Book, 'I will bring it to you in the twinkling of an eye.' Then when Solomon saw it brought to him firmly, he said: 'This is from the grace of my Lord'" (27.40). The miracle that God gave Solomon hints at today's mass-communication devices and technologies. It suggests that the transmission of sound, vision, and even matter is possible and encourages human beings to find them. Various telecommunication systems are mentioned in this verse, which draws attention to a broader frame of scientific development: the transmission of material things surpassing even the speed of light. Although scientists have discussed the possibility of the latter idea, it has not yet been realized. Still, we may draw the principle that the Qur'an elucidates this long-range target for scientists. It not only encourages people to seek the above-mentioned equipment and abilities, but also to transform the earth into a garden of peace, the inhabitants of which can easily communicate with one another, presenting their thankfulness to God, the One who has subjugated all of these comforts to them.

# Jesus: Pioneer of medical sciences

In connection with the story of Jesus, the Qur'an says: "And I heal the blind and the leper, and I quicken the dead, by God's permission" (3:49). According to commentators, this Qur'anic verse indicates that the most evident miracles by which Jesus urged people to follow his way were his healings of illnesses. Accordingly, Jesus is a medical doctor as well as a prophet and messenger of God. By implication, this suggests there is a cure for every illness through the miracles of Jesus. As such, the verse encourages the development of medical sciences in order to find non-miraculous cures for all kinds of diseases. Thus, humans have to search for and discover these treatments, and at the same time they must follow the spirituality of Jesus.

To put it another way, humans should develop the medical sciences, without forgetting God. Following that rubric, medical sciences would then reflect God's beautiful names. Of those, reflections of His name, *al-Shafi* (the Healer), would be reflected through medical development and, through this, research would become meaningful and even sacred. If we advance discussion on the verse's implications, it follows that there must be a cure for cancer and the AIDS virus. It is humanity's responsibility to labor and discover these cures. In the Qur'anic understanding, the earth is like a Divine pharmacy, and the doctors and researchers are like pharmacists, whose purpose is to discover the medicines, which the earth provides. Jesus is considered the pioneer of this concept. Muslim commentators have very beautiful comments about this miracle of Jesus. For our purposes, I have chosen a quote from a spiritual commentary from a modern Islamic scholar. Accordingly, through this verse, God addresses human beings as if God says the following,

O human kind: I [God] gave to Jesus, who left the desires of worldly life for my sake, two gifts. Through them he cures spiritual illnesses as well as physical diseases. Thus, the dead hearts were coming to life by his guidance and the sick who were almost dead were enlivened by his breath and medicine. So, you, O humans, could also find medicine for your illnesses in the pharmacy of My wisdom. Then work hard and find it. If you search, surely you will find it.[2]

# The Prophet of Islam

In addition to the earlier prophets, the Prophet of Islam is also an example to be emulated. Scholars are in agreement that among the most well-known religious figures, Prophet Muhammad's life and actions are the most recorded and accessible. His life was so well documented that we know most, if not all, of his prayers and actions through the various narrations of his companions. As he is an example for believers (33:21), he is also a mercy for all the worlds (21:107). The Qur'an itself speaks of the night prayers of the Prophet (73:20), which for him were prescribed, unlike for his community. Additional information about the prayers of the Prophet comes from his wife, 'Aisha. 'Aisha narrates that the Messenger of God had a mat he would lay out during the day and use as a divider during the night, and he would pray behind it. People learned that the Prophet had long night prayers, and they wanted to pray what the Prophet prayed. They would come to the Prophet and pray as the Prophet did, with only the mat to divide them. The Prophet was afraid for his community and said, "Do of good deeds [prayer] what you are able to do. Surely God does not get tired at all, but you will get tired. The most beloved of deeds in the sight of God are the continuing ones even if they are small." 'Aisha further narrated that because of the fear that people would put too much burden upon themselves, the Prophet left that place of prayer until God took his soul. 'Aisha adds that the Prophet was thorough. When the Prophet did something he would do it completely.[3]

If one were to summarize the life of the Prophet with one word, that word would emphatically be prayer. Besides his prescribed daily prayers, he had voluntary prayers between the morning and noon prayers, as well as between the sunset and evening prayers. The prior is called the Prayer of Duha and the latter is called the Prayer of Awwabin. Besides these *salat*, or prayers that are performed through regimented bodily movements and vocalizations, he also had numerous *dua*, or vocal prayers of supplication. All major hadith collections have sections on his spiritual life, and they present this as an example for believers. To give but one example, al-Bukhari's *Al-Sahih* would perhaps be the best. This collection is also known as the most reliable collection of the sayings of the Prophet because of the strict criteria employed by the author when he collected the sayings. The spiritual life of the Prophet is found in various sections of this collection. Al-Bukhari has sections on the Prophet's first encounter with revelation, the Prophet's fasting, supplications, *raqa'iq* or piety in the life of the Prophet,[4] and *da'awat* or prayers of the Prophet.

In the section on *da'awat*, al-Bukhari records a variety of prayers of the Prophet. For instance, there is a prayer which is known as the best prayer for asking God for forgiveness:

O God, you are my Lord. There is no god other than You. You have created me and I am Your servant and I abide to Your covenant and promise as best as I can. I take refuge in You from the evil I might have committed. I acknowledge Your favor upon me and I acknowledge my sin. Forgive me. Surely none can forgive sin except You.[5]

In the Islamic tradition, prophets are considered innocents and sinless. According to Islamic theology, they have a quality called *isma,* which can be translated as "protected from sin." This is a quality that is given to all prophets of God, and all Muslims believe that God protects His prophets and messengers from sin. Since this is the case, Muslim theologians would ask, why then would the Prophet have this prayer? They would respond that the Prophet wanted to set an example for his community and the believers. The Prophet himself says, "Daily I ask forgiveness from God and repent to God more than seventy times."[6] Similarly, there are some prayers the Prophet said before going to sleep. One is short and says, "My Lord, with Your name I die and in Your name I am resurrected."[7] There is another similar prayer the Prophet said before going to sleep:

My Lord, I have submitted my soul to You. I have trusted my affairs to You. I directed my face to You. And I rely on You in hope and awe of

You completely. Surely, there is no refuge or safe haven from You except with You. I believed in Your Book You have revealed and in the Prophet You have sent.[8]

It is important to note that belief in the Prophet of Islam requires belief in all other prophets of God. Therefore, devout Muslims every evening before sleep renew their belief in the prophets and messengers of God. Resting with such a belief in all messengers of God aims to bring tranquility to the lives of all believers. Likewise, there are many prayers of the Prophet one can say upon awakening. One of them is: "All praises belong to God who gives us life after having taken it. The final return is to God."[9]

Al-Bukhari records that the Prophet one night woke up and prayed eleven units of prayer, during which he said the following: "My Lord make a light in my heart. Make a light in my eyes. Make a light on my right and make a light on my left. Make a light on top of me and make light under me. Make a light in front of me and a light behind me. Make a light for me."[10] The connotations of light in the Islamic tradition are guidance, truthfulness, etc. It is as if the Prophet was saying this against the darkness of the night, asking for the Divine light against darkness, which represents disbelief and hopelessness.

On a variety of occasions, Islamic scholars and mystics have put together the sayings of the Prophet. There are numerous books, websites, and now even apps which collect many of the prayers and supplications of the Prophet. One book in my collection contains 137 prayers on subjects from waking in the morning and going to sleep at night to wearing clothing and eating and drinking to entering a restroom or a house of worship.[11] This genre of vocal prayers of the Prophet is very well known in the Islamic spiritual tradition and in the circles of Muslim mystics. There are a variety of examples of this genre, and perhaps the most well known of them is al-Nawawi's (d. 1277) *Al-Adhkar*, which has been highly esteemed since Ottoman times, and printed and reprinted in various forms. This is considered a book of devotion. For example, al-Nawawi starts his book with the prayers that the Prophet used to say by day and night. Following this, al-Nawawi mentions the Prophet's emphasis of recitations of the Qur'an as a *dhikr*. Al-Nawawi says, "The best of *dhikr* is recitation of the Qur'an."[12] Under this section, al-Nawawi mentions various of the Prophet's sayings with regard to the merits of certain Qur'anic chapters.

The Prophet would encourage his companions to do actions that would help with their spirituality with regard to the needs of individuals. The Prophet had great wisdom regarding what to recommend to whom. For some he would recommend vocal prayers, while for others he would recommend fasting. For example, in a well-known hadith, Abu Umama al-Bahili (d. 700) comes to the Prophet and says, "'O Messenger of God, command me with a command that I take from you and God will make it beneficial for me.' The Messenger of God said: 'Stick to fasting. Surely it has no equivalent.'"[13]

As the Qur'an says, following the Prophet is essential for the love of God. "Say [O Muhammad]: If you love God, then follow me. God will love you and forgive you of your sin, and God is the Most-Forgiving, the Most-Merciful." (3:31) This verse states that following the Prophet of Islam, and for that matter all other prophets of God, results in the love of God. And the love of God is the goal of Islamic spirituality. They are connected to each other, love of God and following the practices of the Prophet. In Islamic spirituality, when one speaks of following the way of the Prophet, it includes following the way of the earlier prophets. Perhaps for this reason Muslims in the daily prayers, after praying for peace and blessings for the Prophet of Islam and his family, immediately pray for Abraham and his family as well.

O God, bestow Your mercy on Muhammad and on the family of Muhammad, as You bestowed Your mercy on Abraham and on the family of Abraham, for You are the Most-Praiseworthy, the Most-Glorious. O God, bestow Your blessings on Muhammad and the family of Muhammad, as You bestowed your blessings on Abraham and on the family of Abraham, for You are the Most-Praiseworthy, the Most-Glorious.

# The *Mi'raj*

Literally, *mi'raj* means ladder for ascension. The Prophet was taken from Mecca to Jerusalem, and from there the Prophet ascended to Heaven, met with God, and came back bringing the five daily prayers as a religious obligation for his community. The event is mentioned briefly in the Qur'an and in a detailed way in the Hadith. Chapter Seventeen of the Qur'an is called "*Al-Isra*" and *al-Isra* or the Night Journey is the name given to the first part of the *Mi'raj*, the departure of the Prophet from Mecca to Jerusalem. The first verse of the chapter states, "Glory be to Whom did take His servant for a Journey by night from the Sacred Mosque [in Mecca] to the farthest Mosque [in Jerusalem], whose precincts We did bless so that We might show him some of Our signs. Surely He is the All-Hearing and All-Seeing" (17:1). There are other verses which indicate the Prophet saw God. Most notable is the first part of chapter 53, "*Al-Najm*" or "The Star" (verses 1-18). Because of the significance of this event, Islamic piety has developed a specific genre on chanting and remembering this experience of the Prophet. In many Islamic countries, *Laylat al-Mi'raj*, which occurs on the twenty-seventh of the month of *Rajab*, the seventh month of the Islamic calendar, is celebrated annually as a holy night. This Prophetic experience is believed to have happened in a very short period of time, and Muslim mystics believe that this is an example of being close to God. Generally it is interpreted to have happened bodily and spiritually, not in this dimension but in another dimension. The angel Gabriel with the Prophet entered that dimension and passed through various levels of heaven, and in each level, the Prophet met with a messenger of God. For example, the Prophet of Islam met with Adam, Enoch, Moses, Jesus, and Abraham. According to this story, Adam was in the first layer of heaven, while Abraham was in the sixth. Whenever the Prophet passed, these messengers of God said, "The wholesome brother and the wholesome Prophet is welcome." This was repeated by each prophet as they saw the Prophet of Islam. It is believed that the Prophet reached a level at which the angel Gabriel said, "I am not allowed to pass this line, but you go ahead because you are invited." That is believed to be the line between Divinity and creation, i.e. necessary and contingent existence. This line in Islamic mysticism is known as *Qab Qawsayn*. Literally, this refers to the distance of two bows, but it is understood to mean the distance of two eyebrows.

The portion of the *Mi'raj* just prior to and during when the Prophet first encounters God is known as the *Tashahhud*. This is believed by some to be the conversation that took place between God and the Prophet during the *Mi'raj*. There are two versions of this prayer, in one of which the Prophet says,

All praises belong to God, and all mercy and all good belong to God. God says, "Peace be upon you, O Prophet, and the mercy of God and His blessings be with you." The Prophet says, "Peace be upon us [Your servants] and upon all righteous servants of God. I bear witness that there is no deity except God and I bear witness that Muhammad is His servant and His Messenger."

This lofty conversation is repeated in every two units of prayers, either prescribed or voluntary. Regarding the prayer, it is believed that when the Prophet said "peace be upon us," he meant angels—specifically archangels— all prophets of God—specifically those he met during his journey—and all saints and other righteous people, which is to say his prayer is encompassing.

During the *Mi'raj* of the Prophet, God commanded the Prophet's community to pray fifty times a day. The hadith has a beautiful and brotherly advisory conversation between Moses and the Prophet of Islam on this. The Prophet narrates his experience,

God prescribed on my community fifty prayers a day and I turned back and I passed by Moses and he asked "What did God prescribe on your community?" I said "fifty." Moses said, "Go back to your Lord. Surely your community will not make it." I went back and God reduced to half . . .

This continues until the number five is reached. At this point, when the Prophet returns to Moses and Moses again tells him to return, the Prophet of Islam tells Moses, "Now I feel shy of asking my Lord again."[14]

*Mi'raj Nameh* has become a literary genre in the Islamic tradition. This includes poems, stories, and illustrations of the Prophet riding a mysterious mount called *al-Buraq* to ascend through the heavens and meet with the Divine. Muslim mystics have wondered if they can have this Prophetic experience to a certain extent via their prayers. The Prophet says, "Prayer is the *mi'raj* of the believer." This is not a well-known hadith, but some scholars and mystics refer to it as such.[15] Within prayer, the position in which one is closest to God is in prostration, *sujud*. Therefore, while there is no way to make the *Mi'raj* of the Prophet, there is a way to make one's own *mi'raj*: through prayer and prostration. The Prophet himself after his *Mi'raj* experience would spend long periods of time in prostration, and he encouraged believers to do more prostrations and to have more requests from God in their prostrations, because this is when they are in the state closest to God. Therefore, *mi'raj* is not something that ever ends. It continues throughout the lives of mystics through constant prostrations.

# Blessings for the Prophet

One of the aspects of the *mi'raj* is frequently asking for blessing for the Prophet of Islam. *Salat* and *salam*, or blessings and peace for the Prophet are an important part of the Islamic tradition. In fact, it is a Qur'anic command for Muslims to request blessings for the Prophet. "God and His angels bless the Prophet. O believers, you should also ask God to bless and give him peace" (33:56). There is also a strong hadith tradition which encourages asking for peace and blessings for the Prophet, and that the Prophet himself becomes aware of such blessings. Muslim mystics have developed their own style of asking for peace and blessings for the Prophet from God.

The scholars of hadith, while compiling the sayings of the Prophet, categorized them and put them into sections. Some of them focus on the prayers of the Prophet. Others focus on the Prophet's fasting or acts of charity, etc. For instance, the most prominent Hadith collector, al-Bukhari, has a section on the depth of faith, which can be found under the title "*Kitab al-Iman*," or "The Book of Faith." He includes religious practices, such as retreat, which as an Islamic practice can be found in "*Kitab al-I'tikaf*" or "The Book of Retreat." While various prayers, both prescribed and voluntary, which include both verbal and actions such as gestures of bowing and prostrating, can be found in the section called "*Kitab al-Salat*," and occasional prayers, especially those practiced by the Prophet, can be found in "*Kitab al-Da'awat*." Likewise, the Prophet's practice of fasting, both prescribed and voluntary, can be found in "*Kitab al-Siyam*," or "The Book of Fasting." The recitation of the Qur'an as a spiritual practice can be found in the section called "*Kitab Fada'il al-Qur'an*." Themes, such as the importance of the afterlife, the deceptive nature of this worldly life, poverty and wealth as a test for human beings, the virtue of patience, the spiritual danger of gossiping, respect for the Divine, shedding tears out of Divine respect, ascetic life, the danger of showing off, the virtue of humbleness, and love and yearning for the meeting with the Divine are all cited and discussed in the Hadith literature under the section called "*Kitab al-Raqa'iq*," or "The Book of Piety."

The Qur'an essentially says that prayer and humble supplications lead to salvation in this life and also in the afterlife. Therefore, the Prophet of Islam, whose life was in total compliance with the Qur'anic ideal, is known as the "Sultan of Worshippers." He would open his hands, turn to his Lord, overflow with thanks and glorification, bow and double himself up in prayer, and constantly pray to God. He did this throughout his life. He woke up every morning and performed his daily prayers, both prescribed and voluntary. He stayed in God's presence at night and spent most of his night in prayer. He would continue his prayer even while eating, going to bed, traveling, returning from a campaign, confronting an enemy, experiencing worldly or heavenly disasters, witnessing miraculous events, and suffering from illnesses or troubles. There are specific books dedicated to the Prophet's prayers, which give more details about all of his supplications. For every occasion, the Prophet used to say a special prayer. These prayers have been used by Muslims throughout the history of Islam.

# 4

# Ideas and concepts

*O believers, remember God very often.*

QUR'AN 33:41

There are many ideas and concepts that could be described in such a chapter. To simplify what could otherwise be a taxing and confusing amount of words and definitions, I would like to give the basic ideas of Islamic spirituality through the analogy of a ladder. In its most basic form, this ladder has three steps. The first is *iman bi Allah*, or faith in God. The second is *ma'rifat Allah*, or the knowledge of God. The third is *mahabbat Allah*, or the love of God. This last step corresponds with the concept of *ihsan*, or doing what is beautiful, as mentioned in the hadith of Gabriel when the angel Gabriel appears to the Prophet of Islam and asks questions about faith, submission, doing what is beautiful, and the final hour.

Most manuals of Islamic spirituality consist of long sections on various important concepts in the Islamic spiritual tradition. One of the early works on the subject, Abd al-Karim al-Qushayri's *Al-Risale al-Qushayriyya*, which has been translated into English as *Principles of Sufism*,[1] describes forty key spiritual themes. These include positive elements—repentance, fear of God, spiritual jihad, that is, striving against earthly desires, hope, contentment, trust in God, thankfulness, patience, sincerity, truthfulness, and remembrance—and negative themes, such as envy, backbiting, and jealousy.

In our era, one of the prominent figures who has elaborated on the theme of Islamic spirituality is Fethullah Gulen. In the first two books of his *Kalbin Zümrüt Tepeleri*, published in English as *Emerald Hills of the Heart: Key Concepts in the Practice of Sufism*, he defines approximately 100 terms and concepts of importance to Islamic spirituality. As this collection spans four volumes, there is a significant amount of information here on Sufism and the Islamic spiritual tradition. In the present chapter, I hope to build upon these sources and bring a new approach to find a way of integrating the themes discussed by mystics with lived experiences. I also hope that what is here is refreshingly brief and easily accessible. My approach then is not to simply list and define concepts, but to integrate them into a discussion of how these ideas can be incorporated into the human experience. In any given day in the life of a human being, these concepts emerge and are experienced in a variety of ways, and can be seen as a key organizing principle of everyday life.

Human beings are made of body and soul, and as such are constantly involved with these concepts. Since the level of human beings in the Islamic pyramid of creation is not static, but is changing constantly, these concepts are experienced in a very real way by each human being.[2] Even in otherwise mundane tasks such as eating, sleeping, and speaking, one can see a variety of these spiritual concepts involved.

## *Shukr* or thankfulness

One of the most important elements to be constantly practiced and felt is thankfulness, or *shukr*. As one Persian poet and mystic, Saadi Shirazi (d. 1291) said, "Every breath contains two blessings, life in the inhalation and the expulsion of stale and useless breath in the exhalation. Thank God, then twice for each breath."[3] Some mystics go even further by saying that for this opportunity to be thankful, another thankfulness is necessary, and therefore the chain of thankfulness continues. This is why it is impossible to fully thank God, the Owner of the gifts. It is also why angels, who constantly praise and worship God, will say in the afterlife, "Lord, you are exalted. We have not worshiped You as You deserve."[4]

The Qur'an frequently mentions the importance of thankfulness. In some verses (e.g., 2:243, 10:60, 12:38, 27:73, and 31:14), it states that people have to be thankful for the bounties of God. It also states that few people are truly thankful to God. "It is God Who has made the night for you to rest and the day for you to see. Indeed, God is the Owner of bounties for human beings, but most people are not thankful to Him" (40:61). These verses indicate the importance of thankfulness in Islamic spirituality as well as for the spiritual well-being of all human beings.

Therefore, even a simple action such as eating requires thankfulness. Prior to eating, the Prophet recommended that one invoke the Divine names and in this there is *dhikr*, remembrance. Generally, one should repeat the formula which is known as the *Bismillah*, and is also the first verse of the first chapter of the Qur'an. It goes as follows: "In the name of God the Most-Compassionate, the Most-Merciful." Here three Divine names are invoked. These are Allah, *al-Rahman*, and *al-Rahim*. The Islamic tradition suggests that at the beginning of everything that is good, one has to say this formula. This is the foundation of the mystical tradition of *dhikr*. Muslim mystics have taken this Islamic principle and added more Divine names and more chants in their circles of remembrance of God. Returning to the example of eating, during the course of eating, one has to contemplate on how the food has been prepared and the processes that the food has passed through from the farm to the table. This contemplation, known also as *tafakkur*, becomes an important theme of Islamic spirituality to the extent that a moment of it may become so reward-worthy as to be the equivalent of many voluntary prayers. Among mystics, it is believed that contemplation of the food that is given by God is more delicious than the food itself. In this, there is a combination of thankfulness, remembrance, and contemplation. When the eating is over, there should be thankfulness to the One who provides it, and that is the real Owner, the real Maker. The Prophet used to say after eating, "Praise be to God, the One who provided us with food and water and made us among those who submitted themselves to God."[5] The Prophet also used to say before going to bed, "Praise be to God, the One who provided us with food and water and sufficed us and sheltered us. How many people don't have enough to suffice themselves and no place to shelter themselves?"[6] Thus regular, simple eating with such beautiful intentions—remembering, contemplating, and being thankful—becomes enlightened, as if it moves from darkness to the light, and become an act of worship. In other words, thankfulness turns regular actions into actions of worship.

# *Tawba* or repentance

Similarly, speaking is an action that involves various Islamic spiritual concepts. Speaking the truth or truthfulness is one of the most important themes of Islamic spirituality. In fact, the Prophet praised the concept of truthfulness, to the point of noting that every truthful person will eventually be in Paradise. That is to say, God will create venues and opportunities for such a person to become a believer and end up in Paradise. Within the concept of speaking, knowingly or unknowingly, human beings may make some mistakes. These mistakes require repentance. If the mistakes involve the rights of others, whether material or spiritual, one has to find the person and ask for his or her forgiveness. For example, mockery, backbiting, and slander are among the most significant elements of human beings' relationships with each other that the Qur'an prohibits.

> O believers, do not let a group of men ridicule another. Perhaps some are better than the others. Do not let women ridicule each other; perhaps one is better than the others. Let not one of you slander another nor call each other by [disgraceful] nicknames. How terrible is such defamation after having true faith. Those who do not repent are certainly wrongdoers. O believers, stay away from conjecture; some conjectures are sin. Do not spy and let not some of you backbite each other. Would you like to eat the flesh of your dead brother? Surely you will find it disgusting. Be pious towards God. Surely God is the Most-Accepting of repentance and the Most-Merciful. (49:11-2)

For the utterances of such negative words, the two Divine names indicate a very important concept in Islamic spirituality. That is *tawba,* or repentance. Repentance is to be practiced for all bad deeds. In fact, some mystics of high spiritual level practice *tawba* for even negative thoughts and imaginings. However, generally speaking, human beings are not held to account for their thoughts so long as they are not put into action.

The Qur'an invites people to repent: "O you who have believed, repent to God with sincere repentance. It is hoped that your Lord will expiate your bad deeds and bring you into Gardens beneath which rivers flow" (66:8). Another verse, relating the story of Jethro, who commanded believers to ask their Lord for forgiveness and to repent to their Lord, says, "Surely my Lord is the Most-Merciful and the Most-Loving" (11:90). There is a similar verse in the story of Noah. Here Noah speaks to his people and says, "Ask forgiveness of your Lord. Surely, He is ever the Most-Forgiving" (71:10). Again the Qur'an speaks of a group of people who intentionally commit bad deeds. The verse says, "And those who, when they commit an immorality or wrong themselves, remember God and seek forgiveness for their sins. And who can forgive sins except God? And they do not knowingly insist on what they did" (3:135).

Relatedly, many anthologies of the sayings of the Prophet have dedicated a section to the concept of repentance. If one counted all of the sayings, there would be more than 100. A few stand out from the hadith on the subject. In one, the Prophet says, "All Children of Adam make mistakes, the best of those who frequently make mistakes are those who frequently repent."[7] In Arabic, this hadith puts a grammatical emphasis, which connotes frequent or constant repenting, on the word that indicates the repenting person. There is another hadith in which the Prophet and his companions saw a woman embracing her child with tremendous compassion and love, to which the Prophet said, "God is more compassionate to His servants than this woman is to her child."[8]

According to the nature of the bad actions and their types, the ways of repentance also differ. If a bad deed involves a transgression on the rights of human beings, whether material or verbal, such as stealing someone's property or backbiting someone, etc., the way of repentance for such an action is to go to the person and sincerely ask for his or her forgiveness. If the transgression relates to a material thing, that thing should also be returned to the rightful owner. This is a type of repentance that is practiced with regard to transgressions on individual's rights. The other group of bad deeds relate to the rights of God, that is, transgressions against God. For these types of transgressions, sincere repentance is necessary. God is happy with the repentance of human beings, regardless of the magnitude of the sin. There is no hopelessness in Islam. As the Qur'an says, "Say [O Muhammad]: 'O My [God's] servants who have been reckless against their souls, do not despair of the mercy of God; surely God forgives all sins; surely He is the Most-Forgiving, the Most-Merciful'" (39:53). Furthermore, in the Islamic spiritual tradition, there are some sinful actions that are considered great sins. In other words, these are sinful actions that can destroy the spiritual lives of individuals. Generally Islamic scholars have mentioned various types of "great sins," which are akin to the Christian concept of the deadly sins. The great sins include murder, dishonoring one's parents, adultery, bearing false witness, etc. A Qur'anic verse says, "If you avoid great sins that have been prohibited to you, We will remove from you your lesser sins and admit you to a noble place [Paradise]" (4:31). There are hundreds of Qur'anic verses that speak of the importance of repentance. Perhaps for this reason, repentance is the first step in Islamic spirituality.

For initiation into the Sufi orders, the first thing that the novice must do is repent. Traditionally, the novice holds the hand of the master and tells him or her in a general way about their desire for repentance, without mentioning the sins or their types. The initiate promises that he or she will never return to those sins that they have committed. That is the first initiation into the mystical path. In the non-attached mystical traditions, because there is no master, there is no holding the hand of the master. Instead, an individual by his or her own initiative repents to God. Once a person repents, it is believed that God removes all the sins of the individual. In the mystical tradition, even if one repents there is no guarantee that the sin was removed. Therefore, one has to remain humble and not act as if one is sinless, and all the while remain hopeful that God accepts the repentance. Repentance does not need to be in the presence of someone else, and individuals are not recommended to mention their sins to others. They are to mention them only to God, and ask only God for forgiveness, as repentance is something between an individual and God. In fact, according to Islamic spirituality, one is not supposed to mention one's sins to others lest they become witnesses in the afterlife against the sinner.

One should ask God for forgiveness on a daily basis to prevent the accumulation of sin in one's spiritual life. The Prophet, to serve as an example for his community, used to ask forgiveness seventy times a day. He would say, "Lord, forgive my sins that I know and my sins that I do not know."[9] God, through one of His ninety-nine names, *al-Tawwab*, accepts repentance from people even if they repent at the last moment of their lives. As a principle, though, people should not delay their *tawba* to the last moment, since they might not have a chance to do it then.

Having said this, there are also conditions for the acceptance of repentance. Mystics have elaborated on the conditions for repentance, but three of them are common to all mystics and theologians. One is to feel really sorry and sad for what has been done. The second is to firmly and decisively quit that bad deed. Third is to steadfastly decide to not return to that bad deed again. Interestingly, there are also some occasions when repentance is much more likely to be accepted, such as during the month of Ramadan and the days of pilgrimage. It is hoped that going on pilgrimage for the sake of God, performing the requirements, and repenting during the pilgrimage results in the removal of sins. The Prophet says, "Anyone who goes on pilgrimage and is not violent and does not violate the rules of pilgrimage, he or she returns [home] as if newly born with no sin."[10] Another statement of the Prophet suggests that repentance is always acceptable until the last moment of a person's life. "Surely God accepts the repentance of His servants until the agony of death."[11]

In other words, though it is highly recommended that one repents as soon as possible, that does not mean a later repentance is not acceptable. Repentance of any sin washes it away, and therefore earlier repentance prevents accumulation of sin. The Prophet mentioned that sins make stains on the heart. If they are not removed by repentance and asking for forgiveness, eventually they cover up the entire heart and the heart loses its capacity of being revived. Every heart is capable of being revived and opened to the spiritual experience. This is why the Prophet says that repentance is acceptable until the last moments of the agony of death. On one occasion, the Prophet explained the concept of repentance to his people with the example of a lost camel. Emphasizing the importance of repentance, he compared the holy joyfulness of the Divine at the repentance of individuals to the joyfulness of a Bedouin who finds his lost camel. The Bedouin falls asleep only to wake up and realize his camel, on the back of which were his food and drink, is gone and the weather is hot and he is unbelievably thirsty. He then goes back to his place, falls asleep, and wakes up to realize that his camel is back. The holy joyfulness of God is greater than even the joyfulness of that person.[12]

Some hadith collections contain a version of a prayer, which is believed to be the best of the prayers for asking for forgiveness, narrated from the Prophet. It is known as the "Master of Forgiveness prayer" which the Prophet used to say in the mornings and in the evenings. This Prophetic prayer that encompasses all aspects of repentance goes as follows:

> My God, You are my Lord. There is no deity except You. You have created me and I am your servant and I keep going to stay on my covenant and my promise to You as much as I can. I take refuge in You from the evil that I may have committed. I confirm to You all the bounties that You have bestowed upon me. And I confess to You my sin. Forgive me. Surely, no one can forgive sins except You.

Of this prayer of repentance, the Prophet said the following: "Anyone who says this in the morning wholeheartedly and dies on that day, he or she will be among the people of Paradise. Anyone who says this prayer in the night wholeheartedly and dies in that night before morning, he or she is among the people of Paradise."[13] Despite the fact that according to Islamic theology the prophets of God are innocent and do not commit sins, the Prophet of Islam says, "I ask forgiveness from God and repent to Him daily more than seventy times."[14] Hadith commentators interpret this as the Prophet wanting to be an example for believers. Because he was a model of repentance, he shows believers that they have to also repent as much as they can and be careful about the burden of sin, being aware so that their sins do not accumulate. On one occasion the Prophet said, "Surely the believer sees his or her bad deeds like a mountain that can fall over them anytime."[15]

All of this begs the question: Is there an unforgivable sin? The Qur'an indicates that all sins are forgivable except the sin of idolatry. "God does not forgive that a partner should be ascribed to Him, but He forgives anything other than that. And whoever ascribes partners to God has surely invented a great sin" (4:48). Even then, if an individual changes his or her mind and believes in God, the previous sin is forgiven. A hadith *Qudsi*, that is, a hadith where the words belong to the Prophet and the meaning belongs to God, reports God as saying, "If My servant comes to Me with the measurement of the span of the hand I will draw near to him with an arm's length. . . . Whoever comes to Me walking, I will come to him running."[16] This suggests that a small attempt on the part of humankind toward reconciliation draws a great response from God. Accordingly, the door for reconciliation between God and His servants remains open. God asks for the reconciliation of human beings because of His encompassing mercy, not because God needs this reconciliation. In fact, it is narrated that if all human beings come together to harm or benefit God, they cannot do either one at any level.[17] Therefore, the Divine willing for reconciliation between human beings and God, as well as between human beings themselves, is something that humankind, not God, needs. That is why the Qur'an says, "If God punishes people because of their actions, He would not leave a living creature on the surface of the earth. But He postpones them to a certain appointed time. When their time comes, [they will absolutely know that] surely God sees [everything concerning] His servants" (35:45).

# The soul, or *al-nafs*

Having said that, now it is significant to focus on the concept of *al-nafs*, or the soul, a part of human nature that if not trained leads to bad deeds. However, if the soul is well trained and rectified, it can be a positive vehicle for spiritual advancement. The Qur'an speaks of the soul in a variety of verses. Occasionally, the Qur'anic word for the soul, *al-nafs*, is mentioned as being identical with the human self (e.g., 25:68, 17:33, and 5:45). This is not what Muslim mystics are speaking of when they refer to the soul. They speak of three main levels of the soul, which are also mentioned in the Qur'an. In the following section, I will discuss this mystical understanding of the soul.

In the mystical tradition of Islam there are three major levels of the soul. These are the evil-commanding soul (*al-nafs al-ammara*), the blaming soul (*al-nafs al-lawwama*), and the satisfied soul or the soul at peace (*al-nafs al-mutma'inna*). The evil-commanding soul is a negative character, always encouraging human beings to commit evil deeds. The Qur'an tells of this in the story of Joseph. Joseph did not accept the amorous request of the wife of the king of Egypt. The Qur'an speaks of her request and Joseph's strong rejection. Later, the king's wife confesses that she actually asked Joseph and wanted to have him, and that Joseph was innocent. In this situation, Joseph speaks of his soul that is looking for desires, and he says, "Surely I do not consider my soul free from all mistakes because the soul commands evil, except for the soul that God has bestowed His mercy upon. Surely my Lord is the Most-Forgiving and the Most-Merciful" (12:53).

Another Qur'anic verse says, "Those who are fearful of God and prevent their soul from unlawful desires to which they are inclined, their place is Paradise" (79:40-41). This is the soul that commands evil and leads human beings to the lowest desires. The Qur'an also speaks of this level of the soul as the one who whispers (50:16). This soul has to be reined in, disciplined, trained, and purified. Through this, the soul becomes a platform for spiritual development.

In the Qur'anic story of Cain and Abel, the evil-commanding soul plays a significant role. Chapter 5 verse 30 speaks of the violent behavior of Cain and the peaceful behavior of Abel. Abel says, "If you extend your hand to me to kill me, I will not extend my hand to kill you. I fear God." Yet, despite the peaceful reaction of Abel, Cain's evil-commanding soul beautified his action of killing for him and he killed his brother. The Qur'an says, "And his evil-commanding soul beautified the killing of his brother and he killed him and became among the losers." In this action of the evil-commanding soul, one can see wrongdoing, envy, and transgression. The final part of the verse implies who the real victim is. The Qur'anic verse states that the killer was among the losers and the killed was among the victorious. The one who was killed was not defeated by his evil-commanding soul, while the one who did the killing was. This verse also indicates that violations of the Ten Commandments come about, at least in part, as a result of the evil-commanding soul's beautification of them.

This *nafs* is the capacity within human beings that encourages all negative attributes. The Prophet says about this *nafs,* "Your greatest enemy is your *nafs* that is inside you."[18] A prominent modern Indian Hadith commentator, Muhammad Abdur-Rahman Mubarakpuri (d. 1925), in his commentary on a hadith speaks of a constant struggle between this *nafs* and spirit: any struggle against *nafs al-ammara* is considered the greatest struggle.[19] The duty of human beings is to rectify the soul from evil characters. The purpose of sending the prophets is the purification of the soul. As the Qur'an emphatically states, "Surely the one who has purified the soul has succeeded" (91:9). It is narrated that Abu Bakr, the first caliph, advised Umar, who would become the second caliph, "The first thing that I strongly warn you about is your evil-commanding soul which is inside you." Hadith commentators speak of this struggle as spiritual jihad. Some contemporary commentators would divide this spiritual jihad into four steps. The first step is to learn religious values. The second is to practice those religious values. The third is to teach those who do not know, and the fourth is invitation to the Divine path or the way of God. However, it is also clear that any individual's own spiritual jihad will differ from others' based on their own strengths and weaknesses.

Many classical Sufis would consider love of the world as the most dangerous characteristic of the soul. However, a more modern approach suggests that one cannot simply abandon the world. Human beings should work hard in the world, yet must not let love of the world into their hearts. While classical or medieval mystics considered love of the world and worldly possessions as part of the efforts of the evil-commanding soul to deceive, more recent Sufi masters like Said Nursi oppose this idea. Nursi suggests that wealth and worldly possessions are not inherently bad. If they are used for the greater good, they are positive. He beautifully says, "One has to abandon the world not through work, but through heart."[20] That is to say, one must work hard, but one must not attach one's heart to worldly possessions. Nursi outlines four reasons for this principle. First he says, "The worldly life is short and goes quickly towards setting. Detachment from worldly possessions will be difficult and perhaps harmful, and therefore it is not good to attach the heart to them in the first place." Second, "Pleasures of worldly life are like poisoned honey. At the level of their pleasures there are pains as well." Third, "The grave that is waiting for people and people are quickening towards does not accept the beautiful worldly possessions as a gift." Fourth, "God asks people to abandon one hour of their worldly pleasures a day for Him. In response they will be with eternal friends [in Paradise]."[21]

The evil-commanding soul has been and will continue to be with human beings until the Day of Judgment, therefore there is no need to search for the enemy outside; the enemy is inside. According to the Qur'an, it was the evil-commanding soul that lead al-Samiri, the Samaritan, to worshiping of the golden calf. The Qur'anic verse quotes the Samaritan when it speaks of the angry Moses, saying, "My soul prompted me" (20:96). It is understood from this Qur'anic verse that what caused the Samaritan to deviate from worshiping God to worshiping the calf was the evil-commanding soul. That the golden calf attracted the soul of the Samaritan also implies that material things and pleasures will always be among the things that will continually attract the soul, drawing human beings from the way of righteousness. Considering the fact that the calf is made of gold, the Qur'an clearly states that the calf cannot be God. Moses, in this story being the Prophet of God, burns the calf and throws its ashes into the sea to illustrate that materialistic things cannot be God or objects of worship. So because the Samaritan listened to the evil-commanding soul he also became an agent of deception and therefore the Qur'an states that "The Samaritan has led them astray" (20:85).

The second level of the soul is called *al-nafs al-lawwama*, or the blaming soul. This is a stage between the soul that commands evil and the soul that is at peace. This level of the soul is mentioned in only one place in the Qur'an, (75:2) and in this verse God swears upon this blaming soul to signify its importance. The blaming soul leads to repentance, asking for forgiveness, and the return to the Divine. It blames itself and regrets the bad deeds it has committed, and the good deeds it has failed to do. If the action is bad, the soul would say, "I wish I had not done that." If the action is good, the soul would say, "I wish I had done more." Some Qur'an commentators would say that this is the soul of believers. According to the prominent commentator al-Alusi, "It [the soul] has been enlightened to a certain extent and woken up. Whenever it commits a bad deed because of its nature, it starts blaming itself and as a result, hates what it has done."[22] Importantly, in the Qur'an immediately after swearing on the soul, God swears upon the Day of Judgment when all deeds become clear. This indicates that the deeds of the blaming soul are committed in this world, but they are rewarded in the afterlife, when the soul reaches a higher level.

The third level of the soul is known as *al-nafs al-mutma'inna*. This is the soul at peace, the soul that is satisfied. It opposes evil actions and is satisfied with what God has given to it. It is mentioned once in the Qur'an (89:27). The name that the Qur'an uses for this level of the soul comes from the same root of the word that is mentioned in the Qur'anic verse on the satisfaction of the heart. "Surely, through the remembrance of God, hearts are satisfied" (13:28). The word that is used for satisfaction comes from the same root as the word used for this soul. This suggests that this level of soul leads to the highest level of certainty of faith as well as the ultimate peace. At the same time, it leads to a high level of feeling the presence of God. One early scholar, al-Mawardi (d. 1058), speaks of seven meanings of *al-nafs al-mutma'inna*. "The believing soul, the soul that responds to God's call, the soul that confirms what God has promised, the soul that is saved, the soul that is pleased, the soul that is satisfied with the world and returns to God, and the soul that is satisfied with God."[23]

At this juncture, we should return to the theme of spiritual jihad. If the struggle against *al-nafs al-ammara* is successful, the result will be the development of good qualities in human beings. The Qur'an in various verses speaks of these qualities. The following example illustrates the qualities of the servants of God, that is, people who have succeeded in increasing the level of their soul.

The servants of the Most-Merciful are those who walk on the earth modestly and who, when the ignorant address them, say, "Peace." And those who pass the night prostrate to their Lord and standing. And those who say, "Our Lord, avert us from the punishment of Hell, surely, its punishment is terrible, surely it is an evil abode and place of dwelling." And those who in their spending are neither extravagant nor stingy but keep to a way between them. And those who invoke no other god with God, nor kill a life which God has forbidden, except in the course of justice, nor commit adultery. (25:63-68)

While speaking of *nafs*, al-Jahiz (d. 868) describes three faculties of the soul. The first is desire, which is common to human beings and animals. The second is anger, which is common again to human beings and animals. The third faculty is intellect, and this faculty is only found in human beings.[24] Like al-Jahiz, Said Nursi in his interpretation of Qur'an 1:6, which says, "guide us to the straight path," also speaks of these three faculties of the soul. For Nursi, each faculty also has three levels. Each level has a positive and negative extreme and a middle, balanced area. Of these three levels, Nursi says that the middle, balanced way is best. According to Nursi, when a believer in his or her daily prayer asks God to be guided to the straight path, what he or she is really asking is to be guided to the path wherein these three faculties of the soul are balanced and used in the proper ways. For Nursi, the proper use of these three faculties leads to courage, chastity, and wisdom. Therefore the Qur'an does not tell people to deny and eliminate their desires, anger, or intellect fully; instead, the verse asks people to balance them, the result of which brings harmony to individuals and society.[25]

In this respect, the Islamic spiritual understanding of the soul and the balancing of the faculties of the soul can be considered akin to contemporary self-help and psychological betterment regimens. Many of these, no matter what their original province, focus on ideas of balance and achieving a middle way. Similar as well is self-help's general dictum to avoid areas and activities that can easily lead away from the middle path and to instead focus on the way of countering it: to remember.

# *Dhikr* as a shield against Satan and the evil-commanding soul

In Islamic Spirituality, Satan and the evil-commanding soul are considered the enemies of human beings. There is a constant struggle in the inner life of human beings in this regard. The Qur'an states that Satan puts animosity and hatred among people and deviates them from the remembrance of God (5:91). It also says that Satan is one who overcomes people and makes people to forget their remembrance of God. "Satan has overcome them and made them forget the remembrance of God" (58:19). These and similar verses of the Qur'an show that one of the tasks of Satan is to prevent human beings from remembering God and that is why it insistently reminds people that they have to remember God. Mystics following this Qur'anic instruction have made the remembrance of God a part of their rituals and chanting. Muslim mystics would consider the remembrance of God or *dhikr* as a shield against Satan and the evil-commanding soul. The goal of Satan and the evil-commanding soul is to distract human beings from the remembrance of God. Yet because God is the Most-Knowledgeable and the One who sees everything, by the remembrance of God one is able to eliminate the impacts of these two enemies.

*Dhikr* is remembrance of God, but more than that it is in itself a Divine bounty. As Abu Talib al-Makki (d. 996) demonstrates, remembrance of the Beloved is one of the signs of love of God. The more one remembers God, the more one loves God. Even more importantly, one of the most meritorious bounties God bestows on His creatures is to help them to remember Him. According to al-Makki, it is narrated that "for God there is bounty for every creature to give away. He has not bestowed upon his servants anything more virtuous or meritorious than inspiring in them His remembrance."[26]

With this in mind, it is important to elaborate on the ways one can have *dhikr*. Since the Prophet is the best example, according to Muslim mystics one must say what the Prophet said. If one zeros in on the sayings of the Prophet about *dhikr*, four key phrases emerge. The first is *Subhan Allah*. This phrase is about exalting and glorifying God. Literally, it means God is exalted.

The second phrase as *Alhamdulillah*. This is more about praising God, and has the connotation of all praises belonging to God.

The third phrase is *La ilaha Illa Allah*. This phrase declares the oneness of God and that there is no deity but God. It implies that all ordinary creatures are not worthy of being God; everything is created by God, and anything that is created cannot be the Creator.

The fourth phrase is *Allahu Akbar*. This is about the greatness of God and the smallness of everything in comparison to God. The things that are great in the realm of creation are great because of God's greatness. Messengers of God are great, but they are great because of their connection to God. These four phrases are the core of the Qur'an and the core of the daily prayers and the core of mystical remembrance of God. The Prophet used to repeat each of these thirty-three times after the prescribed prayers. In the mornings and in the evenings, sometimes the Prophet would repeat this 100 times. Likewise, Muslim mystics have been practicing this tradition for a long time. A Qur'anic verse refers to those who believe and do good deeds as being people who are guided to the beautiful words. Despite the encompassing meaning of this verse, especially the term "beautiful words," some commentators of the Qur'an specifically mention the words "*La ilaha Illa Allah*," the translation of which is, "there is no deity but God," "God is the most exalted," and "God is greater than everything." A Qur'anic verse can be accepted as a reference from the Holy Book of Islam to the Sufi tradition of remembrance of God. The verse says, "And they had been guided [in worldly life] to good speech, and they were guided to the path of the Praiseworthy" (22:24).

The phrase *Alhamdulillah,* or, more phonetically, "*al-Hamdu Lillah,*" is a short phrase, but it is very significant in the Sufi tradition of *dhikr*. It is recommended that one repeat this frequently, because on the Day of Judgment when good and evil deeds are weighed on the scales, this phrase is one of the heaviest items on the side of good. The phrase indicates that God is the source of all bounties that occur through conscious and unconscious causes. Because God is the Cause of causes, all praises go to God automatically, even if people are not aware of it. For example, if someone takes you to a municipal park and you praise the person who takes you to the park, your praise also goes to the municipality itself, because they are the cause of the park. But ultimately your praise goes to God, because it is God who creates trees and grass and flowers, all the beauties of the park.

Another way of remembering God is through the recitation of the Qur'an. The Qur'an itself is a reminder and a remembrance, and therefore reading the Qur'an itself is *dhikr*. Mystics generally read the Qur'an on a daily basis. Even if they are only able to read ten pages, it is still an important element of their daily routines. Prophetic statements suggest that one should read no less than fifty verses from the Qur'an daily. Less than that would be considered abandoning the Qur'an.

In the Holy Book of Islam, God connects people's remembrance of Him to His remembrance of people. "So remember Me, and I will remember you; and be thankful to Me; and do not be ungrateful to Me" (2:152). In his commentary on this verse, al-Tabari the famous Quran commentator says that the verse in question reminds people to be obedient to God and to listen to the Divine commands and the Divine prohibitions. If people remember God in this way, God will remember them by bestowing his mercy and forgiveness upon them.[27] Again in the interpretation of this verse, a prominent commentator, al-Qurtubi, narrates a story involving a conversation between the Prophet and a Bedouin Arab. The Bedouin comes to the Prophet and asks him, "The commandments of Islam are so many for me. Tell me only one of them so that I will practice it." The Prophet said, "Let your tongue always be wet with the remembrance of God."[28] Other commentators of the Qur'an also have elaborated on this verse. It is believed that Moses asked God, "How should I thank you, my Lord?" And God said, "Remember Me and do not forget Me. When you remember Me, you will thank me. When you forget me you will deny Me."[29] A Qur'anic verse states, "Be pious towards God as God truly deserves" (3:102). Some Islamic scholars interpret this as stating that God must be obeyed, and that there should never be a bad deed against God. And God should be remembered and not forgotten. And God should be thanked and not denied. Hasan al-Basri in interpretation of this verse says, "God asks people to remember Him by doing what God has commanded to do and God will remember them about what he promised for them."[30]

Another mystic interprets the verse as saying that if people remember God through their prayers, God will remember them through His forgiveness.[31] Al-Alusi, a prominent commentator of the Qur'an, in his commentary on chapter 2, verse 152 divides *dhikr* into three categories. The first one is called *dhikr* by tongue, and that is to praise God through statements of praise, to exalt God and recite the Qur'an, the Word of God. The second one is *dhikr* by heart. This is contemplation on the responsibilities of human beings with regard to the Divine commands and warnings, as well as contemplation on the attributes and the mysteries of the Divine. The third is *dhikr* by action, and that is to act according to what God has commanded and avoid what God has prohibited.[32]

Since the daily prescribed prayer encompasses various bodily actions of *dhikr*, it has been called *dhikr* in the Qur'an.[33] Al-Qushayri's interpretation of chapter 2, verse 152, especially on the statement, "Remember Me," has valuable points. According to him, the people who look at the external nature of the verse will understand this as obedience to the Divine commands. A group of people who understand the inner meaning of the verse will understand remembering God to be "to abandon every desire other than God." He goes further, interpreting these two Qur'anic statements as saying,

> Remember Me with your humbleness, I will remember you with My bounties. Remember Me with a broken heart, I will remember you with goodness. Remember Me with your tongue, I will remember you with the heart. Remember Me with your heart, I will remember you by fulfilling your requests. Remember Me at the door with your service, I will remember you with my response of fulfilling all My bounties on the rug of closeness to Me. Remember Me by purifying your inner life, I will remember you with my full kindness. Remember Me with your efforts and struggle, I will remember you with My generosity and gifts. Remember Me with My attribute of peace, I will remember you on the Day of Judgment when repentance is no longer valid. Remember Me with awe, I will remember you with fulfilling of your desires.[34]

Another consequence of *dhikr* is found in a hadith Qudsi:

> I treat My servants with their good thoughts of Me and I am with My servants when they remember Me. If they remember Me in their heart, I will remember them too. If they remember Me in the presence of people, I will remember them in the presence of a group that is better than them. If they come to Me with the closeness of the measurement of the span of the hand I will draw near to them with an arm's length. Whoever comes to Me walking, I will come to them running.[35]

Through this hadith Qudsi, we are to understand that if a person remembers God, God will remember that person in a group of angels.

## *Qalb,* or heart

Just as rectification of the soul is necessary for spiritual development, so too is purification of the heart. In fact, heart, or *qalb*, is considered the center of the Sufi tradition. In the following I will discuss the concept of heart and its place in Islamic spirituality. It is important to note that for Islam, heart is also the central element of human existence, both materially and spiritually. In a hadith that speaks of what is allowed and what is prohibited, the Prophet states the following: "Surely in the body there is a piece. When it is wholesome the entire body is wholesome. When it is corrupt, the entire body becomes corrupt. Be aware, that piece is the heart."[36]

There are many Qur'anic verses referring to the importance of heart in Islamic spirituality. The Qur'an speaks of the heart of the Prophet of Islam. It was to his heart that the Qur'an was revealed. In other words, his heart was so pure that the Pure Revelation was able to come to that heart. In reference to this revelation, the Qur'an says, "The Trustworthy Spirit [angel Gabriel] has brought it down upon your heart, [O Muhammad] that you may be one of the warners" (26:193-194). The angel Gabriel's purity and the purity of the Qur'an as a Divine revelation meshed with the purity of the heart of Muhammad. The importance of a pure heart is attested to in that it leads human beings to Paradise.

The Qur'an describes the afterlife as "the day when neither wealth nor progeny shall profit except for whom comes to God with a pure heart" (26:89). With this, the Qur'an states that the first condition for entering Paradise is a pure heart. A pure heart is necessary to receive revelation. For this reason, just as the Prophet possessed a pure heart, so did all previous prophets. For instance, the Qur'an speaks of the heart of Abraham. "Surely among those who followed Noah was Abraham when he came to his Lord with a pure heart" (37:84). Abraham with his pure heart is among the people of Paradise. Pure heart indicates a heart that is free of the diseases of hypocrisy and hatred. As one saying of the Prophet suggests, a group of people will enter Paradise because their hearts are pure and innocent like the hearts of birds. That means their hearts are soft, pure, and peaceful; free of hated and full of love.

Because Islamic spirituality is centered around the purity of heart, when the Prophet was asked about piety he placed his hand on his breast, saying, "piety is here, piety is here, piety is here."[37] Perhaps for this reason the mystics focused on the importance of heart rather than external prayers. For mystics, external prayer is important, but internal piety is more so. Commentaries on chapter 22 verse 35 of the Qur'an refer to a saying of the Prophet, "Saints of my community do not enter Paradise because of their fasting and praying but they enter Paradise because of their peaceful hearts, their generous souls and their sincere advice."[38] Pious hearts are softened when God is mentioned. Therefore, sincerely practiced Islamic rituals such as charity and prayer are directly related to heart as well. The Qur'an says, "And give [O Muhammad] good tidings to the humble those whose hearts quake when God is mentioned, and those who endure patiently whatever afflicts them, and those who perform the prayer, and those who spend from what We have provided them" (22:34-35).

One story in the Qur'an, the story of the mother of Moses, Umm Musa, illustrates that on certain occasions God may support people's hearts so that they can become content and receive strength. In the Qur'an the mother of Moses, is shown to have great compassion for her baby and as well as great love for obeying Divine instruction. Perhaps she had a perplexing moment when she saw that her baby had been found by Pharaoh's fisherman. According to the Qur'anic narrative, baby Moses rejects all milk offered to him. Perhaps out of her compassion, his mother was about to disclose that the baby was hers so that she could suckle him. If she had done so, Moses would have been killed by Pharaoh for being an Israelite boy. The Qur'an says that God made her heart unwavering so she would not disclose the identity of Moses. As a result, she receives confidence and strength in her faith in God, and she is among the believers. The verse says, "And the heart of Moses' mother became empty [of all else]. She was about to disclose [the matter concerning] him had We not bound fast her heart that she would be of the believers" (28:10). Although the story is about the mother of Moses, it can have implications for hearts that are distressed. By Divine intervention, hearts can be made resolute and strengthened. The mother of Moses is a model in this regard. She was not only a believer; some Muslim scholars have said that she was a prophet, since she received a revelation from God. The Qur'an does not specify her prayer here in this verse, yet it is evident that she received *sakina*, a strong feeling of the Divine presence,[39] through which her heart rested in God.

Purity and soundness of heart leads us to the question of what makes hearts impure, stained, or sick. Perhaps the greatest disease that impacts the purity of the heart is arrogance. In the context of Islamic spirituality, sins that come from desire are forgivable. This is because Adam sinned out of desire and God forgave him. Sins that come out of arrogance are not as easily forgiven. Satan, when he claimed that he was better than Adam because Adam was created from soil and he was created from fire, committed the sin of arrogance. We do not know whether Satan ever asked for his sin to be forgiven, and perhaps due to his continued arrogance he did not. What we do know is that Satan's sin was not forgiven. Satan's arrogance is not only one instance of the Qur'an's shunning of arrogance. It states that human beings should not be involved only in the adornments of the world, which leads to arrogance. In the Qur'an, the figure known as Korah or Qarun is known for his extreme wealth and can be seen as the epitome of arrogance.[40] It should be noted that, in principle, wealth is not a negative, per se, in Islam. Wealth only becomes negative when it leads to arrogance. The Qur'an suggests that people should have a balance between worldly things and those that will lead to eternal life, all the while acknowledging that eternal life is greater. Verses 60-61 in chapter 28 suggest that those who have received the promise of the afterlife can look forward to eternal paradise, and thus should be able to recognize the superiority of the eternal to the ephemeral. The afterlife is eternal and the worldly life is ephemeral.

As the Qur'an states, "What is with God is better and more sustainable" (28:60). Addressing Qarun, the Qur'an further states, "And with that which God has given you, pursue the abode of the Hereafter and do not forget your portion in this world. Be good to others as God has been good to you, and do not pursue corruption on earth for God does not love the corrupt" (28:77). This Qur'anic verse infers two important elements of Islamic spirituality. The first element is related to doing what is beautiful, because God asks Qarun to do good to other people as God has done good to him. The second important element is to avoid corruption, or *fasad,* on earth. *Fasad* is a generic term which includes all types of physical and spiritual impurities. The verse ends with a kind of oxymoron by mentioning love and corruption in the same sentence, by extrapolating that God loves, but in this case does not love the corrupt.

One of the antidotes for arrogance is forgiveness. Individuals must ask Divine Grace for purification of their heart and use their free will to remain vigilant for the deceptions of Satan and the evil-commanding soul. At this point, mention should be made of the nature of Divine Grace in Islam. Though one might work very hard to blot out his or her past corruption, it is Divine Grace which plays the ultimate role in deciding one's fate. Therefore, it is Divine will and not human activity which leads to Paradise. That said, an important aspect of human free will is the ability to better oneself and the world in the hopes that the Divine Grace will come to that individual. As we have mentioned, the right use of one's capacities is in itself a form of thankfulness to God for what has given already. Regarding forgiveness specifically, the Prophet has given human beings a model prayer. In his frequent prayers, as the Prophet's wife 'Aisha narrates, the Prophet would say, "O God, [You are] the One who changes hearts. Steadfast my heart in faith."[41] Another prayer of the Prophet relates to asking for the enlightenment of the heart. Similarly, there are many prayers of the Prophet that have to do with faith and hearts, such as, "Lord make faith beloved to us and make it beautiful in our hearts."[42]

Having said this, it is important to focus on the metaphorical third step of the ladder and that is love of God. The love of God comes through the purity of heart and the rectification of the soul. God loves and is beloved. The love of God is the real love, *ishq haqiqi.* As an example, one can refer to a part of the prophet Abraham's story as narrated in the Qur'an. Here, according to commentators, he is speaking with his astrologers. Speaking of a star, he says "this is a bright thing. It might be my lord." When the star sets, he says "I do not love those who fade away" (6:76). Following this, he says similar things about the moon and the sun. He sums this up by saying, "O my people, surely I have quit that which you associate [with God]. Surely I have turned my face towards the One Who has created the heavens and the earth, as a man of pure faith. And I am not one of the idolaters" (6:78-79). A prominent scholar, referring to this story and the statement of Abraham said, "O my soul, since the truth is this, and since you are from the people of Abraham, peace be upon him, be like Abraham and say, 'I do not love those who fade away.' Turn your face to the Eternal Beloved."[43]

All love for things other than God have to ultimately be for His love. If they are not for God's love, they are derivative love or *ishq majazi*. The Prophet used to ask for the love of God. "Lord, bestow upon me Your love and the love of the things that make me closer to You." People may love their spouses, parents, friends, property, and so on, yet this love has to be for the love of God, because without God none of them would exist. If one loves worldly things for God's sake, that love becomes eternal and reward-worthy. The sign of loving something for God—for example, the love between spouses—is that their love for each other increases as they get older. This is because in old age, physical beauty is decreased but love continues. One may love a beautiful panorama, but the panorama does not know the loving person; one may love the stars of the night, but the stars do not know the person who loves them. Many of these beloveds, like youth and wealth, leave without ever saying goodbye. The following quote illustrates the encompassing nature of love and how love is a central theme in Islamic spirituality.

> Love is a reason for the creation of this universe. It is also a connection between the elements of the universe. It is also the light and the life of the universe. Since human beings are the most comprehensive fruits of the tree of the universe, the love which has been put in the nucleus of this fruit, the heart, encompasses the whole universe. Thus, the One who deserves such unlimited love must be the One who is Unlimitedly Perfect.[44]

This alludes to the famous hadith Qudsi, "I was a hidden treasure. I loved to be known. I created the world so that I would be known." This evidently shows that love is the foundation of the creation of the universe.

One has to love God, but the question that comes to mind is what is the way one must follow to result in God's love in return. The Qur'an answers this question that if one wants to be beloved, then one must follow the ways of the beloved of God, that is, the prophets, the saints, the pious, etc. And therefore God asks the Prophet to say, "If you love God, follow me. He will love you" (3:31).

Historically, shunning the world or the love of the world was an important element of Islamic mysticism. Due to this fact, many modernist scholars criticized Islamic mysticism for negligence of the importance of this world and focusing solely on the afterlife. Many went further and considered this to be a reason contributing to the stagnation of the Islamic world in science and technology as well as in economic arenas. It can be argued that emphasis on shunning the world for mystics ended with Said Nursi. He said that the world has three faces. Two faces of the world are admirable, desirable, and lovable, while the third is shunned.

The first face is that the world is a place where God's beautiful names are reflected and believers can contemplate on them. In other words, the world is an exhibition displaying the beautiful names of God.

The second face of the world is understood through an analogy that the Prophet himself used. That is, the world is a farm for the afterlife. Individuals must sow in order to reap in the afterlife. With this, the world becomes a fertile ground for the fruits of the afterlife. For these reasons, the world is beloved and should be loved.

The third face of the world is the aspect that is shunned in Islamic mysticism. This is the face of indulgence in worldly desires. When early mystics spoke of the deceptive world, they meant this dimension, but because they used vague language, perhaps this was understood by others as total rejection of worldliness. Such a misunderstanding, instead of leading people to abandon worldliness with their hearts, led some people to abandon it with their actions. This is not what is actually meant in the mystical tradition. If so, how is it that work or serving others are considered acts of worship by the Prophet? Nursi beautifully describes the loss and the gain that can result from these various approaches to the world. He says,

> If humans, deceived by indulging in the world of multiplicity through the love of the world, are drowned, definitely they will have an unlimited loss. They will execute themselves spiritually. If humans raise their heads and listen to the message of the Qur'an through the ears of the heart and direct themselves to Unity, they can ascend through the ladder of worship, go to the throne of perfection, and then can become eternal.[45]

# *Sabr* or patience

As we have seen, the spiritual struggle against the evil-commanding soul, the endeavor to purify it to reach the level of blaming and finally the level of the soul at peace, is a significant challenge that requires patience. The Qur'an speaks of *sabr*, or patience, as one of the most important qualities that the human spirit can attain. There are many categories of patience. Some Islamic scholars divide it into three categories. First is patience against difficulties and calamities—sorrow and grief. Second is patience in actions, that is, patience against sin and bad deeds. Third is the patience that is required to continuously perform good deeds and prayers.

Although these three categories are different, they all require a certain level of perseverance because of the challenges that they involve. Regarding the first, if there is a natural disaster, famine, or grave illness, one should search for all possible ways to rectify the situation, but in the end one has to be patient and remain thankful to God. One can even petition God for an alleviation of the situation, but one should not complain to other people about the difficulties. The Qur'an describes the servants of God as those who are patient in times of both prosperity and adversity. Addressing several challenging situations, the Qur'an says,

> And hurry for forgiveness from your Lord and for a Paradise as wide as are the heavens and the earth, it is prepared for the pious who give charity for the cause of God in prosperity and in adversity and those who control their anger and those who forgive people. God loves [and will reward] those who do what is beautiful. (3:133-134)

As for the second category, although it is intertwined with the first to a certain extent, more specifically it is about the patience to withstand things that are attractive but harmful. If one looks at everyday life, one can see how the ease of committing desirable bad deeds requires a high degree of patience to prevent them from becoming part of one's life. It is mentioned in one of the sayings of the Prophet that the way to Hell is covered with prohibited, desirable things, while the way to Paradise is lined with things that are seemingly difficult.[46]

The third category of patience is related to prayer, fasting, and other good deeds, such as charity, community service, etc. There is no doubt that praying five times a day with the required ablution, that is, washing one's hands, face, arms, feet, is not an easy task. Similarly, fasting for the entire month of Ramadan, abstaining from both eating and drinking sunup to sundown, is a challenge. These spiritual exercises require a tremendous amount of patience. In addition to this, Muslim mystics will add voluntary prayers, such as midnight prayers, prayers after and before the prescribed prayers, and many other prayers that the Prophet highly recommended, as a part of their daily lives. In the Islamic tradition, one can find hundreds of examples that involve patience, both direct and indirect. Because of the importance of patience, the Qur'an speaks of it as a quality possessed by good people: "They are those who believe and advise each other to patience and advise each other to compassion. They are those of the Right Hand" (90:17-18) and "By the time! Surely, human beings are in loss except those who believe, and do wholesome deeds, and advise each other with the truth and patience" (103:1-3).

One verse directly addresses the Prophet and asks him to be patient and respond in a positive way to people who have insulted him. Interestingly, the verse does not suggest passivism; rather, it advises the Prophet not to respond in the same way that he was insulted, but to actively respond by praising God more. Through such patience, one will reach a spiritual level that God is pleased with. "Be patient with what they say and exalt God, your Lord, with praise before the rising of the sun and before its setting and during periods of the night and at the corners of the day, that you may be pleased [with what you are given as a reward]" (20:130). After this, the Qur'an describes patience in prayer by saying, "And command your people to pray and be patient in it. We ask of you no provision, but We give you sustenance and the end [Paradise] is for [the people of] piety" (20:132).

In his commentary on the third verse of chapter 103, al-Qushayri says, "Patience with [the actions of] God is the most difficult one." [47] Because human beings may not always understand the meaning of the actions of God, they question God about His intentions. They want God to show results immediately, but God postpones them until a certain time and occasion. God never forgets and never abandons, but for some reasons might postpone. People become impatient as a result. Indicating that God never forgets, the Prophet of Islam says, "God accepts prayer, but one has to be patient and should not say 'I prayed, but my prayer was not accepted.'" [48]

To do justice to the concept of patience, several volumes would be needed. For present purposes, I will refer to just a few Qur'anic verses that give a sense of how patience more broadly is presented in the Qur'an, and as a result in the Islamic spiritual tradition. At least twelve times, the Qur'an uses the active participle of the word "patience," with most of these being plural, that is, "God is with the patient ones." For example, 2:153 refers to patience with prayer and difficulties as an aid in gaining the afterlife: "O believers, seek help through patience and prayer. Surely God is with the patient ones."

The Qur'an instructs the Prophet to give good news to people who are patient. In this case, the patient are those who show patience during fear, famine, and loss. The Qur'an suggests that all of these should be considered tests. People have to do all they can to prevent them, but at the same time when they occur they must be patient. The Prophet is instructed to give good news of Paradise to those that are patient. "Surely We shall test you through fear, hunger, loss of wealth, lives, and fruits. [O Muhammad], give good news to the patient ones" (2:155). Also, in chapter 2 verse 45 implies that patience is not an easy task: "Seek help in patience and prayer; and surely it is hard except for those who are humble."

A similar verse describes people who have patience by mentioning them as being first in the categories of good people. This suggests that patience results in other good behaviors, such as truthfulness, obedience, charity, and worship. "Those who say: 'Our Lord! We believe. Forgive us of our sins and guard us from the punishment of Fire,' are the patient, and the truthful, and the obedient, and those who give charity and those who ask forgiveness in the early mornings" (3:16-7).

In another verse, the Qur'an makes a connection between patience and the struggle for social harmony. It suggests that quarreling results in the weakening of society, and commands that believers be patient, for God is with the patient. To restrain anger during discussions which can result in violent conflicts requires a great amount of patience. By commanding this, the Qur'an lays the foundations for social harmony, itself an essential element of Islamic spirituality. "And obey God and His messenger, and do not clash with each other or else you will lose courage and your strength will depart. And be patient. Surely God is with the patient ones" (8:46).

Patience in the Qur'an is also presented as a marker of steadfastness. In the story of Luqman, when he is advising his son he tells him to pray, to command what is good and forbid what is evil, and to be patient regarding the things that afflict him. The Qur'an presents this quality as a part of steadfastness. "O my son, establish the prayer and enjoin that which is good and forbid that which is evil, and bear patiently that which befalls you. Surely this is among the elements of steadfastness" (31:17). Steadfastness is also a quality that is related to prophets. This is particularly true for the five elite prophets, but some commentators believe that it is not limited to them. In one verse, the Qur'an commands the Prophet of Islam to be steadfast like the earlier prophets.

Be patient [O Muhammad] as the possessors of steadfastness of the messengers God had patience, and do not hasten [punishment] for them [your people]. When they see what they were promised, it would seem to them that they had not stayed but for an hour of the day. This [the Qur'an] is a Divine message then none will be punished except those who disbelieve. (46:35)

It is understood from this verse that the Prophet was frustrated because of the persecution he received from his own people, and he wanted a quick Divine judgment against those who had wronged him and his followers.

As mentioned in chapter two, in the Qur'an the prophet Job is known as the hero of patience. The Qur'an does not describe the details of his sickness and disease, but many Muslim commentators have provided details of his diseases to the extent that we know that they prevented him from the remembrance of God through his heart and through his tongue. In this desperate situation, the Qur'anic Job never complained. He praised God and remained patient, even when the diseases impacted his heart and his tongue and started to prevent him from praising and worshipping God. He supplicated to God and asked for healing. He did this not for his comfort, but for the ability to continue his praising of God. He said, "My Lord, harm has afflicted me and You are the Most-Merciful of the mercifuls" (21:83). For his sincere prayer, God immediately responded and cured his diseases.

In the Qur'an at least seventeen times believers are commanded by God, through the Prophet of Islam, to be patient. This Divine command addresses all believers of all time periods and asks for their patience: "And follow what is revealed to you, [O Muhammad], and be patient until God judges. And He is the Best of Judges" (10:109). The reward for being patient is awarded by God, because patience is a beautiful action and God does not forget rewards for what is beautiful: "And be patient, surely God does not forgo reward for those who do good" (11:115). Again, a Qur'anic verse addresses the Prophet and asks him to be patient despite plans and tricks against him, and to ask for grace from God for this patience. "And be patient, and your patience is only with the help of God. And do not grieve for them, and do not be distressed by what they plan against you" (16:127).

Another verse addresses the Prophet, telling him to be patient, and in this case it seems to be telling him to be with the pious, the poor who are seeking to please God rather than looking at the world's ornaments and following those who are heedless of God's remembrance:

> And keep yourself patient with those who call upon their Lord in the morning and the evening, seeking His face [i.e. for the sake of God]. And do not let your eyes pass beyond them, while you desire adornments of the worldly life, and do not obey the one whose heart We have made heedless of Our remembrance and who follows his desire and whose affair is wasting. (18:28)

One commentator suggests that the occasion of the revelation of the verse was related to the desire of the nobles of Quraysh, the Prophet's tribe, for the Prophet of Islam to sit with them only, and not sit with the weakest of his companions, including Bilal, the Ethiopian; Suhayb, the Roman; Ibn Mas'ud, and Ammar. The Divine command prevented the Prophet from acceding to their request, and it forced his soul to be patient in sitting with the weakest of his companions.[49] Part of the difficulty for the Prophet was his desire that these elites would accept the Divine revelation.

Near the end of chapter fifty-two, the Qur'an again addresses the Prophet and tells him to be patient with being persecuted by the people of Mecca, as he is under the protection of God and God will protect him from them. "And be patient, [O Muhammad], for the decision of your Lord, for surely, you are under Our eyes. And exalt God with His praise when you stand up" (52:48).[50] At the end of this verse, there are two things that are emphasized. One is exalting God, which the Prophet is commanded to do. This is related to the Divine name al-Jalil, which has a connotation of majesty and power. The other aspect is praising God, which is related to the Divine name al-Jamil, having something to do with beauty, compassion, and mercy. So when the Prophet is commanded to exalt God with His praise, he was commanded to combine the reflection of these two apparently opposite Divine names. Since this requires effort and constant prayer, the Prophet was commanded to be patient in the face of being persecuted by his own people.

One final verse to mention asks the Prophet to be patient in waiting for Divine help. At the revelation, the pagans of Mecca were strong and tormented the Prophet. The Qur'an therefore enjoins the Prophet to be patient, and not to respond to his adversaries impatiently: "So be patient. Surely the promise of God is truth. And do not let those who have no certainty make you impatient" (30:60). What is the reward for one's patience? The Qur'an is clear on this. It says that God rewards people with Paradise and its beauties because they remained patient in their lives on earth: "And they were rewarded for their patience with a Garden [Paradise] and silk" (76:12).

# *Tafakkur,* or contemplation

In the beginning, I mentioned that there are three levels of Islamic spirituality: to believe in God, to know God, and to love God. One of the most important components of Islamic spirituality with regard to the knowledge of God is *tafakkur,* meaning reflection or contemplation. This is a principle that elevates human beings first to the knowledge of God and then to the spiritual enjoyment of loving God. Through contemplation, one can recognize the arts of God in the realm of creation. There is a distinction between looking and seeing. One can look, but still may not be able to see. The Qur'an refers to the realm of creation and says everything exalts God, but you do not understand their exaltations, stating that, "The seven heavens, the earth and what is in them are glorifying Him. In fact, there is nothing which does not glorify God with His praise, but you do not understand their glorification" (17:44).

The Prophet himself says, "One hour of contemplation is better than the voluntary prayer of one [full] night."[51] Sometimes a moment of contemplation becomes a remarkable step in the understanding of God and may make a big change in the life of an individual. Many Qur'anic verses end with phrases such as "why do you/they not see," "why do you/they not look," or "why do you/they not contemplate." One of the most well-known passages on contemplation in the Qur'an is in chapter three, and in it a verb derivative of the word *tafakkur* is directly used.

> Surely in the creation of the heavens and the earth and the changing of the night and the day are signs for those of understanding who remember God, standing or sitting or reclining, and contemplate upon the creation of the heavens and the earth: 'Our Lord, You have not created this for vanity. Glory be to You! Guard us against the chastisement of the Fire.' (3:190-191)

A similar verse again invites human beings to the contemplation of the heavens and earth, but adds,

> The ships which sail through the sea with that which benefits people, and the rain that God has sent down from the heavens, reviving the earth after it is dead and the scattering of animals on it, and directing the winds and the clouds subjugated between the heavens and the earth are signs for people who use their reason. (2:164)

There are many other verses that contain the word *tafakkur* and words derived from it. Occasionally the Qur'an complains about people's lack of reflection: "Do they not reflect upon themselves?" (30:8) This verse strongly suggests that human beings should contemplate on their inner lives as well as on physical creation. Also, the Qur'an invites believers to contemplate on the creation of human beings. In the sight of God, human beings are the most important of God's creatures. Contemplation on the creation of human beings leads to spiritual elevation. First, it speaks of the beginning of the creation of human beings as a family and the beginning of the creation of humanity, and then it draws our attention to the creation of every individual human being, how they develop from a sperm into a full human being, and invites people to contemplate their creation. The Qur'anic verse says,

> We have created the human being from an extraction of clay, then We set him/her, a drop, in a receptacle secure, then We created of the drop a clot then We created of the clot a tissue then We created of the tissue bones then We clothed the bones in flesh; thereafter We produced him/her as another creature. So blessed be God, the Most-Beautiful of creators! (23:12-14)

Therefore, human beings' lives cannot be purposeless. There is purpose to all aspects of everyones' lives. This Qur'anic emphasis on contemplation leads to the discovery of the nature of the lives of human beings. This is why the following Qur'anic verse seems to be inviting human beings to contemplate in a questioning manner, "Do human beings think that they will be abandoned [without purpose]? Were they not a drop of fluid which was poured out? Then they became a clot; then He shaped and fashioned and He made of them two kinds, male and female. Is He not able to bring the dead to life?" (75:36-40)

Importantly, the Qur'an invites people to contemplate on the history of earlier generations and learn lessons from them: "Tell them the story so they may reflect" (7:176). There are similar verses which ask human beings to contemplate on their own death and life: "God takes the souls at the time of their death, and those which have not died, in their sleep. He keeps those for whom He has decreed death, but frees the others until a determined time. Surely in that are signs for people who reflect" (39:42). The Qur'an also makes a connection between the Qur'an itself and contemplation on the Qur'an: "[We sent them] with the clear proofs and books. And We have sent down to you the Remembrance [the Qur'an] that you may make clear to human beings what was sent down to them, so that hopefully they will reflect" (16:44). This invitation from the Qur'an to contemplate on it and its verses ascertains that contemplation is a form of worship in Islam.

Additionally, there are Qur'anic verses that are considered an invitation to contemplation on the cycle of day and night:

> Say, "Have you considered if God should make for you the night continuous until the Day of Resurrection, what deity other than God could bring you light? Then will you not hear?" Say, "Have you considered if God should make for you the day continuous until the Day of Resurrection, what deity other than God could bring you a night in which you may rest?

Then will you not see? And out of His mercy He made for you the night and the day that you may rest therein and seek from His bounty and hopefully you will be grateful?" (28:71-73)

According to these Qur'anic verses, contemplation must lead to the understanding of Divine mercy, since the cycle of day and night is the result of the mercy of God. In other words, night and day are the work of God's mercy, and therefore, as the Qur'an indicates, such an event is not random. Through contemplation, one will see this as owing to the mercy of God. As we understand from this Qur'anic verse, the eyes of thought or heart will open to the mercy of God through contemplation. Such an important contemplation and reflection on the works of God will lead to knowledge of God. Therefore, the end of the verse suggests that if human beings hear and see the art of God in the circle of day and night, they will become more aware of the Divine presence and be grateful.

There are many verses that encourage contemplation on the realm of nature. Verses from chapter sixteen invite human beings to contemplate on certain foods and the qualities they possess.

And your Lord inspired the bee "Make you houses in the mountains and in the trees and in what people have erected. Then eat from all of the fruit and follow the ways that are made easy for you by your Lord [in your search of the fields to make honey]." Then there comes forth from out of their bellies a drink of diverse colors wherein there is healing for people. Surely in that is a sign for people who contemplate. (16:68-9)

And,

It is God who has sent down water for you from which you drink and by which trees grow and in which you grow your livestock and by which He grows crops for you, and the olive and the date-palm and grapes and all kinds of fruit. Surely herein is indeed a sign [in the Oneness of God] for people who contemplate [on His art]. (16:10-1)

Despite a myriad technological advances, human beings have not been able to produce something as majestic and beneficial as honey, nor grow crops or raise livestock without water. It is in this that human beings are invited to contemplate. There is also a passage about subjugating what is in the skies and on the earth:

God is the One who subjugated to you the sea so that ships may go on it with His command and that you may seek of His bounty and hopefully you will be thankful [to God]. And He has subjugated to you what is in the heavens and what is on the earth, all from Him. Surely in this are signs for people who contemplate. (45:12-13)

The Qur'an also asks people to contemplate on what is around them: "Do they not consider how the camel was created and the heaven, how it is raised? And how the mountains were erected? And how the earth was spread out?" (88:17-20)

Contemplation encourages us to remember that when we see of the works of God in nature we should not consider them purely mechanical actions. If one saw a tree which was growing chocolate or a river flowing with gold, he or she would find these things amazing and consider them miracles. Why then should human beings not be surprised when they see a tree growing an apple or find a pure spring bubbling up from a mountain? These things, which are great gifts of God, have come to be taken for granted and seen as commonplace. It is through contemplation that human beings are able to truly see the wonder and majesty in these Divine arts.

Love of God brings people together and creates a social cohesion to human existence. Let me end this chapter with a quote from the farewell sermon of the Prophet. The Prophet gave his sermon in Mina, a suburb of Mecca, during the feast of sacrifice and said,

> O human beings! Surely your Lord is One and your father [Adam] is one. Be aware there is no superiority of an Arab over a non-Arab and there is no superiority of a non-Arab over an Arab. And there is no superiority of black over red and red over black except for in piety and good conduct. Surely the best of you is the best in conduct.

After his sermon, the Prophet asked, "Did I convey the message?" and his companions said, "Yes, O Messenger of God." Then the Prophet said, "Let those who are present convey the message to those who are absent."[52]

# PART TWO

# Theology and spirituality

# 5

# Al-Ghazali

Abu Hamid Muhammad bin Muhammad al-Ghazali (d. 1111) was a Muslim philosopher, jurist, theologian, and mystic. He is considered one of the *mujaddid,* or renewers of the religion of Islam. He was born in the city of Tus in modern-day Iran. He visited major intellectual centers of the time—Baghdad, Damascus, and Jerusalem—to learn both religious and natural sciences. Due to his attainment of deep knowledge in these fields, at a young age he was appointed as the head of the Nizamiyya schools in Baghdad. One of the dangers to the spiritual life is the love of worldly positions and possessions. Al-Ghazali felt himself thus endangered, because the position for him was becoming an obstacle, making him so busy that he forgot his connection with the Divine and with the way of the Prophet. An individual may be consumed with his or her daily life—job, family, etc.—but this should never block them from their connection with the Divine. Al-Ghazali later would say, "The issues of this world would not prevent the Messenger of God from making his heart constantly with God, due to his high spiritual level."[1] Al-Ghazali then raises the example of people who are in business. They concentrate on their business life so much that things such as the call of nature will not take their hearts from their aims, goals, or anything that is important for their business. Al-Ghazali suggests that one's connection with the Divine should be at least as strong as this. It is evident that al-Ghazali was afraid of such a danger for him, that his life as the head of such a prestigious institution might cause him to forget his connection to the Divine.

As he became closer to the Seljuk rulers and received worldly rewards, he felt the danger even more. The position of being the head of the Nizamiyya schools not only failed to satisfy him, but was becoming a spiritual obstacle to him. Al-Ghazali uses this reasoning when he explains why Jesus did not marry. "Perhaps his situation was a case that required him to become too busy and it was hard to find an allowed [*halal*] environment or it was not even possible to combine marriage and worship so he preferred dedication to worship rather than marriage."[2] Perhaps for a similar reason al-Ghazali thought that combining his position and dedication to worship, at least under his circumstances, was not possible. While he was thinking this, the pull of worldly desires was also attacking. Al-Ghazali describes this spiritual crisis as follows:

> Then I contemplated into my intention of teaching, I realized that it was not pure enough to be for the sake of God. On the contrary, the reason and motivation was to seek worldly position and to have fame. It became certain to me that I was on the edge of danger and I was about to fall into the fire if I were too busy to change my situation. I continued to contemplate in this. I put together my steadfastness to get out of Baghdad and to leave those situations there. But the next day my steadfastness dissolved. I put forward one step and put backward another. Whenever in the morning desire for the seeking of the afterlife comes, in the evening the host of passion attacks it and dissolves it. Mundane desires were pulling me with their chains to remain as I was, however the caller of faith was calling

> > "depart, depart. There is nothing left of your life, but a little and there is a long journey in front of you. And all of what you have known of knowledge and practice in which you are engrossed is pompousness and imagination. If you do not prepare now for the afterlife, when will you prepare? If you do not cut your connections, when will you cut them?"

> At that moment the steadfastness on escaping and getting away became strong. Satan came and said: "This is a temporary situation. Be careful not to listen to it. It goes away quick. If you listen to it and leave this fame and position . . . you may not get it again." For almost six months I wavered between the pulling of the desires of the world and the callers of the afterlife.[3]

As a result of this spiritual crisis and a desire for self-discovery, he resigned and went into seclusion for at least seven years, and by the end he had decided that the spiritual path was the best way to follow. The famous historian and Hadith scholar al-Dhahabi (d. 1348) describes al-Ghazali as "the master, the leader, the ocean [of knowledge], the proof of Islam, the wonder of the time, and the ornament of religion."[4] Al-Dhahabi describes al-Ghazali further, saying,

> His deep investigations in the sciences and other areas of knowledge lead him to be more concerned with asceticism and this lead him to reject the presidency [of the school] and return to the eternal abode and the path of God [through] sincerity and rectification of the soul. He went to pilgrimage, visited the Dome of the Rock. . . . He rectified his soul and made jihad against it. He rejected Satan and wore the clothing of the pious and after years returned to his hometown sticking to his way, using his time, and focusing on knowledge.[5]

According to al-Dhahabi, al-Ghazali took his spiritual path from Abu Ali al-Farmadhi (d. 1084). More famously, his theological teacher was Imam al-Haramayn al-Juwayni (d. 1085), who was the imam of the two holy mosques in Mecca and Medina. As a Sufi initiate, he did what he was assigned to do of compulsory prayers, voluntary prayers, chanting of the Divine names as remembrance of God [or invocations]. In the last period of his life, his writing focused on the Hadith collections, particularly those of al-Bukhari and Muslim bin al-Hajjaj. Qadi Abu Barkr bin al-Arabi (d. 1148), the famous jurist and theologian, indicates the importance and popularity of al-Ghazali by saying, "I used to see him in Baghdad with 400 dignitaries with turbans from the community attending his lectures and taking knowledge from him."[6]

Al-Ghazali was a great mind who wrote more than 200 books and treatises. His magnum opus, *Ihya 'Ulum al-Din* or *Revival of the Religious Sciences*, is his greatest book on Islamic spirituality and still of great relevance today. Al-Ghazali also wrote a book criticizing philosophers called *Tahafut al-Falasifa*, which is widely translated and has been published as *The Incoherence of the Philosophers*. In this work he criticizes philosophers on twenty points, but also agrees with them on some. He brought counter-arguments to the claims of Muslim philosophers, such as al-Farabi (d. 950) and Avicenna (d. 1037). His major concern was philosophers' views on metaphysics. He found three teachings of the philosophers to be theologically problematic. The first is the claim that the resurrection of human beings will be only in soul and not in body and soul, and their rejection of the fact that there will be bodily punishment and rewards. The second is that philosophers limit God's knowledge to only groups of beings, and not individuals. He responds to this philosophical idea by quoting this Qur'anic verse:

And those who disbelieve say: "The hour shall not come upon us." Say: "Yes by my Lord, the Knower of the unseen, it shall certainly come upon you; not the weight of an atom becomes absent from Him, in the heavens or in the earth, and neither less than that nor greater, but (all) is in a clear book." (34:3)

Third is the philosophers' belief in the eternity of the world. As a theologian, he strongly supported the idea that the world is created and not eternal. According to al-Ghazali, "these three problems do not reconcile with Islam in any way. The believers in these are believers in a lie."[7] He also criticized the philosophers' view of denying the attributes of God.

Al-Ghazali himself was criticized by some of his contemporaries and by later scholars for including some weak hadith in *Ihya 'Ulum al-Din*. He was also criticized for some of his mystical ideas. Some also have criticized his famous statement about logic: "Logic is the prerequisite of all sciences. For anyone who does not know logic, there is no trust in anything he knows." Al-Ghazali was also both criticized by some and praised by others for his famous statement, "There is in possibility nothing more wondrous than what is." This can be understood as an invitation to contemplate in the world of nature. This is to show the wisdom and the beauty of the Divine arts in the realm of creation, which are considered the reflection of God's beautiful names, the unlimited sources of beauty. This statement by al-Ghazali should not be understood, as some philosophers have, that God cannot create something more wondrous than this, to which medieval Muslim theologians have responded.

Always, al-Ghazali avoided extremism in his theology and his mystical understandings. He understood the Qur'anic term "the straight path," which is found in the first chapter of the Qur'an as "the balanced one." He wrote his famous book on theology called *Al-Iqtisad fi al-I'tiqad*, which can be translated as "the balance in belief." In his *Mishkat al-Anwar,* or *The Niche of Light*, he criticized two groups with extreme ideas, namely al-Batiniyya (the Esotericists) and al-Hashawiyya (the Literalists). Al-Ghazali kept to a middle ground between esotericism and literalism, arguing that this is the straight path of the Qur'an. Additionally, he sharply criticizes the Esotericists in his book *Fada'ih al-Batiniyya, or The Infamies of the Esotericists*.[8]

In his autobiographical *al-Munqidh min al-Dalal* or *The Deliverer from Error*, he describes his experience and how he finally settled in the mystical tradition. He divides people into four groups. The first group he calls theologians: "God established the group of theologians and moved them to their calls."[9] It seems that he praises theologians, but he does not find theology satisfactory for himself. He says: "The science of theology for me was not enough and for the disease that I was complaining of, it was not a healer."[10] The theologians he refers to are generally scholars of dialectical theology, known in the Islamic tradition as *mutakallimun*. To him, these people are involved with debates to defend the way of the Prophet, but engage in pointless hair-splitting by focusing on the incoherence of opposing groups. Al-Ghazali argues that for the improvement of faith, this is not a requisite. For him, knowledge of the complex arguments made by theologians is not necessary for faith. He says, "They plunged into the study of substances and accidents and their principles. But since that was not the aim of their own science, their discussion of the subject was not thoroughgoing; therefore it did not provide an effective means of dispelling entirely the darkness due to the bewilderment about the differences dividing men [people]."[11] Muslim philosophers are the second group. He accuses them of being followers of Greek philosophy and not the creed of Islam. Third are the esotericists, who he considers as distorters of the religious texts.

According to al-Ghazali, philosophers and theologians are far from finding the truth of faith which is attained through Islamic spirituality or mysticism. It is interesting to see that al-Ghazali in his arguments was not against the natural sciences. Further, he did not see a contradiction between theology and mathematics, logic, politics, ethics, etc. What he was opposing was the philosophers' metaphysical views. Regarding philosophy, al-Ghazali says,

> I devoted myself to that in the moments I had free from writing and lecturing on the legal sciences—and I was then burdened with the teaching and instruction of three hundred students in Baghdad. As it turned out, through mere reading in those embezzled moments, God Most High gave me an insight into the farthest reaches of the philosophers' sciences in less than two years. Then, having understood their doctrine, I continued to reflect assiduously on it for nearly a year, coming back to it constantly and repeatedly reexamining its intricacies and profundities. Finally I became so familiar with the measure of its deceit and deception, and its precision and delusion, that I had no doubt about my thorough grasp of it.[12]

According to his categorization, the final group are the mystics. This group found the truth. After a long period of seclusion and contemplation, he came to the conclusion that Sufism, or Islamic spirituality, is the only way among these four to find the truth and gain eternal bliss.

> When I had finished with all those kinds of lore, I brought my mind to bear on the way of the Sufis. I knew that their particular Way is consummated [realized] only by knowledge and by activity [by the union of theory and practice]. The aim of their knowledge is to lop off the obstacles present in the soul and to rid oneself of its reprehensible habits and vicious qualities in order to attain thereby a heart empty of all save God and adorned with the constant remembrance of God.[13]

He further says, "how great a difference there is between your knowing the definition of drunkenness—viz., that it is a term denoting a state resulting from the predominance of vapors which rise from the stomach to the centers of thought—and your actually being drunk!"[14] After coming to this understanding, he seems to have begun studying the early mystics:

> Therefore I began to learn their lore from the perusal of their books, such as *The Food of Hearts* by Abu Talib al-Makki (God's mercy be upon him!) and the writings of al-Harith al-Muhasibi, and the miscellaneous items handed down from al-Junayd and al-Shibli and Abu Yazid al-Bistami (God hallow their spirits) and others of their masters. As a result I came to know the core of their theoretical aims and I learned all that could be learned of their way by study and hearing.[15]

According to al-Ghazali, human beings are veiled from the Divine light because of their negative practices. Human beings must prepare to receive the gift of Divine revelation. They can do this by cutting their ties to earthliness and worldliness and making their connection with the Divine of supreme importance in every part of their being. This can be done by withdrawing from the world and engaging in the instructional exercise of *dhikr* in addition to the prescribed prayers. The purer the soul, the more it sees the Divine light. Knowing philosophy or theology is not enough to get rid of vicious qualities, and therefore it is through spirituality that the purification of the soul increases and the door of Divine light opens. He makes a distinction between knowing and experiencing. While knowing may not be able to pierce the veils of Divine light, experiencing can.

Al-Ghazali in *Mishkat al-Anwar* speaks of veils that prevent human beings from seeing the Divine light. These veils, according to al-Ghazali, are selfish appetites (*al-shahwa*), anger (*al-ghadab*), corrupt beliefs (*al-i'tiqadat al-batila*), negative imagination (*al-khayalat*), and corrupt rational analogy (*al-muqayasat*). The result of these veils is that human beings worship deities of their own desires rather than God, as the Qur'an commands. To defeat these veils, there has to be a cleanliness of faculties and sincere religious practice. One has to actualize the prophetic spirit, which is considered the highest faculty. Eventually, one will reach the level of *fana* (annihilation of one's ego in the presence of God), which is the highest possible position to attain in Islamic spirituality.

Since the Sufi path is the way to follow, al-Ghazali elaborates on how to perceive the Divine light. It is important to note that one of the ninety-nine names of God is *al-Nur,* which means the Light. God is the Light and the One who lights the light. As a name when it is used for God, it is used in a real sense, because the real light is God's light. When the word is used for human beings, it is used in a metaphorical sense. When one thinks of the reflection of the Divine name *al-Nur*, the sun—earth's most powerful source of light—comes to mind. Despite the greatness of the sun's light, it is but a shadowy reflection of the Divine name *al-Nur*. In his discussion of the Divine light, al-Ghazali argues the goal of human existence is to be close to God through an inward transformation of the soul. The result will be knowledge of the cosmos, then one's self, and finally knowledge of God, which is the highest level of knowledge. Once an individual reaches the knowledge of God, that person will have inner purification.

Al-Ghazali speaks of the Divine light in his interpretation of what is called the "the Verse of Light," which itself is the namesake of chapter twenty-four "The Light." The verse says,

> God is the light of the heavens and the earth. The similitude of His light is as a niche wherein there is a lamp and the lamp in a glass. The glass is as if it was a glittering star, kindled from a blessed tree, an olive that is neither of the east nor of the west, whose oil would shine even if it were not touched by any fire. Light upon light, God guides to His light whom He pleases. God strikes similitudes for people, and God has knowledge of everything. (24:35)

Al-Ghazali has a unique interpretation of the Verse of Light. He states that the equivalent of the lamp found in the Qur'an are the five senses. The equivalent of the niche is human imagination. Glass is equivalent to reflection. The tree is equivalent to rational faculty. The olive is equivalent to the prophetic faculty.

When such spiritual qualities are attained, the inner eyes become open. Just as human beings have two eyes through which they can see materials, they also have two eyes of the heart. While the material eyes are weak, the eyes of the heart are sharper. Once they are open, they can see the reality of things as they are. They can see the unseen world. In a comparison between the inner eyes and the outward eyes, al-Ghazali lists seven imperfections of the outward eyes. These are that the eye cannot see itself, does not see what is far from it or what is extremely close to it, does not perceive what is behind veils, perceives only the surface of things, sees only some existent things, does not see what is infinite, and sees large things as small. All of these prove that the vision of the naked eye is limited. The inner eyes, however, are free from these imperfections. The outer eye derives from the world of sensation and visibility, and the inner eye derives from another world, namely, the world of *Malakut,* or the world of dominion, which is the invisible spiritual world.

In his book *Kimya-i Saadat,* translated as *The Alchemy of Happiness,* he discusses another important element of the spiritual tradition: heart, or *qalb.* He says of heart in connection to the human soul, "He who neglects it and suffers its capacities to rust or to degenerate must necessarily be the loser in this world and in the next."[16] Heart is central to everything for al-Ghazali. On heart's significance, al-Ghazali says,

> The first step to self-knowledge is to know that thou are composed of an outward shape, called the body, and an inward entity called the heart or soul. By "heart" I do not mean the piece of flesh that is situated in the left of our bodies, but that which uses all the other faculties as its instruments and servants. In truth it does not belong to the visible world, but to the invisible, and has come to this world as a traveler visits a foreign country for the sake of merchandise, and it will presently return to its native land. It is the knowledge of this entity and its attributes which is the key to the knowledge of God.[17]

Further, al-Ghazali describes how knowledge of God is the highest purpose of the soul, and through this tacitly makes reference to Qur'an 13:28, which says that hearts rest in the remembrance of God:

> Anyone who will look into the matter will see that happiness is necessarily linked with the knowledge of God. Each faculty of ours delights in that for which it was created: lust delights in accomplishing desire, anger in taking vengeance, the eye in seeing beautiful objects, and the ear in

hearing harmonious sounds. The highest function of the soul of man is the perception of the truth; in this accordingly, it finds its special delight. Even in trifling matters, such as learning chess, this holds good, and the higher the subject-matter of the knowledge obtained, the greater the delight. A man would be pleased at being admitted to the confidence of a prime minister, but how much more if the king makes an intimate of him and discloses state secrets to him.[18]

For a variety of reasons, *Ihya 'Ulum al-Din* is the most important of al-Ghazali's writings on Islamic spirituality. It is to this work that we now turn. The book is divided into four-quarters, and it is generally printed in four volumes. The first is about prayers. In this section, al-Ghazali describes various types of remembrances of God and prayers, and how to categorize the daily prayers. Recitation of the Qur'an and the secrets of pilgrimage, charity, and fasting, as well as giving details on how one can revive their nights through prayer are also discussed. When he describes the remembrance of God, he describes the merits of remembering God based on the Qur'an and the Hadith. Following this, he speaks about the merits and etiquette of prayer, the merits of asking forgiveness from God, and the merits of asking blessings from God to the Prophet. He also describes the prayers that it is believed the Prophet said in the mornings and in the evenings, and after each prescribed prayer. He also speaks about the prayer that is narrated from the Prophet and his companions, and he gives instructions on how to perform prayers. For example, he says,

If you are of those who are looking for the harvest of the afterlife and those who are following the Prophet (peace and blessing be upon him) in what he did of prayers, say in the beginning of every prayer, "Exalted my Lord, the Highest of the high, the Giver" and the end of your prescribed prayers say, "there is no deity but God. He is the One, has no partners, all that is visible [*mulk*] belongs to Him and praise belongs to Him, he is powerful over everything." And say "I am pleased with God as the Lord and with Islam as the religion and with Muhammad as the Prophet." [Repeat this] three times. And also say, "My Lord the Creator of heavens and earth, the Knower of unseen and visible, the Lord and the King of everything, I testify that there is no deity except You. I take refuge in You from the evil of my soul and from the evil of Satan and his partners." [Again al-Ghazali says] say "My Lord, I ask you for forgiveness and health in my religion in my worldly life, in my family, and in my possessions. My Lord cover my mistakes, give me safety from my fears, and decrease my blunders, and protect me from any danger in front of me and from the back of me and from danger right and left, from above and I take refuge in you for dangers that come from below me."[19]

Then al-Ghazali refers to the prayers of the Prophet on various occasions, from entering a mosque to wearing new clothes. For example, al-Ghazali says: "When you wear new clothes say, 'My Lord You have clothed me in these clothes. Thanks be to You. I ask You of the goodness of it and the best of what has been made for it. I take refuge in You from the evil of it and from the evil that is made for it.'"[20] Next al-Ghazali gives details on how an individual can revive their nights. Nights are the time of sleeping, and sleeping is the sister of death.[21] Since the Prophet spent a significant amount of his night in prayer, it has become a tradition in Islamic spirituality that people wake up after midnight or before dawn and perform prayers as frequently as they can. Al-Ghazali says,

> People in this world are travelers. Their first station is the cradle and their last station is the grave. The home is Paradise or Hell. The span of life is the distance of this travel. The years of this are different stations and the months of it shorter rest areas and the days of it are the miles and the breaths of it are the steps of it. And obedience to the Divine is the real possession and the time of it is its capital [money]. And the desires and inclinations of it are the robbers on the way. And the profit of it is accomplishment of the triumph of meeting with God in Paradise with a large property and eternal bounties. And the loss of it is to be away from God.[22]

Here he also speaks of the time from the beginning of the day through the end of the day, and what types of prayers are to be done. Then he has a specific emphasis on the prayers that are said at night. Though there is much emphasis on prayer at night and the Prophet spent much of his own night in prayer,[23] al-Ghazali makes it clear that prayer is not to be done at the expense of sleeping. He quotes from the Prophet to show that the Prophet prohibited his followers from forcing themselves awake to pray at night, saying that those who only pray and fast are not part of the Prophet's community. Al-Ghazali divides the nights into four periods. The period that he calls the fourth period starts with the passing of the first half of the night until one-sixth of the night remains. This is the time of night prayer. This is a time that all are asleep except the Most-Living and the Most-Sustaining. Al-Ghazali recounts narrations from David and the Prophet of Islam. The Prophet of Islam was asked, "Which part of the night is most heard when the prayers are performed?" And the Prophet responded, "the middle of the night." According to al-Ghazali, David, the prophet of God asked God: "My Lord, I love to worship You. What is the best time of worship?" God sent him a revelation saying, "O David. Do not wake up at the beginning of the night and at the end of the night because anyone who wakes up at the beginning of the night will sleep at the end. Therefore, wake up at the middle of the night."[24]

In a section of *Ihya 'Ulum al-Din* called "Al-Muhlikat," or "The Things that Destroy," al-Ghazali lists such defects as anger, rancor, envy, worldliness, love of wealth, arrogance, conceit, etc. as things that can destroy a person's spiritual life, and he provides remedies for them. While mentioning the danger of bodily appetites, particularly satiation and lust, he provides remedies in the form of abstinence and hunger.[25] After this, al-Ghazali sees following the appetite of the stomach as the greatest of the destructive forces. According to al-Ghazali, the chain of destructive characters starts with the stomach. These destroy the spirit and are a pain on the spirit. Al-Ghazali refers to a saying of the Prophet, which says, "The best of you before God is the one who stays hungry longer and contemplates longer."[26] It is evident that there is a strong connection between physical health and eating habits. Al-Ghazali finds this important for the spirit as well.

In this section, he describes the soul, spirit, heart, and reason. After this, he speaks of the rectification of the soul, the beautification of ethics, and the treatment of the diseases of the heart. As was noted above, for al-Ghazali, the heart is the center of everything. When he speaks of the heart he uses two meanings. One is the physical heart that is on the left side of the human chest cavity, similar to pine cones. Al-Ghazali notes that this is not his intention when he speaks of heart. He calls this heart just a piece of meat from the visible world, that even animals can see with their eyes. He speaks of heart as follows:

> It is a subtle Divine spiritual faculty. It has a connection to the physical heart. This subtle faculty is the essence of humanity. It is this the one who perceives, the one who knows, and the one who comprehends in human beings. It is this the one who is accountable, punished, blamed, and requested. It has connections to the physical heart, many people's minds have been perplexed in understanding the way of this connection.[27]

In his book, it is not his goal to speak about the nature or essence of the heart, which even the Prophet did not describe, but only to deal with its qualities.

Elsewhere in his magnum opus, al-Ghazali outlines the themes that are considered deliverances, al-munjiyat, or literally savers. These are things that will save people from Hell and deliver them to Paradise. For al-Ghazali, like many mystics, repentance is the first in this group of savers. Repentance from sins means a return to the One who knows everything and covers all shameful things and mistakes. It has to be noted that one of the Divine names is al-Sattar, the All-Covering, that is, the One who covers the sins of people and does not embarrass them. According to al-Ghazali, repentance is "the beginning of the way of the salikun [those who undertake a spiritual journey] and it is the capital of those who have succeeded."[28] Al-Ghazali further describes human beings as being made of a mixture of both good and evil, and for rectification there is a need to burn with the fire of regret; in order to have a precious jewel, there is a need for heat and fire. Similarly, in order to rectify and purify the essence of human beings from the ugliness of Satan, there is a need for the fire of repentance. He suggests that if the

sins are not cleaned with the fire of regret and repentance, in the afterlife
they will be cleaned with another fire, which is much harsher than the fire
of repentance. Al-Ghazali refers to a saying of the Prophet which states that
repentance is not something ritual, but something found deeper in the heart.
The Prophet says, "regret is repentance."[29]

Religiously speaking, repentance is a necessity. Repentance is what
connects people to the Divine. Without repentance, there is no possibility
of being in the presence of God and seeing the beauty of God. Al-Ghazali
illustrates the necessity of repentance beautifully as follows:

> What is meant by necessity is what is necessary to reach the eternal bliss
> and to be saved from eternal damnation. If the eternal bliss and eternal
> damnation are based on an action, that action becomes necessary . . . .
> When the meaning of religious necessity is understood and it is also
> understood that this necessity is the vehicle to eternal bliss and there is
> no eternal bliss without meeting the Divine and anyone who is veiled
> from the meeting of the Divine is miserable and also understood that
> following carnal desires and being attached to this transient world are
> the things that are moving individuals away from the presence of the
> Divine.[30]

For all this, repentance seems to be the best way to reach the presence of
the Divine, and it has to be done as soon as possible. Otherwise, there is the
possibility of accumulation of sins, which can cover the face of the heart
to the extent that it will no longer be a mirror for the Divine. Al-Ghazali
emphasizes that the repentance must be done quickly. However, he does
not close the door of hope. Rather, regret and repentance are doors that
individuals can enter anywhere and at any time. Here al-Ghazali makes
reference to two verses from the Qur'an. The first says, "O you who have
believed, repent to God with sincere repentance. It is hoped that your Lord
will expiate your bad deeds and bring you into gardens beneath which
rivers flow" (66:8). The second is a concluding part of a long verse which
says, "And repent all of you to God, O believers so that you may succeed"
(24:31). He also refers to a saying of the Prophet, "The repenter is the
beloved of God. The one who repents from sins is like the one who has no
sins."[31]

When al-Ghazali describes the importance of repentance, he discusses the
levels of faith. For him, faith has many doors, from the lowest to the highest.
As an example, al-Ghazali gives the highest door of faith to be the testimony
of faith: "There is no deity but God." This, therefore, is the most important
element of the faith. The lowest is to remove from people's way things that could
harm them, like thorns. Therefore, a connection exists between committing
sin and one's level of faith. In theory, the higher the level of one's faith, the less
sin that person commits. In the same way, al-Ghazali sees in human beings
not only one existence, but many of them. The highest of these are the

heart and the spirit. The lowest is that which removes dirt and hair from the body, distinguishing humans beings from animals.[32]

Al-Ghazali sees repentance as a cure that is made of two things. One is sweet and the other is bitter. It is similar to the sweetness of honey and the bitterness of vinegar. In this case, he speaks of the sweetness of knowledge and the bitterness of patience as the two major components of repentance. This way, repentance becomes an elixir that cures the diseases of the heart. It is repentance that can defeat addiction, which is a disease of the heart. In response to a question about the relationship between the diseases of the spiritual heart and the diseases of the body, al-Ghazali says, "The diseases of the heart are more than the diseases of the body."[33] In explaining why this is so, al-Ghazali relates three major reasons, which also show the danger of the diseases of the heart. First, the sick person who has a disease of the heart does not know that he or she is sick. Second, the consequences of diseases of the heart are not seen in this world, unlike diseases of body, the consequences of which manifest themselves in the form of illness and death. The consequences of the diseases of the heart can lead to the death of the heart, but they still might not be seen in this world. The third is the lack of a proper doctor for the diseases of the heart. By doctor, al-Ghazali refers to the spiritual masters that were frequently available in earlier eras of Islam. Al-Ghazali complains, "The disease has become much stronger and the doctors who were going to cure it have become sick so that they cannot cure it. Therefore they deceive people. They act as if they are curing it, but in reality are unable to cure it."[34] One cannot stand but to wonder, if masters of spirituality were scarce in the time of al-Ghazali, what he would have thought had he lived in our time. But perhaps due to the proliferation of information in the modern age, people might gain access to knowledge, possibly finding cures through knowledge of spirituality and patience that al-Ghazali describes as sweetness and bitterness.

Because patience is one of the components of repentance, al-Ghazali dedicates a section to patience, describing it as half of faith. He divides patience into two elements. One is related to the body, such as bodily difficulties that one must become patient about, e.g. bodily prayers that are hard to perform or sickness. Physical patience is a positive dimension, but for al-Ghazali even more important is spiritual patience, that is, patience against carnal desires. This could have a variety of names, such as chastity, self-control, etc. According to al-Ghazali, the Prophet once was asked about faith: "'What is faith?' The Messenger of God replied, 'faith is patience.'"[35] For al-Ghazali, patience is also a cure. The components of patience are knowledge and action, which make a mixture to cure the diseases of heart. This medicine changes according to the nature of the disease. For some people, patience in fasting is most important. For others, it may be something else. He says, "Anyone who trains their soul on opposing desires will overcome it whenever they want,"[36] and he sees this as an essential element of patience.

Another among the things that are considered savers in the teachings of al-Ghazali is thankfulness. Interestingly, al-Ghazali starts with the nature of Satan and his conversation with the Divine, observing that he will deceive people by closing the way of thankfulness and making most of them unthankful to God: "Then I shall come to them from their fronts and from their backs and from their rights and from their lefts, and You will not find most of them thankful" (7:17). Al-Ghazali also states, "Know that God equated thankfulness with His remembrance in His Holy Book, even though He said the remembrance of God is greater."[37] In reference to Qur'an 14:7, according to al-Ghazali, God increases His bounties to the thankful without exception. The verse says, "And when your Lord proclaimed, 'If you are thankful, surely I will give you more, but if you are not thankful, My punishment is surely terrible.'"

Al-Ghazali sees thankfulness as one of the stages of the travelers in the way of Islamic spirituality. It is made of three components. One is knowledge, the second is exposition, and the third is action. As for knowledge, it is to understand the bounties as coming from the Giver of the bounties, *al-Mun'im*. What is meant by exposition is the joy that happens because of the bounties that come from the Giver of the bounties. As for action, it is to do what is the goal of the Giver of the bounties and what is loved by the Giver. In describing thankfulness, al-Ghazali makes reference to Shibli (d. 946), an important mystic who says, "thankfulness is to see the Giver in the bounties."[38] He also refers to Moses in this regard, narrating that Moses in his supplication to God said, "'My Lord, You created Adam with Your own hands and You gave him such and such [many bounties]. How did he thank You?' God responded to Moses 'He knew that all these bounties were from Me. That knowledge from him was thankfulness.'"[39] Based on this story, al-Ghazali surmises: "Therefore you do not thank unless you know that everything is from Him. If any doubts intervene you cannot be knowledgeable neither about the bounty nor about the Giver of the bounty."[40]

Further, al-Ghazali refers to the following hadith:

It is narrated that on one occasion, the Prophet asked a person, "How is your morning?" The person responded, "my morning is good." The Prophet repeated that and the person repeated it was good. The Prophet repeated this a third time and the person responded, "my morning is good and I praise God and thank God for that." The Prophet responded, "That is what I wanted from you."[41]

Thankful action are divided into three categories, according to al-Ghazali: actions of the heart, actions of the tongue, and actions of the extremities. Furthermore, al-Ghazali says that one of the thankfulnesses of the eyes is that when one sees the weaknesses of a believer, one does not disclose them, and one of the thankfulnesses of the ears is to not disclose the deficits of the believers if you hear them. In other words, one should be respectful of people and must avoid embarrassing them. This principle seems compatible with the teachings of Jesus when he says,

> Judge not, that you be not judged. For with the judgment you pronounce you will be judged, and the measure you give will be the measure you get. Why do you see the speck that is in your brother's eye, but do not notice the log that is in your own eye? (Mt. 7:1-3)

Theologically speaking, the opposite of thankfulness is denial. Using God's bounties in a way that is not what they were created for is considered unthankfulness. For example, eyes are created to see and contemplate on the wonders of creation, not as a vehicle for lust. Hands are created to build up, not destroy. This is also true for the inner organs, even if their exact function is not known. Therefore, al-Ghazali says,

> Anyone who uses anything in a direction that is not the direction that it is created for and that it is meant for surely has denied the bounties of God. For example, the one who strikes others with his hands has denied the bounties of the hands because hands are created for the person to defend himself against something that could destroy him and to take what is beneficial to him and not to harm others with his hands.[42]

Again in al-Ghazali's teachings, among the themes that are considered savers are being fearful and being hopeful; he considers hopefulness and fearfulness to be medicines for the diseases of the heart. Hopefulness is to be hopeful about God. He compares this to someone who farms and sows seeds and is hopeful to harvest them when the time comes. Needless to say, before this, one has to have fertile land and good seeds to sow. If the land is not good for sowing seeds, such hope becomes incompatible with what al-Ghazali is describing. According to him, such hope would be the hope of fools and of deception.

He gives an analogy to indicate the role of the heart in faith and actions:

> Accordingly this world is a farm for the afterlife. The heart is the land and faith is the seed and the prayers and rituals are comparable to tilling and cleaning of the soil. The heart that is not dedicated is like a land that is incapable of farming. In that land seeds cannot grow. The day of judgement is like the day of the harvest. People harvest only what they have sown.[43]

Seemingly, al-Ghazali responds to a question of whether hopefulness or fearfulness is more important. He suggests that hopefulness is related to love, and love indicates closeness to God. Also, when there is love, there is hope. Because of this, in the Islamic teaching, to be hopeless is essentially prohibited; always one has to be hopeful about God. Al-Ghazali refers to a statement of Ali, who refers to a man whose sins led him to hopelessness. Ali told the man: "Your hopelessness from the mercy of God is greater as a sin than your entire sins."[44] Ali therefore is suggesting to this person that although he has many sins, he should not be hopeless about God. Al-Ghazali also recounts a narration from the Prophet:

> A man was in Hell for one thousand years and he used to still say the Divine names, *al-Hannan* [the One who shows mercy] and *al-Mannan* [the Most-Gracious], and God said to Gabriel: "Take My servant to Me." Angel Gabriel took this person to the Divine and God asked the person: "How did you find that place?" The man said: "That place is the worst of all places" God commands Gabriel to take the man back to his place. As he walked away, he looked behind him and God asked: "Why did you look back?" The man said: "I had hoped that You would not return me to Hell after You had removed me." God then told Gabriel to take him to Paradise.

Al-Ghazali says, after citing this, "His hope was the reason for his salvation."[45]

For al-Ghazali, fearing God is also medicine for the diseases of the heart. He describes two types of fearfulness and gives several analogies of these. First, he says, imagine a child in a house, and a savage animal or a snake enters the house. Most probably the child will show no fear, and perhaps will try to catch the snake and play with it. But if the father of the child is with him, he will be afraid of the snake and will try to escape, and the child also will follow his father. In this case, the fear of the father is informed by knowledge, and the fear of the son is in imitation of his father. In the same way, fearing God has two dimensions. One is the fear of the punishment of God and the second is the fear of the "people of hearts," that is, people who have knowledge of the attributes of God. This has something to do with respect and awe that is mixed with a certain amount of fear of being separated from something that is very beloved. This is why the second fear is more important for Muslim mystics. For them, the first fear is small and superficial. Al-Ghazali refers to a statement of Dhu al-Nun al-Misri (d. 859), an Egyptian Muslim saint, which says, "The fear of fire in comparison to the fear of separation [from God] is like a drop [of water] to the ocean." In al-Ghazali's understanding, this second meaning is what the Qur'an means when it says, "And surely knowledgeable people are those who fear God" (35:28). The fear of the general believers is similar to the fear of the child that follows his father. There is no doubt that this fear is not the ideal for mystics.

According to al-Ghazali, poverty and asceticism are also among the savers. In relation to poverty, he refers to Qur'an 47:38, which says that people are called upon to spend in the way of God, and that God is rich and human beings are poor. For our contemporary society, what is important here is not being poor per se, as al-Ghazali and other early mystics believed and acted upon, but to use what wealth one is given to do good deeds without attaching one's heart to that wealth. As the Qur'an says, "O human beings, you are the poor before God. God is the Rich and the Praiseworthy" (35:15). Regarding asceticism, al-Ghazali essentially sees it as leaving one thing for something that is more worthy. In other words, it is to prefer the afterlife, which has far more worth than this life; it is to prefer the ornaments of Paradise to those of this life.

As with other savers al-Ghazali focuses on three dimensions of asceticism: knowledge, exposition, and action. As for knowledge, it is knowing that what is with God is more sustainable and more valuable than worldly things. It is like preferring jewels over snow. As al-Ghazali puts it,

> It is not difficult for the owner of the snow [in summer] to sell it in return for jewels and pearls. This is the story of the world and the afterlife. The world is like the snow before the sun, constantly melting before it comes to the end, and the afterlife is like a jewel that does not become annihilated.[46]

Al-Ghazali in this regard refers to the story of Qarun, saying that those who had knowledge were the ascetics from the people of Moses. As the Qur'an says, "Those who had been given knowledge said: 'Woe unto you. The reward of God is much greater for those who believe and do good deeds. And only those who are patient can receive this reward'" (28:80). Importantly, al-Ghazali does not say that simply abandoning wealth is asceticism. Indeed, for him, this would be a form of showing off and would go against the very principles of asceticism.

Another of the themes that al-Ghazali considers savers is trust in God. It is something that is beloved by God. Therefore, the one who trusts in God is also the one who receives the love of God. Al-Ghazali makes a connection between believing in the oneness of God, *tawhid*, and trusting in God by referencing a saying of the Prophet: "If you had trust in God in a true way, He would have given you sustenance as birds are given sustenance."[47] For al-Ghazali, the essence of trust is the belief that God is the One who reigns over everything. Without His permission, nothing can happen. This is the meaning of *tawhid* for Sufis. Similarly, the Sufi understanding of annihilation in God is to see only God in the realm of existence. The keys to everything are in the hands of God. The individual is fully immersed in God, and this is trust in God. Once a person has full trust in God, the person's strength in God becomes even greater. It is to see God as the Cause of causes.

As a master of analogy, al-Ghazali once again uses a beautiful metaphor: a person is forgiven by the king and receives a proclamation signed by the king for his forgiveness and for his release from the prison. This person looks at the ink and the paper and the pen of which the signature has been made, and he says, "If it were not for the pen, I would have not been released." He forgets the mover of the pen and focuses on the pen itself. Al-Ghazali says, "This is an utmost level of ignorance. The one who knows the pen has no

power in itself, it is subjugated to the hands of the writer, does not praise the
pen. Instead such a person praises the writer."[48]

Other savers include: love of God, yearning for the Divine meeting,
pleasure with what God wills, and friendship in God. In al-Ghazali's work,
these four elements have a singular connotation of delivery and derive from
the love of God. For al-Ghazali, love of God is the highest of all the stages
of spirituality. He refers to a Qur'anic verse which says, "God will bring a
people whom He loves and who love Him" (5:54). According to al-Ghazali,
to love anything other than God without relating it to God shows ignorance
and a lack of knowledge of God. Love for scholars, saints, and the pious are
all in reference to the origin of love, and that is the love of God. Therefore,
things other than God can be loved, but this love must be for the sake of
God. Also, according to al-Ghazali, the happiest person in the afterlife is the
one who loves God the most. One of the important elements here shows that
true love of God is being pleased with what God wills. Al-Ghazali illustrates
this with a hadith.

> The Prophet asked a group of his companions: "What are you?" And they
> said "We are believers." And the Prophet said, "What is the sign of your
> belief?" They said: "We are patient against the difficulties and we thank
> God for the bounties and we are pleased with whatever God wills." The
> prophet said: "By God almighty, Lord of the Ka'ba, you are the believers."[49]

Three additional savers for al-Ghazali are good intention, sincerity, and
truthfulness. Sincerity and truthfulness are part of good intention, and this
is essential in everything. Even if one is with the Prophet of God, if one's
intention is not pure, it does not contribute to one's spiritual well-being. In
fact, al-Ghazali refers to a hadith regarding some people who migrated with
the Prophet from Mecca to Medina, but whose intentions were for worldly
things, specifically for women to marry. Hence, their migration was for these
things only, and not for the sake of God. He also refers to a saying of the
Prophet which says, "God does not look at your shapes or properties, but
He looks at your hearts and actions."[50] Heart is the center of intention, and
everything starts with heart.

The final two themes that al-Ghazali considers savers are *muraqaba*,
which has a connotation of meditation, and *muhasaba*, or self-interrogation.
For mystics, an important aspect of meditation is meditation on the afterlife.
This includes meditating on the Day of Judgment, on the intercession, on the
aspects of Paradise and Hell, and on seeing the beauty of God in the afterlife.
All of these actions are *muraqaba*, and this is what leads to *muhasaba*.

To conclude, it is worth mentioning how al-Ghazali describes the vast
aspects of Divine mercy. He does so by reiterating a saying of the Prophet:
"For God there are 100 mercies. He sent one of these to the *jinn*, human
beings, birds, animals, and insects. Because of this mercy they show each
other kindness and compassion. Ninety-nine of these mercies, God will

show to His servants on the Day of Judgment."[51] Elsewhere, al-Ghazali describes mercy as follows:

> The full mercy is the distribution of goodness to the needy and God's willing for the needy is caring for them. The encompassing mercy is the one that is bestowed upon those who deserved and those who do not deserve. God's mercy is both complete and encompassing. It is complete because God willed to fulfill the needs of the needy and fulfilled them. As for its encompassing aspect, it is because it covers those who deserve and those who do not deserve. It encompasses the world and the afterlife. It includes indispensable needs and just needs and many additional things beyond the needs. Therefore, He is the true Most-Merciful, unconditionally, truly in the deepest way.[52]

This is what gives hope to all human beings.

# 6

# Bediuzzaman Said Nursi

In March 1960, despite the restrictions the government placed on his travel, an ill, 83-year-old man asked his students to drive him from Isparta, a city in western Turkey, to Urfa, a city nearly 600 miles to the east. Urfa, or Sanliurfa as it is known today, is situated near Turkey's border with Syria and is believed by some to be the birthplace of Abraham. He arrived there and settled in a hotel. The government commanded him to leave the city immediately and return to Isparta, but his students informed the officials that they would follow the instructions of their master, who was not planning to go back. The Minister of the Interior insisted that the local governor use whatever means necessary to remove him from the city, but the public responded to the government, saying that they would not allow their guest to be kicked out of the city. This was a man who had never married, who had chosen a life of poverty, but was spiritually one of the richest men on earth. During his second night in the city, the man passed on to the afterlife. The date was March 23, 1960, or Ramadan 25, 1379 in the Islamic calendar. This man was Bediuzzaman Said Nursi, a man who shaped the mind of millions.

At a young age Said Nursi had a dream, and in this dream a figure—some would say it was the Prophet and others the fourth caliph Ali, who is also known as the Sultan of Saints—commanded him, "Explain the truthfulness of the Qur'an." Of this dream, Nursi once said that despite his lack of ability he understood that a person like himself would be a candidate for such an important task. Although he had begun his readings and memorizations earlier, perhaps this was the real beginning of Nursi's spiritual journey.

When he started to search for guidance for his own journey, Nursi studied the various Muslim mystics who held a great place in Islamic spirituality. He was attracted to them, but he was not satisfied; he was looking for something more. One day, looking for guidance, Nursi opened the great mystic Abd al-Qadir al-Jilani's (d. 1166) book *Futuh al-Ghayb*, or *The Revelations of the Unseen* and read the following: "You are in the house of wisdom. Look for a doctor to cure your heart." Nursi says that at that time he was a member of the Islamic House of Wisdom, the highest religious institution of the Ottoman Empire. He says that it is as if he was attempting to cure the ills of the community, but he himself was in need of a doctor. In fact, he believed that his diseases were the worst of all; how could such a sick person cure the spiritual ills of others? He understood that al-Jilani was telling him that he was sick and should look for a spiritual doctor. Nursi accepted al-Jilani as his doctor and he began reading *Futuh al-Ghayb*. According to Nursi, the book was so powerful that it performed surgery on his soul. The book's curing power was so strong that Nursi could not originally read the whole book. From then on, Nursi considered himself a student of Abd al-Qadir al-Jilani. Nursi also considered the poems and prayers of Imam Ali, known as *Qasida Jaljalutiyya*, to be instructions for him. One can see how Nursi takes his spiritual instruction from these two great masters of Islam.

In his early life, what he called his "Old Said" period, Nursi attempted to find his way through politics "to serve religion and knowledge," but then he realized that, in practice, political Islam was not compatible with the core teachings of Islam which, for Nursi, are based on sincerity, justice, and compassion. Together he abandoned two great evils—smoking and politics based on polarization and self-interest—and coined his famous statement, "I take refuge in God from Satan and politics." Elsewhere, he also likened someone mixing politics and Islam to a man carrying a light and a hammer. He dedicated himself to the light of Islam rather than the hammer of politics.

After abandoning politics, he found a new way to serve humanity, rooted in the mystical tradition of Islam, yet divergent from traditional Sufism. He established his new way on four steps, which I call "the four noble truths of Nursi." He says, paralleling his steps to the way of the Naqshabandi order, which also has four principles, "abandoning the world, abandoning the hereafter, abandoning the body, and abandoning this 'abandoning.'"[1] that his humble way has four things. Nursi's ways are absolute weakness, absolute poverty, absolute enthusiasm, and absolute thankfulness. Elsewhere, compassion and contemplation are the two major principles of his way, and based on his writings in sum, it seems the four truths are weakness, poverty, compassion, and contemplation. These are rooted in his understanding of the Qur'an.

Weakness, or *'ajz*, means to understand that people are not able to meet their needs for themselves; they are reliant on God. As he says,

Yes, human beings can be defeated by a blind scorpion and a footless snake. Therefore, it is not humans' own power, but instead it is the fruit of their weakness that the subjugation of the Divine and the generosity of the Most-Merciful dresses humans in silk from a tiny worm and gives honey to them from a poisonous insect. O Human beings, since this is true, abandon arrogance and egoism. Declare at the door of the Divine your weaknesses and deficits by asking for help and your poverty and your needs by prayer and supplications and show that you are a servant and say this, "God is Sufficient for us. He, in Whom we trust, is the Most-Excellent," [Qur'an 3:173] and elevate [in the realm of spirituality].[2]

Poverty, or *faqr*, means to consider oneself poor before God, not before people. It is God who made this planet which sustains human beings. This truth requires human beings to understand the limits of their ability to provide life's necessities.

Compassion, or *shafaqa*, means to show kindness toward human beings and nature. It is compassion that has beautified the universe. This is the reflection of the Divine names that are repeated frequently in the Qur'an and daily prayers by Muslims: *al-Rahman, al-Rahim*, the Most-Compassionate, the Most-Merciful.

Contemplation, or *tafakkur*, means to contemplate the realm of creation and find the reflections of the Divine names in the realm of nature. With this, Nursi distinguishes himself from prominent Muslim mystics, such as Ibn al-Arabi (d. 1240), who promote the idea of the oneness of being, or *wahdat al-wujud*, and consider the realm of nature a shadow. Nursi considers the realm of nature real and capable of providing a deep understanding of the Divine names that are reflected in it. In other words, *tafakkur* means to think of the created things not on their behalf, but on the behalf of their Creator, and investigate them as the reflection and the mirror of the beautiful names of God.

These principles therefore constitute Nursi's way of spirituality. Nursi calls it "the Qur'anic way." He made these pillars of his methodology and they can be considered the foundation of a new understanding of Islamic spirituality. This is a spirituality that is based on compassion, and today humanity needs compassion more than ever. Moreover, Nursi's methodology is one that can be practiced by everyone. Nursi himself compares his way of spirituality to that of Ibn al-Arabi, noting that while Ibn al-Arabi considered his way of knowing God superior to that of theologians like al-Razi (d. 1209), from a Qur'anic perspective even Ibn al-Arabi's detached spirituality is lacking and has deficits. For Nursi, it is the intimate connection to the world that defines spirituality, as well as knowledge and experience of the Divine real. Nursi refers to a poem of Saadi Shirazi (d. 1291), which says, "For the awakened one, every leaf is a notebook of the Divine." Nursi explains this as follows: "Faith is not only knowledge. In faith there are shares of many subtleties. . . . When issues of faith enter into the stomach of reason, they are divided into various faculties such as spirit, heart, soul, and many other subtle faculties. Each takes a share and absorbs it. If there is no sharing of those subtle faculties, that is considered incomplete. That is what Ibn al-Arabi wanted to remind al-Razi."[3] Though the way of Ibn al-Arabi is higher than that of the theologians, it is impractical for most people. The Qur'anic way of Nursi is both higher than that of even Ibn al-Arabi and it is shorter, which allows everyone the ability to follow it.

# Nursi on Sufism

Before further exploring the path that Nursi took, it is worthwhile to describe how Nursi himself understood that path. In a section in the Twenty-Ninth Letter, he has a detailed description of what Sufism is for him. He starts this section with this verse from the Qur'an: "Surely for the Friends of God there is no fear upon them and they do not grieve" (10:62). For Nursi, when he answers the question, "What is *tariqa* [the path]?" instead of giving a technical definition, he says,

> The goal and the aim of *tariqa* is the knowledge and the discovery of the truths of faith. Under the shadow of the *Mi'raj* of the Prophet through the feet of heart, in a spiritual journey to get the truth of faith and the Qur'an to a certain degree in an experiential and feeling way that is what is called *tariqa* or *tasawwuf* which are a mystery of human beings and perfection of humanity.[4]

In this part, Nursi describes human beings as "the encompassing index of the universe" and the hearts of human beings as "a spiritual map of thousands of realms." He also considers the heart a "seed of the unlimited truth of the universe."

Following this, Nursi says that *dhikr* and *tafakkur* are the keys to the journey of the heart and to spiritual development. For Nursi, the beauty of *dhikr* and *tafakkur* are unlimited. Regardless of their many unlimited benefits in the afterlife, only in this world, in such a stressful and burdensome life, does the heart need to rest and find a refuge of spiritual joy. Not all people are able to reach this level of joy through human social interactions. On the contrary, sometimes human social interactions can lead to the opposite and indeed become a burden. In this case, it is *dhikr* and *tafakkur* which can lead to a refuge. Nursi carefully responds to the accusations against Sufism by saying that there might be some charlatans who falsely claim to be Sufis, but this should not detract from real Sufism. He notes that as in any profession, there might be some people who are misusing Sufism. Therefore, "accusations against Sufi orders and mysticism by some esoterically minded Sunni scholars and narrow-minded politicians who attempt to close up this great treasure, this fountain of life, are unacceptable."[5]

Nursi also describes some of the dangers of a high level of spirituality. To counter this, one has to be knowledgeable about the Qur'an and Sunnah, i.e. the path of the Prophet and follow them without extremism. For instance, he describes what is called the "Level of the Mahdi." When one reaches this level, he or she might think him or herself to actually be the Mahdi, when in reality he or she is just passing in the shadow of that state. This can lead to arrogance and disrespect toward the earlier saints who have achieved such a level of spirituality. For Nursi, to get rid of these risks in the journey of spirituality one has to follow the principles of the essence of the scholars of Islamic theology and the guidance of Islamic law, particularly the guidance of such scholars as al-Ghazali and Ahmad Sirhindi. People should always be humble and accuse their soul so that they will not be misled while completing their spiritual journey. It is to the ways of doing this that we will now turn.

# The Divine names

Nursi's spirituality is reflected in his prayers and in his understanding of the Divine names. His personal life was one that was full of prayer. His disciples describe his level of devotion in terms of his prayer and supplications. He would read on a daily basis the supplications of early saints. One example of his daily reading is the compilation of many prayers of prophets and prominent saints, *Majmuat al-Ahzab*, which despite being over 1,800 pages Nursi would finish in fifteen days. His night prayers are also very famous, and were often referred to by his disciples.

Based on his own understanding the of Qur'an and Sunnah of the Prophet, he developed new supplications, which are said after the five daily prayers in addition to the Prophetic ones. Prophetic supplications include praising God with the phrases "*Subhan Allah,*" or "God is exalted," thirty-three times; "*Alhamdulillah,*" or "Praise be to God," thirty-three times; and "*Allahu Akbar,*" or "God is Greater than anything" thirty-three times. For Nursi, These are followed by asking God to bestow peace and blessings on the Prophet of Islam, his family, and other earlier prophets. Then the beautiful names of God are said or chanted. These are repeated after morning, noon, afternoon, sunset, and evening prayers. Similarly, after each prayer a short, designated section from the Qur'an is recited. Today, the spiritual path of Nursi is practiced by millions of Muslims, individually and in congregation. Because according to Nursi's teaching, sincerity is the spirit of prayer, and without sincerity any prayer is dead, he asked his students to read his *Treatise on Sincerity* at least once every fifteen days.[6] He also compiled a book of prayer in which he included a number of prayers and supplications from the Qur'an, as well as the supplication from the Prophet known as *al-Jawshan al-Kabir*, which contains 1,001 names of God and prayers of early mystics, including Uwais al-Qarani (d. 657) and Muhammad Baha al-Din al-Naqshabandi (d. 1389). There is also a section of the book called *sakina*, which means feeling the presence of God that brings calmness and tranquility. A last element is the section on his own supplications which shows his close relationship to the Divine.[7]

Nursi's main focus is on the Divine names. Following the Prophetic Hadith, he chose as a part of his daily scheduled prayers to recite a section from chapter fifty-nine of the Qur'an. This generally took place after morning and sunset prayers. The section from chapter fifty-nine contains fourteen names of God in a row, and it is the only place in the Qur'an where so many of God's names are mentioned together.

> He is God, there is no deity other than Him, the Knower of the invisible and the visible. He is the Most-Compassionate, Most-Merciful.
> He is Allah, other than Whom there is no deity, the Sovereign Lord, the Holy One, the Peace, the Keeper of Faith, the Guardian, the Majestic, the Compeller, the Superb. Glorified be God from all that they ascribe as partners (unto Him).
> He is Allah, the Creator, the Initiator from out of nothing, the Fashioner. His are the most beautiful names. All that is in the heavens and the earth glorifies Him, and He is the Mighty, the Wise. (59:22-4)

All of Nursi's spiritual writings have some connection to the Divine names. Even when he addresses the afterlife, he makes a connection to the Divine names. For example, according to Nursi, the Divine name *al-Adl*, or the Most-Just, necessitates the coming of the Day of Judgment where justice will be thoroughly fulfilled. He would say often oppressors and murderers dye without having punishment for their crimes. Therefore, Divine justice necessitates that there must be a place where oppressors and criminals who have not received their punishment in this world receive their punishment. That is the requirement of the Divine name *al-Adl*. It is well-known aphorism in Islam that in the afterlife, justice will be so thoroughly applied that if a goat with horns harmed a goat with no horns, the justice between them will be fulfilled.

Nursi makes a strong connection between the knowledge of God and the Divine names. The more one knows of the Divine names, the deeper one's knowledge is of God. Perhaps because of *al-Jawshan al-Kabir*, sometimes Nursi talks about 1,001 names of God, but this is not to limit the Divine names. Inspired by the Qur'an, Nursi does not give a specific number to the Divine names, because the Qur'an does not give such a number, but instead just uses the plural. To better understand the variety of Divine names, Nursi offers the parable of a ruler who has many attributes. The ruler of a country has the attributes of a just ruler in the circle of justice, and the title of the commander-in-chief in the circle of the military. Therefore, one person may have many titles, in accordance with many duties.

Similarly, for God there are a variety of names and attributes. These are called the most beautiful names of God, or *al-Asma al-Husna*. Each name has superiority in a circle of God's creation. The Other Divine names are also secondarily reflected in each specific circle of the other circles. Every creature has a direct relationship at the individual level with the related Divine name/s, despite the fact that the same name has a general reflection in all similar creatures. To give an example, one of the beautiful names of God is *al-Hayy*, "the Most-Living," which is to say

that the source of life is God. The reflection of this Divine name is found
in all creatures that have life: humans, animals, and plants. In other
words, every living thing takes its life from the Most-Living. Despite this
general reflection, every creature, a bird in the air or a fish in the sea, has
a direct connection to the Divine name *al-Hayy*. Each individual creature
has two positions. One is in direct relation to God's name. The other
position is a general state, which is a reflection of the Divine name that
is within all living creatures.

In the mystical understanding of Nursi, this remarkable contemplation
is known as *ehadiyyet tecellisi* and *wahidiyyet tecellisi* (*tajally al-ahadiyyah*
and *tajally al-wahidiyyah* in Arabic). The first is specific, the latter is general.
For example, all human beings share major characteristics. They have two
eyes, two ears, two hands, two feet. But at the same time, every individual
has distinctive characteristics that make him or her unique. As the Qur'an
says, every human being has unique fingerprints: "Do human beings think
that We shall never be able to reassemble their bones? Surely We are able to
remake their fingertips" (75:3-4).

Every creature may reflect a variety of Divine names. Divine names are
seen within one another. Each Divine name helps the other names to be
known. For example, when God's name *al-Khaliq*, "the Creator," reflects in
a thing, it becomes created. After the creation, *al-Musawwir*, "the Fashioner
or the One who gives form," reflects in order to give form to the creature
in the best possible way. If it is meant to be a living creature, *al-Hayy*, "the
Most-Living," reflects onto it and it becomes a living creature. Then *al-
Razzaq*, "the Sustainer," reflects in order to give all that the living creature
will need, like the sun, air, food, etc. Then, the name *al-Rabb*, "the Lord,"
comes to give proper education as to the conditions of the creature's life
and its environment. For example, a fish living in the sea or a duck which
has just hatched must know how to swim. Learning how to swim then is
a reflection of *al-Rabb*. At the same time, within all of these names, *al-
Qadir*, "the Most-Powerful," is reflected by giving the power of movement
and action. Another Divine name, *al-Alim*, "the Most-Knowledgeable," is
reflected in the creation of every creature created by Divine knowledge. Nursi
states, "Thus human beings are an antique art of God and a very sensitive,
vulnerable miracle of His power. He creates human beings in a way that
they become a mirror for all His names and a center for all His embroidery
and a small sample of the universe."[8] According to Nursi, because human
beings are the art of God, they are intrinsically valuable. Faith in God makes
people aware of this value and disbelief disconnects awareness of this value.
By being the reflection of the Divine names, human beings become worthy
of Paradise. He says,

Through the light of belief, human beings rise to the highest of the high
and acquire a value worthy of Paradise. And through the darkness of
unbelief, they descend to the lowest of the low and fall to a position fit

for Hell. That is because belief connects human beings to the All-Glorious Maker; belief is a relationship. Thus, human beings acquire value by virtue of the Divine art and inscriptions of the Dominical Names which become apparent in them through belief. Unbelief severs the relation, and due to that severance the Dominical art is concealed. Their value then is only in respect to the matter of their physical being. And since this matter has only a transitory, passing, temporary animal life, its value is virtually nothing.[9]

To further reflect on the Divine names, Nursi invites human beings to contemplate on the elements of nature and to see various Divine names chanted by creatures on their tongues of disposition.

> If you would like to view these lofty truths more closely, go and listen to the stormy seas and the quaking earth, and ask them what they are saying. Definitely they will respond to you and you will hear them say, "*Ya Jalil, Ya Jalil, Ya Aziz, Ya Jabbar* [O Majestic One, O Majestic One, O Mighty One, O Omnipotent One]." And then go and ask human and animal babies who are well cared for with great compassion who dwell in the sea and on the face of the earth, and ask them, "What are you saying?" Definitely, they will respond to you with the following Divine names: "*Ya Jamil, Ya Jamil, Ya Rahim, Ya Rahim* [O the Most-Beautiful, O the Most-Beautiful, O the Most-Compassionate, O the Most-Compassionate]." And then go and listen to the sky and you will see how the sky says, "*Ya Jalil dhu al-Jamal* [O the Majestic Who has the Most-Beauty]." And listen to the earth. You will see how it says, "*Ya Jamil dhu al-Jalal* [O the Most-Beautiful Who has the Most-Majesty]." And then look carefully at animals. You will see how they repeat "*Ya Rahman, Ya Razzaq* [O the Most-Compassionate, O the Sustainer]." And then go and ask the spring, and see how it says, "*Ya Hannan, Ya Rahman, Ya Rahim, Ya Karim, Ya Latif, Ya Atuf, Ya Musawwir, Ya Munawwir, Ya Muhsin, Ya Muzayyin* [O the Most-Tender, O the Most-Compassionate, O the Most-Merciful, O the Most-Generous, O the Bestower of bounties, O the Most-Loving, O the Fashioner, O the Giver of Light, O the One who bestows all beauties, O the One who beautifies everything]." And then go and ask a human being who is really a human being and see how he [or she] reads all of beautiful Divine names and also see how all these beautiful Divine names are written on his [or her] forehead. If you look carefully, you can read them. As if the whole universe is a majestic band of *dhikr*. The smallest melody is mixed with the strongest, by which a majestic tenderness comes out.[10]

Additionally, Nursi on several occasions describes how even the seasons are reflections of the Divine names. Hence, contemplation of the seasons can be a form of contemplation of the Divine names. Moreover, it is strongly emphasized in the Qur'an that human beings should contemplate the heavens and the earth: "Surely in the creation of the heavens and earth and in the alternating of night and day there are signs for people of understanding" (3:190). In one passage from his work *The Words,* Nursi beautifully illustrates this in detail.

> Thus, just as the day shows the light, and the light the sun, the great value together with the utter profusion; and the boundless intermingling and intermixing together with the utmost differentiation and separation within the utter profusion; and the great distance together with the utmost conformity and resemblance within the limitless differentiation and separation; and the infinite ease and facility together with the infinite care in the making within the utmost resemblance; and the absolute speed and rapidity together with the total equilibrium and balance and lack of waste within the most beautiful making; and the infinite abundance and multiplicity together with the highest degree of beauty of art within utter lack of waste; and the utmost munificence together with absolute order within the highest degree of beauty of art, all testify to the necessary existence, perfect power, beautiful Lordship, and oneness and uniqueness of a Most-Powerful Who has Majesty, a Most-Wise Who has Perfection, a Most-Compassionate Who has Beauty. They demonstrate the mystery of the verse: "His are the Most-Beautiful names." (Qur'an 20:8 and 59:24)[11]

Elsewhere, Nursi describes the sun as a reflection of the "eight greatest Divine names" and he calls it a "page of light for reflection in the Divine names."[12]

In the mystical Islamic tradition, one can spiritually develop by contemplating or following the reflection of a certain name of God. Some prophets mentioned in the Qur'an are known among mystics as reflections of certain divine names. In fact, the wide variety of the Divine names has caused the diversity of human beings. For example, Jesus is known as the reflection of many Divine names, particularly the Divine name *al-Qadir,* "the Most-Powerful." Because of this reflection, he was able to perform miracles, such as bringing the dead to life and healing the sick, that were not possible for regular human beings. He was supported by God and made close to God, but he was not God; he was a reflection of the names of God. Similarly, some mystics are known as the reflection of the Divine name, *al-Wadud,* the "Most-Loving," "the Lover," or "the Beloved." In Islamic spirituality, the concept of love is centered on this Divine name. All loves in the realm of creation are the reflection of this Divine name, just as all beauty in the realm of creation is the reflection of the Divine name *al-Jamil,* the Most-Beautiful.

## *Al-Ism al-A'zam*, the Greatest Name of God

At this point, it is necessary to discuss Nursi's unique interpretation of the Greatest Name of God, *al-Ism al-A'zam*. However, first some general information about the Greatest Name of God must be given. This is a topic that many Muslim mystics have spoken about, and it is an idea that is first found in the sayings of the Prophet. Specifically, one of the companions of the Prophet narrates that he was sitting in the mosque with the Prophet, when they saw a man praying by saying, "My Lord, I ask You and surely all praises belong to You. There is no deity but You. You are the Most-Bountiful, the Creator of heavens and earth. You are the Most-Majestic Who has kindness. I ask You O You who are the Most-Living, the Most-Sustaining." The Prophet asked his companions, "Do you know what this prayer is?" They responded, "God and His Messenger know and we do not know." Then the Prophet said, "He prayed to God with God's Greatest Name. Such a name that when God is called by this name, He surely responds and when He is asked with this name, He surely gives."[13]

It is this last portion of the hadith that makes the Greatest Name of God so significant. It is believed by Muslim mystics and others that if one addresses God with this name, God will fulfill the request. Hence, there have been many interpretations as to what the Greatest Name of God is. Al-Razi cites at least three common interpretations. Two of these see Divine names from the preceding hadith as the Greatest Name. The first interpretation considers the Divine name *Dhul Jalal wa al-Ikram*, "the Most-Majestic Who has kindness," to be the greatest. The second considers *al-Hayy al-Qayyum*, "the Most-Living, the Most-Sustaining," to be the greatest.

A third interpretation, according to al-Razi, is that all Divine names are holy and great. Thus, a combination of all the Divine names is the greatest name of God. This interpretation, which appears to be favored by al-Razi, seems to be saying that Allah is the Greatest Name of God, since this is the proper name of God and therefore includes all other names of God.[14] Elsewhere, al-Razi also discusses why the Greatest Name of God is hidden. He argues that as there is wisdom in hiding the Night of Honor, there is wisdom in hiding the Greatest Name of God. Likewise, the saints are hidden in the community and which prayers are accepted is hidden. He says, "The Greatest Name of God is hidden among the Divine names so that people will glorify all the names of God."[15]

There are other opinions that al-Razi did not discuss as well. According to some Muslim scholars and mystics, it is believed that the Prophet referred to the following verses as the Greatest Name of God: "Your God is One God; there is no deity but Him, the Most-Merciful, the Most-Compassionate," (2:163) and "Alif Lam Mim. God, there is no deity but Him, the Most-Living, the Most-Sustaining" (3:1-2). For some mystics, the Greatest Name of God would be *al-Wadud*, while for others, the Greatest Name of God would be *al-Hakim*, the Most-Wise. All told, there are at least forty understandings of what the Greatest Name of God is.

A mystic and commentator of the Qur'an, Ismail Hakki Bursevi, narrates a story about how the Greatest Name of God is taught and what kind of people are qualified to be given knowledge of the Greatest Name of God. According to this story, a student of Islamic spirituality comes to a saint and starts serving him. One day the student asks his master to teach him the Greatest Name of God. The master asks him if he is qualified for that, and he responds yes. The master then asks him to go to the main gate of the city and come back and let him know what he sees there. The student goes to the gate and sees an old man carrying wood on his donkey coming toward the gate. A soldier appears, beats the man, and takes his wood. The student returns to the master and tells him the story. The master asks him what he would have done had he known the Greatest Name of God. The student says that he would have asked God to destroy the soldier. The master responds that the old man was the one who taught him the greatest name of God, and then he says, "Know that the Greatest Name of God is given only to those who have the qualities of patience, mercy, and compassion towards creatures."[16]

Nursi has a different understanding regarding the greatest name of God. His approach is that the Greatest Name of God is a combination of six Divine names: al-Quddus, "the Most-Holy;" al-Hayy, "the Most-Living;" al-Hakam, "the Final Judge;" al-Fard, "the Most-Unique;" al-Qayyum, "the Most-Sustaining;" and al-Adl, "the Most-Just." One can see the reflection of these Divine names in the Universe and in human beings. The following will provide an example of the purity of nature as a reflection of the Divine name al-Quddus.

The reflection of this Divine name is seen in all purity and cleanliness that is found in the universe, including on the Earth. In fact, the whole universe, particularly the Earth, is similar to a factory. There is a great deal of work taking place which under normal conditions should result in a messy environment. If it is not cleaned up very carefully, it will not be possible for human beings to live on it. It is evident that the planet, when not polluted by human beings, is clean in every way. Nothing can be found on the Earth that is not in some way not beneficial. If we see some temporary ugliness, it disappears very soon as a result of the Divine name of al-Quddus. Nursi interpreted this Divine name through analogy:

A human being who does not wash his [or her] body for one month, or does not clean up his [or her] room, will find it very dirty and ugly. Therefore, this cleanliness and purity that is found in the palace of the universe always comes from a wise cleansing and a careful purifying. If there were no such cleansing and purification, all the animals who come to the Earth would drown and die in one year because of its dirtiness. Also, if there were no such cleansing, the remnants of the stars and moons would break our heads and the heads of other animals, and in fact, even the head of the whole planet Earth by sending meteors the size of mountains upon us and this would cause us to be exiled from our earthly homeland. However, there is no evidence that many meteors were dropped from the skies, only a few meteors have come as lessons for humanity, which did not harm anyone.[17]

All this cleanliness in the universe is a result of the divine name, *al-Quddus*. A great reflection of *al-Quddus* is seen in this Divine action of purification. The Qur'an draws our attention to the contemplation of this. Every creature shares in the reflection of this name. A fly, by cleaning its small face, shows a reflection of the name *al-Quddus*, as does as a bird cleaning its wings. Even creatures of the seas and the Earth that eat dead animals are working in this Divine factory to immediately clean up any ugliness in any part of it. Even individual cells in our bodies are listening to the Divine command of *al-Quddus*. As the lids of our eyes heed this divine command, clouds are also heeding it and working as a reflection of this Divine name. Nursi says, "A cloud that looks like a sponge distributes water to the garden of the Earth and settles the dust, and in order to not affect the cleanliness of the sky, it leaves immediately and helps show the clean and shining face of the sky."[18] This reflection that is evident in our body, our planet, and our universe comes from the largest circle of the Divine name *al-Quddus*. This action of cleansing is evidence of the existence of the Divine, just as the light of the Sun is evidence of the existence of the Sun. As the praises of all creatures go to the name *al-Quddus*, likewise the action of cleansing of all creatures goes to the same name. Therefore, when a person washes, he or she is reflecting the Divine name of *al-Quddus* in a meaningful way. The Qur'anic verse says, "God loves those who repent [doing spiritual cleansing] and those who keep themselves clean [physical cleanliness]," (2:222) and the Prophet said, "Cleanliness is half of faith."[19]

# Prayer and supplication

It is appropriate now to discuss Nursi's spiritual practice. As prayer was central to this, it is critical to include several of Nursi's important prayers. The first one is known as "Jonah's supplication," a well-known prayer from the Qur'an. Nursi would say this prayer daily thirty-three times between sunset and evening prayers. The supplication is as follows: "There is no deity but You. Glory be to You. Indeed, I was among the wrongdoers" (21:87). Following this supplication, Jonah was saved from the belly of the whale. Jonah understood that under the circumstance of being inside the whale, the only one who could rescue him was the One whose command could constrain the whale, the sea, the night, and the sky. From the perspective of cause and effect, there was no way for Jonah to be saved. Darkness upon darkness, but the Cause of causes saved him because of his supplication. The whale became a vehicle, a submarine for Jonah, and the sea and night became peaceful environments.

For Nursi, our situation in this world is more dangerous than that of Jonah. Our night is our future, which through the eyes of heedlessness is darker than the night of Jonah. Our sea is the planet Earth, which seems to aimlessly wander. Our sea is thousands of times more frightening than Jonah's sea. Nursi suggests that human beings should say the same supplication frequently:

> With the first sentence, "There is no deity but You," we have to draw the eyes of the of mercy of God upon our future. With the sentence, "Glory be unto You," we must draw the mercy of God upon our world. With the sentence, "Indeed I was among the wrongdoers," we must draw the mercy of God upon our soul. So that through the light of faith and the light and the moonlike luminosity of the Qur'an, the wilderness and terror of the night will be transformed into joy and friendship.[20]

After he repeated the supplication of Jonah, Nursi repeated the Qur'anic supplication of Job. The Qur'an asks the Prophet to remember the supplication of Job who said, "My Lord, harm has afflicted me and You are the Most-Merciful of the mercifuls" (21:83). Nursi suggests that Job's wounds and losses were physical and material, while our wounds are inner, spiritual, and invisible. If our inner life were inverted, it would be seen that we have more wounds than Job did. His physical diseases were threatening his worldly life, while our spiritual wounds are threatening our eternal life. Therefore, "we need that supplication of Job, one thousand times more than that holy man."[21]

In many sayings of the Prophet, one can see an encompassing prayer formula that includes the Divine names and offers support for the human spirit. The Prophet would frequently repeat this after his prescribed daily prayers. Following the path of the Prophet, Nursi also would repeat this formula after morning and sunset prayers ten times, and thirty-three times between sunset and evening prayers. It became so significant in Nursi's practice of spirituality that he dedicated a section of his *Treatises of Light* to this formula of prayer and his explanation of it, phrase by phrase. Frequently, while explaining this formula, he would say, "O human being," indicating that the restless spirit of human beings can rest in God through this formula. There are various versions of it in the Hadith literature, and the following is the one that Nursi himself chose and frequently repeated:

> There is no deity but God. He is One. He has no partner. His is the dominion and His is the praise. He alone gives life, He alone gives death, and He is the Most-Living who never dies. All good is in His hands and He is the Most-Powerful over everything. And to Him is the return.[22]

In the following, I will discuss Nursi's writings on a few of the phrases of this formula in which not just Muslims but all human beings are addressed.[23]

In regard to the first phrase, "There is no deity but God," Nursi says that through this the human soul with its many needs finds rest, and that through this phrase the doors to the greatness of God's mercy are opened to humanity. Specifically, "This phrase rescues the heart from an unlimited wilderness and the soul from a painful sadness and provides an eternal joy and an eternal happiness."

According to Nursi, through the second phrase, "He is One," the spirit and the heart of human beings find a remarkable refuge in the face of various elements of the universe that human beings encounter. This phrase becomes a rescuer of the human spirit from the confusions and miseries one might face. If one thinks deeply on the meaning of this phrase, it asks human spirits not to beg the causes, but to return to the Cause of causes. It says the following:

> God is One. Do not wear yourself out having recourse to other things. Do not demean yourself and feel indebted to them. And do not bow down before them and humiliate yourself. Do not run after them and make things difficult for yourself. Do not fear them and tremble before them. For the King of the universe is One, the key to all things is with Him, the reins of all things are in His hand, everything is resolved by His command. If you find Him, you will be saved from endless indebtedness and countless fears.

In any given society, one will encounter people in difficult situations such as sickness, disease, old age, etc. Among the most visible places where these difficulties are encountered are hospitals and elderly care facilities. Interestingly, Nursi has two treatises in his magnum opus which deal with just these two groups, "The Treatise for the Sick" and "The Treatise for the Elders." My hope is that a discussion of these will be useful for people facing these obstacles, and for those who are aiding them. It is not surprising that in both of these Nursi uses an encompassing and general language that can be applied to a variety of situations.

In "The Treatise for the Sick," he offers remarkable comfort to people who are suffering sickness. In twenty-five remedies, Nursi gives a great deal of psychological support. I would hasten to say that many professional psychologists today would consider these remedies to be comfort for those who are sick, and look to them for spiritual support in their time of suffering. To discuss the entirety of these remedies would go beyond the scope of this chapter, but I will give two as an example of how through these remedies Nursi can impact the spiritual lives of those who suffer. The treatise starts with this: "This is written to be an ointment, a comfort, a spiritual prescription, and a visit and well wish to the sick."[24] In the first remedy, Nursi speaks of the virtue of patience. He also suggests that sickness makes life more fruitful and longer through patience and thankfulness to God, since the times of difficulties pass slower than the times of joy. In the second remedy, he divides worship into two types: positive worship and negative worship. Nursi says,

> O impatient sick, be patient and thank. Your illness may transform each of the minutes of your life that pass in illness into one hour of worship. For worship is of two sorts. One is positive worship that is performed such as daily prayers and supplications. The other is negative worship, of the sort which is not actually performed, but is suffered and thus leads to sincere supplication. Illnesses and disasters are examples of this sort. By means of these, those afflicted deeply feel their innate impotence and weakness. They take refuge in their All-Compassionate Creator and ask for help, thus being able to perform sincere worship without showing off. There are authenticated Hadith that a life which passes in illness is counted as worship, provided there is no complaint about God. It is also reliably narrated from the Prophet and there are narrations from saints based on their spiritual experiences that one minute of illness of some patients who show patience and thankfulness equals one hour of worship, and a minute of illness of certain spiritually perfected individuals, equals to one day of worship. Therefore, rather than complaining, be thankful for the illness, which makes one minute of your life the equivalent of a thousand minutes and gains for you a long life.[25]

And in the tenth remedy Nursi warns that worrying doubles the illness. Therefore, one should avoid excess worrying during sickness. He says,

> Your worry is because of the severity of your illness, but your worries make your illness more severe. If you want your illness to be less severe, try not to worry about it. That is, think about the benefits of your illness, the spiritual rewards it brings, and that it will pass quickly. Give up worrying and cut off the illness at the root. Indeed, worry doubles the burden of illness. In addition to your physical illness, it causes an immaterial illness in your heart, upon which the physical illness depends and through which it persists. If that worry vanishes through submission [to the Divine plan], *rida* [being pleased with the Divine plan], and thinking of the wisdom inherent in the illness, one of the important roots of the physical illness will be severed. It becomes less severe and in part disappears. Sometimes a minor physical illness becomes tenfold just through worries and hypochondria. When worries and hypochondria cease, nine tenths of the illness disappears. As worries increase illness, worrying is also an accusation against Divine wisdom, a criticism of Divine mercy, and a complaint about the All-Compassionate Creator. It causes counter-healing and increases illness. Indeed, just as thankfulness increases Divine bounties, so too do complaints increase illnesses and suffering. Furthermore, worry itself is an illness. The cure for it is to know the wisdom inherent in illness. Since you are now aware of the wisdom

in illness and its benefits, apply that ointment to the sickness of worry and be relieved. [Express your joy and] say "Ha!" instead of [expressing your grief by saying], "Alas!" and say "All praise be to God for every situation!"[26]

Against the suffering of the sick members of society, Nursi continues to provide remedies, most of which aim to strengthen the psychology of the sick through trust in God and contemplation of the afterlife. All remedies that Nursi provides have something to do with the importance of patience, prayer, consideration of Divine gifts, eternal vision, and respect and compassion for human beings. Nursi also notes the importance of caregivers, stating that God will reward them for taking care of those who are sick. In some of these remedies, he speaks of the importance of thankfulness and the danger of complaints. Sickness can be a reflection of one or more of the Beautiful names of God, specifically the Divine name al-Shafi, "the Healer," which when reflected on the patient allows the patient to be cured. As a result, a spiritual joy comes. Sickness can be an important step in the fight against the evil-commanding soul and in fact is a powerful scaffold for spiritual development. All these important themes can be fulfilled through relying on and trusting God, the One who is the Most-Compassionate and the Most-Merciful, as indicated in the first two phrases of the formula in question. Now we should return to that formula.

The third phrase, "He has no partner," suggests that any human being can directly talk to the Divine, and no one can be prevented from talking directly to God. Also, if there is no direct command from God, nothing can be moved and nothing can be affected. Nursi says,

The human spirit which has already attained faith may, without any hindrance, interference, barrier, or obstacle in any situation, with any wish, at any time and in any place, enter the presence of the Most-Beautiful Who has Majesty, the Most-Powerful Who has Perfection, who is the Pre-Eternal and Post-Eternal Owner of the treasuries of mercy, and the mines of bliss, and may present its needs. Discovering His mercy and relying on His power, it will find perfect joy and happiness.[27]

The fourth phrase, "His is the dominion," shows that everything that can be imagined belongs to God. This phrase suggests that the entire realm of creation belongs to God, and human beings live and work in His dominion. This also provides the human spirit rest and elevates the heavy burden that frequently leads to hopelessness and stress in life. According to Nursi, this phrase addresses human beings, saying,

O human being! Do not consider yourself your own owner. You have no control over your own governance, such a load would be heavy. You are unable to protect yourself on your own, to avoid calamities, or to do the things that you must. Thus, do not fall into pain and do not suffer torment for no reason. The dominion belongs to someone else. The Owner is both Most-Powerful and the Most-Merciful. Rely on His power and do not indict His mercy. Forgo sadness and get joy. Abandon your troubles and find happiness.[28]

The fifth phrase, "His is the praise," suggests that whatever we have by way of bounties are from God. These are from the eternal Divine treasures. The phrase provides support for the human spirit, which can be disturbed by the ephemeral nature of the bounties. According to Nursi, this phrase addresses human beings by saying,

O human being! Do not suffer from the withering of the bounties because the treasure of Divine mercy is inexhaustible. Do not wail because of your thinking about the loss of the pleasures which causes pain, for the fruit of the bounty is the result of the unlimited mercy. If the tree is eternal, when the fruit is gone, there will be another one to replace it. Think, through praising within the pleasure of the Divine bounties, of something that is one hundred times more pleasing than that fruit. This is the sweet treat of Divine mercy. With this, you will be able to increase your pleasure from the first level to the hundredth.[29]

The sixth phrase, "He alone gives life," suggests that the life that living creatures have comes from the Divine name, *al-Hayy*, and all of life's necessities are also provided by God. The greatest goals of life are related to the Divine. For Nursi, ninety-nine percent of the results of life are directly connected to the Divine. This phrase provides support for the spirit of human beings, which can be overwhelmed by the burdens of life, and shows that the rewards of this life can be added to a person's record in the afterlife. Nursi interprets this phrase as follows:

O human being, do not trouble yourself by shouldering the heavy burdens of life. Do not be sad thinking of the transient nature of life. Do not regret that you came to this world thinking only of its worldly and unimportant fruits. On the contrary, the machine of life in the ship of your body belongs to the Most-Living and Most-Sustaining. It is He who provides for all the machine's expenses and necessities. That life has a great many goals and results that are all belong to Him. You are a helmsman in His ship. Perform your duty well, get your wage, and enjoy it. Think how that ship of life is valuable and how it gives beautiful benefits and how the One who owns that ship is the Most-Generous, the Most-Merciful and be happy and thankful. Understand that if you do your duty rightfully, all of the results that come from that ship will in some way be added to the record of your deeds and will provide an eternal life for you and will enliven you eternally.[30]

The seventh phrase is "He alone gives death." This phrase suggests that death is the soul's honorable discharge from this life to the realm of eternity, and it is God who is changing the place. Therefore, this phrase addresses the spirit of human beings, saying death is:

good news for you! Death is neither execution, nor nothingness, nor annihilation, nor ending, nor being put out. It is not eternal separation, extinction, and is not coincidence. It is not an authorless process towards nothingness. On the contrary, it is an honorable discharge by the Maker who is the Most-Wise and the Most-Merciful. It is a change of location. It is a dispatching to eternal bliss and to your original homeland. It is a door of union to the realm of Barzakh where ninety-nine percent of friends are gathered.[31]

The eighth phrase is "He is the Most-Living and never dies." This phrase suggests that God is perfect and nothing negative can happen to God. He is too exalted to have deficits. The phrase provides a source for the human spirit, because the Perfect can provide necessities, while the needy themselves cannot provide. Therefore, this phrase, according to Nursi, addresses human beings, *jinn*, angels, etc. as follows:

Here is good news for you. There exists an Everlasting Beloved for you who can cure and salve your wounds that are caused by countless separations from the ones you love. Since He exists and is eternal, do not worry about whatever happens to others. On the contrary, what caused your love for beauty and benevolence, virtue and perfection in your loved ones is considerably weak and a shadow of a shadow of a reflection of the Eternal Beloved's eternal beauty that passed through many veils. Do not let their disappearance hurt you for they are kinds of mirrors. The change of the mirrors renews and embellishes the manifestation of the radiance of Beauty. Since He exists, everything exists.[32]

The ninth phrase, "All good is in His hands," again suggests that nothing is lost. Everything good that one performs is recorded and will be seen. Therefore, there is no need for hopelessness or worry. According to Nursi, this phrase addresses human beings and *jinn* by giving them good news, saying,

O helpless ones, when you depart for the grave do not say, "Our house is destroyed, all our labors are wasted. We have left the beautiful broad world and entered the narrow earth." Do not cry out and become hopeless because everything of yours is recorded; all your actions have been written down, every service you have rendered has been recorded. The One with great majesty in whose hands is all good and who is able to bring all good to fruition, will reward your service. Drawing yourself to Himself, He will keep you only temporarily in the grave. Later, He will bring you to His presence. Blessed are you who have completed your service and duty. Your trouble is finished. You are heading toward comfort and mercy. Service and toil are over. You are going to receive your rewards.[33]

The tenth phrase, "He is the Most-Powerful over everything," indicates the unlimited power of God, and that with God everything is possible. To create Paradise is as easy as creating a spring. To create a spring is as easy as creating a flower. The limitless arts of God are unlimited testimonies of His unlimited power. According to Nursi, again this phrase gives good news to the human spirit:

O human being, the service you have offered and the worship you have performed are not in vain. There is a house of reward, an abode of bliss, which has been prepared for you. An eternal paradise is awaiting you in place of this ephemeral world of yours. Believe and trust in the promise of your Majestic Creator whom you know and to whom you worship. It is impossible for Him to break His promise. There is not any deficiency in His power. Weakness cannot interfere with His works. Just as He creates your tiny garden, so too He is able to create Paradise for you and He has created and promised it to you. And because He has promised, He shall, surely, admit you to it.[34]

The eleventh and last phrase is "to Him is the return." This phrase suggests that this world is a place of testing and a spiritual marketplace. People will do their duties, and when they finish they will go for their reward and return to their Creator. In time, they will return to their Most-Generous Master. They will be honored in the presence of the Divine with no veils. All will directly know and find their Master, their Owner, and their Creator. Nursi interprets this phrase as saying,

O human beings, do you know where you are going and to where you are dispatched? A thousand years of happy life in this world cannot be compared to one hour of life in Paradise. And a thousand years of life of Paradise cannot be compared to one hour of seeing the beauty of the Most-Beautiful Who has great glory. You are going to the realm of His mercy, and to the level of His presence. All beauty and loveliness in the derivative beloveds in all the creatures of this world for which you are so addicted and captivated and for which you are longing, are but a sort of shadow of reflection of His beauty and the beauty of His names. And you are going to the sphere of the presence of the Eternally Worshipped and everlastingly Beloved one whose Paradise with all of its subtle beauties is one reflection of His mercy. And all longings and lovings and attachments and captivations, are nothing but a flash of His love. You are being summoned to the eternal feast of Paradise. Thus, enter the grave not weeping, but laughing.[35]

One important and apparently novel aspect of Nursi's spirituality is a concept derived from chapter one, verse five of the Qur'an, "You alone we worship." Nursi, while contemplating this chapter, focused on the use of the plural pronoun "we" and not the singular "I" and why even when praying alone, the plural form is used. Nursi takes the plural form here to indicate that, unlike in the material world where there is a fixed amount of value and benefit, in the spiritual realm, there can be an unlimited increasing of spiritual worth.

This can be described through an analogy of a series of mirrors. Every human being has a mirror which can reflect light without lessening the light of the other mirrors. Thus, the more mirrors, the more light can be reflected and the greater the benefit to all. For Nursi, all that is required to be a holder of one of these mirrors is sincerity. Through this collectivity, then, one's worship and spiritual gains can be available for the benefit of all people who are sincere in their spiritual practice. This is a very important concept for Nursi, because here he includes not only Muslims, but all monotheists. This group of people is vast, and the spiritual power of this one single word "we" is tremendous.

Nursi, referring to what he calls an "enlightened situation and truthful imagination" that he experienced while praying in a congregation at the Bayezid Mosque in Istanbul, says:

> I saw that the congregation of which I was a part was divided into three circles: The first circle was all of the believers on the face of the earth and the vast congregation of monotheists.
>
> The second circle: I saw that I was part of a congregation consisting of all beings, all of which were in a great prayer and in a great glorification [of God]. Each group was occupied with special benediction prayers and glorifications that were particular to its kind. The title of their worship is what is called "The Duties of Creatures" and these are the services of creatures that are witnessed. In this state declaring, "Allahu Akbar," I bowed my head in bewilderment and looked at myself [in the third circle].
>
> Within a third circle I saw an astonishing microcosm which was apparently and qualitatively small, but truthfully, numerically, and dutifully great. I saw a congregation in which every group from atoms of my body to my external senses were preoccupied with duties of worship and thankfulness. In this circle, the dominical subtlety in my heart was on behalf of the congregation saying: "You alone do we worship and from You alone do we seek help," just as my tongue said earlier intending to be on behalf of the two former congregations.[36]

Next, we should turn to another of Nursi's famous supplications, which is found in several forms. He notes that he wrote down this supplication so that even when his tongue is silenced by death, it could still be said and could thereby continue to supplicate for him. In this supplication, Nursi addresses

God with terms including, "O my Compassionate Lord and my Generous Creator," "O Necessarily Existent, O the One of the Unity," "O Omnipotent Lord Who has Glory, O the One hidden in the intensity of His manifestation and concealed in the magnificence of His grandeur. O the One of Absolute Power," "O Lord of land and sea," "O the Creator of everything," etc. In the last section of this long supplication, Nursi addresses God as, "the Lord of the prophets and righteous ones," and says,

> O My Lord and the Lord of the heavens and earth! O My Creator and the Creator of all things! For the sake of Your power, will, wisdom, sovereignty, and mercy, which subjugate the heavens and their stars, the earth and all it contains, and all creatures together with all their attributes and acts, subjugate my soul to me and subjugate to me my request. Subjugate the hearts of people to the Risale-i Nur, so they may serve the Qur'an and faith. And grant me and my brothers perfect belief and a beautiful ending. As You subjugated the sea to Moses (Peace be upon him), fire to Abraham (Peace be upon him), the mountains and iron to David (Peace be upon him), *jinn* and men to Solomon (Peace be upon him), and the sun and moon to Muhammad (Peace and blessings be upon him), subjugate hearts and minds to the Risale-i Nur. Protect me and all the students of the Risale-i Nur from the evil of the soul and Satan, and the torment of the grave and Hell-fire, and grant us happiness in Paradise. Amen. Amen. Amen.[37]

Nursi presents this supplication as a method of prayer through contemplation, and he takes this methodology from the prophetic supplications and from the Qur'an. He is humble and asks God for forgiveness if he has made any mistakes in his supplication: "If I have been at fault in offering to the court of my Compassionate Sustainer this lesson which I have taken from the Qur'an and *al-Jawshan al-Kabir*, as a contemplative prayer making the Qur'an and the *Jawshan* my intercessors, I beseech forgiveness for my fault from His mercy."[38]

Nursi wants to make human beings aware and mindful of their real situation in this world, namely that the life of this world is transient, though it may seem broad and eternal. He compares the past and the future of human beings to two mirrors facing each other. When one looks through the prism of mirrors, a small place becomes as large as a town, but in fact it is still small. Nursi would say it is as small as a grave. Still, there is a way to make this world in reality a large place, by reaching the level of the life of heart and spirit. Should this be achieved, human beings would no longer be constrained by biological limits, and this is why he encourages people to strive for this:

> Since the worldly life and this corporal living and this animalistic life are thus, get out of animalistic constraints, leave corporality and enter into

the level of the life of heart and spirit. You will find a large circle of life, much larger than the world you have imagined and you will find a world of light. Thus, the key to that world is the knowledge of God and making heart saying and spirit working through the Holy phrase of: "There is no deity but God." Which contains many mysteries of the unity of God.[39]

It would be good to conclude this chapter with a brief passage from Nursi, which helps to encapsulate some of the beauty and power of his spirituality as it is found in his writings. Here Nursi "converses" with a prominent early mystic, Abd al-Rahman al-Jami, who is known as one of the poets of love for the Divine in the Islamic tradition:

'To turn the face of people from a multiplicity of causes to the unity of the Divine, see how well Mawlana Jami expressed it, whose nature was kneaded with love and who was intoxicated with the cup of love:

[Nursi gives Jami's poem in the original Farsi] *Yaki khwah, Yaki khwan, Yaki ju, Yaki bin, Yaki daan, Yaki guuy.*

That is,

Want One: the rest are not worth wanting.
Call to One: the others will not come to your assistance.
Seek out One: the rest are not worth it.
See One: the others are not seen all the time; they hide themselves
    behind the veil of ephemerality.
Know One: knowledge other than that, which does not assist
    knowledge of Him, is without benefit.
Speak of One: words that are not related to the One might be
    considered in vain.

Yes, O Jami, you have said the truth. The Truly Sought, the Truly Beloved, the Truly Desired, the One to be Truly Worshiped is only Him, because the entire universe with its various creatures and various languages and various melodies in the greatest circle of the Divine *dhikr* all together say, "*La ilaha illa Hu*" [there is no deity but Him] and bear witness to the Oneness of God. It cures the wounds that come from: "I do not love the things that fade away" [Q 6:76] and shows the eternal Beloved who still remains after derivative, earthly beloveds prove to be ephemeral.'[40]

# 7

# Fethullah Gulen

Fethullah Gulen is one of the most influential and impactful Turkish Muslim scholars of the last several decades. Besides his important scholarship, particularly in the area of Islamic spirituality, he is also a gifted poet, and his poetry forms an important element of his mystical thought. According to official Turkish records, Fethullah Gulen was born in eastern Anatolia in 1941, was educated in the local institutions, and received his spiritual formation from the local mystics, most of whom, including his father, belonged to the Naqshabandi Sufi order. While still a young man, he encountered the writings of Said Nursi. He found them profoundly important, embraced Nursi's writings, and built his spirituality on his background with Naqshabandi Sufi order and Nursi's writings. He is well-versed in Islamic sciences, such as the science of Hadith, the science of commentary on the Qur'an, as well as the science of Islamic jurisprudence. It is true that he has great charisma, but it is his piety and spirituality that attract people to him. His spirituality exceeds his charisma by far, and perhaps this is the least known part of Gulen's life, especially given his portrayal by the Turkish media today.

His writings on spiritual life are all centered on how one can go beyond the imperfections of the body and reach the level of spirit and heart, hence becoming a reflection of the mystical, perfect human being. He has dedicated four volumes under the title of *The Emerald Hills of the Heart* to spiritual themes. Arguably, his mystical writings are all a response to the invitation by Muslim mystics to go beyond the body and reach the level of spirit and heart, as it is formulated in Nursi's statement: "Leave the level of physicality and enter into the level of the life of spirit and heart."[1] In his writings, Gulen, like earlier mystics, including al-Qushayri, describes the Sufi terms through a series of short articles. Most of these descriptions were in the form of unique monthly periodical editorials. His goal was to make people aware of the Sufi terms and internalize them by making them a part of their nature. In this way, his readers and admirers would be able to more easily incorporate these ideas into their lives and practices. He not only wrote of the Sufi terms, but also sincerely practiced them. This constitutes his understanding of Islamic spirituality. In one of his writings he says,

> The Emerald hills of heart are a goal to be achieved. In order to reach that one has to believe and one has to follow the path without hastening, without giving up, and without getting tired. Yes, as it is described in the words of Nursi, "get out of animalistic constraints, leave the level of physicality and enter into the level of the life of heart and spirit." *The Emerald Hills of the Heart* always show the path to this achievement.[2]

As I have written elsewhere, Gulen practices the principles of Islamic spirituality, yet he is not attached to a formal Sufi order. Thus, despite the influence of the Sufi orders from his youth, his path of spirituality can best be called "a non-attached Sufi tradition."[3] It seems that his goal is to think outside of the box. He emphasizes this in his poems. He compares and highlights his themes so that people will not focus solely on the epistemological dimensions. He says that one has to learn the terminology, but this is not sufficient. One also has to contemplate, to internalize those lofty realities in one's heart. He says, "In *The Emerald Hills of the Heart*, there is a journey and transition from terminology and description to the hearing and the feeling."[4]

In order to get a sense of his *Emerald Hills of the Heart*, it is important to know what is mentioned in this series of books. For mystics, repentance is the beginning, and as such Fethullah Gulen starts the first book in his series with repentance, or *tawba*. Subjects that follow include *muhasaba* or self-criticism, *tafakkur*, *taqwa*, and many others. In the first volume, he dedicates one of the largest sections to the importance of *qalb* or heart, as it is the center of Islamic spirituality. When he speaks of heart, he refers to a prominent personality of Islamic spirituality and a popular saint in Turkey, Ibrahim Haqqi of Erzurum (d. 1780), who said, "The heart is the home of God; purify it from whatever is other than Him. So that the All-Merciful may descend into His palace at night." Gulen continues, "It is one's heart that God addresses and that undertakes responsibilities, suffers punishment or is rewarded, is elevated through true guidance or debased through deviation, and is honored or humiliated. The heart is also the 'polished mirror' in which Divine knowledge is reflected." Gulen also refers to a verse from the Qur'an, "Our Lord! Do not cause our hearts to swerve after You have guided us" (3:8), and a Prophetic hadith, "O God, O Converter of hearts! Establish our hearts firmly on Your religion, remind us of the absolute need to preserve the heart."[5]

In this writing, it appears that Gulen addresses his own soul. When asked who his audience is, he says that he could not say, but that he wrote it for his soul and the sacrificing souls, the term he uses for those souls who serve humanity by sacrificing their own comfort. Elaborating on the basic Sufi terms, he makes an interesting distinction between *tasawwuf* and *tariqa*. For him, *tasawwuf* is the spiritual life of Islam, while *tariqa* is the system and the schools of individuals who represent this spiritual life. Therefore, there is no rivalry in *tasawwuf*, but there could be rivalry between the members of different *tariqa*s, that is, Sufi orders. For example,

> The followers of the Qadiri mystical order say, "Chanting the Divine names with a loud voice is better than what Naqshabandis do silently." While Naqshabandis, who prefer silent chanting of the Divine names would say, "Since everything is related to the heart, there is no need for declaration of the Divine names loudly." This differentiation of them is understandable. [6]

The essence of Islamic spirituality has been described as "an Islamic way of transcending one's own soul, that is, of letting one's spirit rise above oneself, and it is where human self ends and the heavenly mysterious begins."[7] In other words, Islamic spirituality is based on abandoning one's physical form in order to gain a spiritual nature. This transformation is expressed in the phrase "annihilation of ego in God's presence." Through this annihilation, one realizes oneself in God. While there are four necessary steps and principles in the Naqshabandi order, "abandoning the world, abandoning the hereafter, abandoning the body, and abandoning this 'abandoning,'"[8] it should be noted that reaching this level is a long journey. In order to understand Gulen's spirituality, one has to understand how Gulen defines the principles of Islamic spirituality. He summarizes these in the introduction to his book on Sufism.

> Reaching true belief in God's Divine Oneness and living in accordance with its demands. Heeding the Divine Speech (the Qur'an), discerning and then obeying the commands of the Divine Power and Will as they relate to the universe (the laws of creation and life). Overflowing with Divine Love and getting along with all other beings in the realization (originating from Divine Love) that the universe is a cradle of brotherhood. Giving preference or precedence to the well-being and happiness of others. Acting in accord with the demands of the Divine Will not with the demands of our own will and living in a manner that reflects our self-annihilation in God and subsistence with Him. Being open to love, spiritual yearning, delight, and ecstasy. Being able to discern what is in hearts or minds through facial expressions and the inner, Divine mysteries and meanings of surface events. Visiting spiritual places and associating with people who encourage the avoidance of sin and striving in the way of God. Being content with permitted pleasures, and not taking even a single step toward that which is not permitted. Struggling continuously against worldly ambitions and illusions, which lead us to believe that this world is eternal. Ever forgetting that salvation is possible only through certainty or conviction of the truth of religious beliefs and conduct, sincerity or purity of intention, and the sole desire to please God.[9]

The powerful spiritual message of the Prophet of Islam is the source of Gulen's own spirituality. Even before the revelation of the Qur'an, the Prophet used to go to the cave of Hira and isolate himself from the worldly life in order to focus on his spirituality. Gulen calls this experience "Hira *sultanligi*," or the sultanate of Hira. Then one day the angel Gabriel appeared to the Prophet. This was the spark that set off the Prophet's prophethood and his long spiritual journey. The revelation of the Qur'an came to the Prophet on various occasions, encouraging him and his companions to follow a spiritual path in life.

Gulen refers to this saying of the Prophet as a foundation of his spiritual development. The Prophet says, "Be respectful of God wherever you are. Follow each bad thing with a good thing so that that good thing will delete the bad thing. And deal with all people with beautiful, moral behaviors."[10] That is to say, never abandon moral behaviors in your dealings with human beings. According to Gulen, this saying of the Prophet illustrates a principle of the spiritual journey that can be explained with volumes of books, a principle that one must follow and live by. He says, "There is nothing that elevates humans spiritually more than beautiful manners. Beautiful manners are the ethics of God. That means human beings become provided with the ethics of God."[11]

Starting from the very beginning of its revelation, the Qur'an has promoted and encouraged piety and purification of heart. While at the same time, it has been addressing the experience of the Prophet himself regarding *Alam al-Ghayb*, the unseen world that human eyes cannot see, the realm of angels. The Prophet's *Mi'raj* is an example of this dimension. The Qur'an states that the Prophet took a night journey from Mecca to Jerusalem, and that he ascended from Jerusalem to the heavens, accompanied by the archangel Gabriel. Finally, he met God beyond the realm of physicality, in the realm of the unseen. The event is embedded in the Hadith in well-documented details. The Qur'an calls the level where the Prophet was lead *Qab Qawsayn* (53:9). Literally, this means the space between two bows, and it indicates the closeness of the Prophet and the angel Gabriel, and this level is where the physical world separates from the eternal one.[12] *Qab Qawsayn* is used frequently by Sufis to indicate their closeness to God. Through his ascension, the Prophet opened a way for Muslims into the world of the unseen. The Prophet brought back to his community the gift of the five daily prayers, which indicates that believers, through prayers, are able to follow the path of spirituality taken by the Prophet during this journey of ascension. The Prophet said, "The servants' nearest position to God is when they are in prostration. Therefore supplicate a lot [while in prostration]."[13] Thus, prostration in prayers is the *mi'raj* of the believers.

Having received such instructions from the Prophet, his companions and the generations after them became models of prayer and prostration. Gulen in his youth read about the lives of the companions and early mystics who explored the areas of Qur'anic spirituality and asceticism that constituted a paradigm for Gulen. These companions and early mystics borrowed key terms from the Qur'an, which they applied to their spiritual experience and teachings. The terms, including ones we have mentioned before—*qalb*, *tawba*, *dhikr*, *ikhlas*, and *sabr*—and others like *khawf* (fear of God), *baqa* (eternity), *baraka* (blessing), *rida* (contentment), *haqq* (the real), *reja* (hope), *ma'rifa* (mystical knowledge), *qurb* (nearness to God), *tawakkul* (trust in God), and *yaqin* (certainty) constitute the heart of the Sufi tradition in general and the core of Gulen's spirituality in particular.

At the same time, the companions of the Prophet borrowed some negative terms to describe the temptations with which they struggled, such as *al-nafs al-ammara*, *ghafla* (heedlessness), *riya* (showing off), and *shirk* (idolatry). These are also the themes that are frequently referred to in Gulen's spirituality. There is no doubt that Gulen follows the spirituality of early mystics, such as Hasan al-Basri (d. 728), the famous woman saint Rabia al-Adawiyya (d. 801), Harith al-Muhasibi (d. 857), Abu Yazid al-Bistami (d. 874), and Junayd al-Baghdadi (d. 910), who took the Qur'an and the sayings of the Prophet as their primary reference for their spiritual teachings and practices. Despite many negative statements and unfounded charges against Gulen by some Political Islamist politicians, the present author, based on his knowledge of Gulen's writings and personal communications with Gulen, argues that Fethullah Gulen can be considered a Rumi of our time, in both his spirituality and understanding. Indeed, when I was honored to translate and edit Sefik Can's (d. 2005) important work *Fundamentals of Rumi's Thought*, Gulen graciously agreed to write a foreword for the book in which he says, "He [Rumi] was a balanced man of ecstasy who sprang alive love and excitement. He did this to such an extent that he inspired in others these significant feelings and continues to do so."[14] The same, I think, can be said of Gulen himself.

## Gulen on *tasawwuf*

At this point it is important to explore Gulen's definition of the spiritual path, *tasawwuf*. Taking from Junayd (d. 910), Shibli (d. 946), and other early mystics, Gulen defines the spiritual path as:

> the path followed by an individual who, having been able to free himself or herself from human vices and weaknesses in order to acquire angelic qualities and conduct pleasing to God, lives in accordance with the requirements of God's knowledge and love, and in the resulting spiritual delight that ensues.[15]

According to Gulen, and as the definition states, to receive the great benefits of spirituality, following the path and the example of the Prophet is crucial. Therefore, the path should be in concert with the teachings of the Qur'an and with the Sunnah of the Prophet, which are the primary sources for Muslim mystics. Gulen divides the followers of the Islamic spiritual path into two categories: "Those who stress knowledge and seek to reach their destination through knowledge of God (*ma'rifa*), and those who follow the path of yearning, spiritual ecstasy, and spiritual discovery."[16] Even though he himself is not attached to a mystical order, Gulen favors the first group.

In examining Gulen's understanding of Islamic spirituality, we encounter a rich account of Gulen's explanation of key mystical themes. Some of the most important of these which Gulen elucidates in his books on the subject are the beautiful names of God, the attributes of God, *tawba, zuhd* (asceticism), *muhasaba, tafakkur, sayr ila Allah* (journey to God), *hudur* (feeling the Divine presence), *nafs, ihsan* (doing what is beautiful), *waqt* (time), *mujahada* (spiritual striving or jihad), *tawhid* (unity), *fana fi Allah* (annihilation in God), *riyada* (austerity), *khulla* (sincere friendship), *'aql* (reason), and *rida* (contentment).

The first step in the spiritual path is *tawba,* or repentance, and it is with this that Gulen begins his book. Gulen's definition of this term is larger than the traditional Sufi one. In the traditional understanding, repentance should be done not just for words but also for feelings, thoughts, ideas, and all behaviors committed against the will of God. Again echoing some of the earliest mystics, Gulen goes even further, dividing repentance into three levels. The first stage is *tawba,* which is the common repentance of most people. The second stage is *inaba.* If *tawba* is the journey to God, *inaba* is a journey in God. The third stage is *awba,* which is a journey from God. In other words, *tawba* is refuge in God, *inaba* is annihilation in God in order to maintain the spiritual levels that one has attained, and *awba* is having one's heart closed to everything except God.[17]

Resistance against bodily desires, that is, asceticism, is called *zuhd,* and for Gulen, *zuhd* is an important moral practice. Although *zuhd* is a central element for many Sufis, it should also be a significant virtue for every Muslim. Its importance to Islam and spirituality more broadly comes from the fact that the Prophet's life defined the meaning and spirit of asceticism. Hence, *zuhd,* especially in this present age of materialism cannot be forgotten. It can be very difficult to resist the materialistic lures of society, but the principle of *zuhd* requires this. However, Gulen suggests that even if we start with just small things, *zuhd* will become an inseparable virtue for us.

Gulen believes that to follow the path of *tasawwuf,* a person must practice *muhasaba,* or, "the self-criticism of a believer who constantly analyzes his or her deeds and thoughts in the hope that correcting them will bring him or her closer to God."[18] Gulen calls it *muhasaba-i nafs,* which is basically grounded in the second Caliph Umar's statement, "O people, question yourselves, before being questioned."[19] People must discover themselves within their inner depths. Gulen completely reflects al-Ghazali's ideas, as expressed in his *The Alchemy of Happiness* about the knowledge of the self. Knowledge of the self is the key to the knowledge of God: "He who knows himself knows God." [20] On the subject of *muhasaba,* Gulen refers to a verse in the Qur'an, "Surely those who fear God, when a glimmer from Satan touches them, they remember [God] and then they see clearly [the Truth and return]" (7:201). This, for Gulen, is to be aware of one's desires, even if one is sometimes pulled down by them. Furthermore, he describes *muhasaba* as "a lamp in the heart of a believer, a warner and a well-wishing adviser in his or her conscience."[21] He also refers to a saying of the Prophet of Islam: "If you only knew what I knew, you would laugh a little and weep much."[22] The people who are aware of this way of Islamic spirituality always think of the verse, "To God belongs all that is in the heavens and on the earth. Whether you show what is in your souls or conceal it, God will question you for it." (2:284) Gulen says that whoever does not question themselves will be unable to evaluate their time, or to make any difference in their future, and their tomorrow will be no better than their today.[23]

In Gulen's view, contemplation is the light of the heart, the sustenance of the soul, and the spirit of knowledge. For those who have this sense of contemplation, the universe is a book to be read, which does not require a specific time, space, or definite position. The Qur'anic verse on contemplation refers to the continuous nature of remembering God: "those who remember God, while standing, sitting, and lying down on their sides, and contemplate on the wonder of creation in the heavens and on the earth" (3:191). Indeed, the gaining of all knowledge is a form of contemplation. As Gulen states,

> Since everything in the heavens and Earth are the property and kingdom of God, studying every incident, item, and quality also means studying how the exalted Creator deals with existence. The believer who studies and accurately comprehends this book of existence, and then designs his or her life accordingly will follow the way of guidance and righteousness all the way to the final station of Paradise.[24]

This contemplation brings tranquility, which is also known as *hudur*.

For Gulen, the term *hudur*, or feeling the Divine presence, means a feeling of being with God, to be filled with Him, and to find Him in one's conscience. By continuously maintaining this, one achieves a state of being in His light. Even though, as Gulen says, "the feeling of Divine presence emanates from Him," it changes according to one's personal level and abilities. Gulen views attaining the higher level of *hudur* as having spiritual enjoyment.[25]

As we indicated above, *qalb*, or heart, is one of the most distinguished terms in Sufism, and it is of paramount importance in Gulen's teaching. For Gulen, *qalb* does not mean the material heart in the human body, but the spiritual one, the heart which is the place of faith and the mirror of God. According to Gulen, *qalb* is a subtle essence from the Divine called, "the reality of humanity" by mystics, and the spirit is the ineffable essence from the Divine. While the biological heart is its vessel, heart is the essence of human beings. As the Prophet says, "God does not look at your appearance, but He looks at your heart."[26]

Another element of the heart for Gulen is that it is "a fortress in which one can maintain sound reasoning and thinking, as well as a healthy spirit and body. As all human feelings and emotions take shelter and seek protection in this fortress, the heart must be protected and kept safe from infection." The life of one's spiritual and physical body is connected to the life of the heart. If the heart is alive, then the other elements are alive and vice versa. Furthermore, Gulen says,

> God considers one's heart. He treats men and women according to the quality of their hearts, as the heart is the stronghold of many elements vital to the believer's spiritual life and humanity: reason, knowledge, knowledge of God, intention, belief, wisdom, and nearness to God Almighty. If the heart is alive, all of these elements and faculties are alive; if the heart is diseased, it is difficult for the elements and faculties mentioned to remain sound. The truthful and confirmed one [the Prophet], upon him be peace and blessings, declared: There is a fleshy part in the body. If it is healthy, then the whole of the body is healthy. If it is corrupted, then all the body is corrupted. Beware! That part is heart. This saying shows the importance of the heart for one's [spiritual] health.[27]

As noted in previous chapters, the aim of Islamic spirituality is to reach the level of *ihsan*, to worship God as if one sees God. For many mystics, this amounts to a transformation into being a perfected human. However, Gulen holds that love is the vital condition for reaching this level. Even if one is in constant *dhikr* and has mastered all of the other steps on the path, if love is not part of that person's path he or she cannot reach perfection. Even if that person lived hundreds of years, he or she would be stuck on the path reaching for perfection. For Gulen, the most important form of love and the one that leads to God is 'ashq (in Arabic *ishq*; passion). As Gulen describes it:

> 'Ashq, which the spirit feels without the intervention of free will, cannot be controlled by the person so affected, for its real source is God, Who loves Himself in a way special to His Sacred Essence and is essentially independent of the created. In addition, it is essentially different from the love felt by the created for the created or the Creator. This sacred, essential love of God for Himself, including His Attributes and Names, is the reason why He created the universe and why He caused humanity to appear in the world. It is also this love that manifests itself in human beings as love of God, as the most essential center of humanity's relationship with God.[28]

These are but a few of the critical steps in Gulen's way of *tasawwuf*. The details of his doctrine are explored in his books on Sufi concepts.[29]

# Gulen's spirituality

Though he shares many elements with other Islamic mystics—constant devotion, modest living, celibacy, etc.—Gulen's way of practicing Sufism is different from that of Islamic mystical orders which tend to have a more ritualistic focus. It will give a better sense of his spirituality if we elaborate on one day in his spiritual life. Almost without exception, he prays his five daily prayers in congregation with his students and others. For Gulen, prayer is central to the organization of his day to day activities, and he spends many hours each day in the recitation and performance of prayer. He wakes up very early and reads his *dhikr* or *awrad* (prayer books). Though Gulen memorized the whole Qur'an at a young age, for him a devotion to constant recitation of the Qur'an is still significant. Therefore, every day he recites a significant section from the Qur'an. Supplication and recitation of the Qur'an and application of the prayers in his own life influenced his interpretation of Qur'anic verses and his approach toward a variety of faiths. In his prayers, especially the prayer that he himself formulated and added to the end of the prayer book that he edited called *Al-Qulub al-Daria,* or *The Yearning Hearts,* he mentions all known prophets by name and asks God for blessings for them. In this prayer, he includes Mary, the mother of Jesus. This fact sets him apart from other mystics. For example, he believes that both intrareligious and interreligious dialogue, particularly among Jews, Christians, and Muslims, is commanded by Qur'anic teaching. Accordingly, he seeks to establish good relations with scholars and spiritual leaders of diverse religious groups, and he follows Rumi in pursuing the path of love, opening his arms to people of all faiths.

Gulen has spent and continues to spend much of his life secluded, in the form of constant retreat. Though his health has deteriorated as he has gotten older, his daily activities have not changed much. After having breakfast, when his health allows, he speaks to his students or visitors for about half an hour, during which he responds to questions, discusses religious topics, and teaches elements of the Qur'an and Hadith to the people around him. Next, he often spends time in writing and editing. Afterwards, he takes a short nap before the noon prayer. In the afternoon until the *asr* or afternoon prayer time, his activities are similar to those in the morning. After he performs the *asr* prayer, he recites or read more of his regular *awrad* and, as his health allows, takes in a bit of exercise. It is then time for the sunset prayer. After preforming the *maghrib* prayer, he eats and then responds to questions or reads. Finally, there is the evening prayer, after which he goes to bed, only to wake up shortly thereafter for his night prayer, *tahajjud.* Despite his advanced age and frail stature, Gulen sleeps and eats less than most. Indeed, Gulen's life is filled with only three things: prayer, recitations, and reading. Consistent with his many writings on the subject, Gulen's life clearly shows his belief that humankind was created in this world to prepare for the hereafter, the Paradise which God prepared for the believers. As a hadith Qudsi says, "I prepared for my pious servants what no eyes have seen, no ears have heard, and no minds have ever conceived." The narrator of the hadith Abu Huraira says, "If you wish read this verse: 'No soul knows what is kept for them of what makes their eye joyful, as a reward for what they have done.' [32:17]"[30]

Gulen chooses to not call himself a Sufi. As we have seen, whether or not someone calls themselves a Sufi is not important; what is important is if that person is a Sufi in spirit and in heart. As Rumi says, "The [true] Sufi is he who has become a seeker of purity: [it is] not from [wearing] the garment of wool and patching [it] and [committing] sodomy."[31] Gulen's understanding emphasizes humbleness, and this can be accomplished by seeking to annihilate oneself in God. Thus, the most trying obstacle on the journey is arrogance. As the Qur'an states, "God does not love the arrogant" (4:36 and 31:18). Similarly, the Prophet speaks of the importance of humbleness by saying that people who humble themselves, God will elevate. Those who act arrogantly, God will lower them.[32]

While Gulen's spirituality centers on individual development, he also gives paramount importance to the happiness of others. In his teachings, individual spiritual development leads to concern for others. Therefore, altruism is an important dimension of his spirituality. Still, even such good efforts should not flatter egoism. According to Gulen, such humbleness and concern for others eventually leads to an individual's elevation to the level of sainthood. In this regard, offering food to the needy is "a virtue and a characteristic of truly pious, saintly people."[33] For Gulen, however, one must be humble and consider this a favor from God and a Divine bounty, to the extent that one forgets what good one has done. Indeed "this virtue is particular to those with considerable nearness to God, who take far greater pleasure in giving than receiving."[34] Furthermore, Gulen raises the bar by suggesting that such sincerity should lead individuals to look only for the pleasing of God, and even spiritual pleasures and the gaining of Paradise should not be their goal. He says, "Without expecting any return, even in the form of spiritual pleasures, for all that one does for God's sake, always being aware of Him and experiencing the shadow of the light of His existence."[35]

Once one has reached the level of relating all achievements to God, one will find oneself in union with God, what is also called self-annihilation in God. Like many mystics, Gulen calls this *fana fi Allah*. What makes Gulen unique in this regard is that he uses social work, such as charity and helping others, as part of spiritual development. He describes self-annihilation in God in this way:

> A person of truth who has reached the point of attaining a new existence in which all the directions are united into one direction falls into such a state that he or she cannot help but utter, "There is no really existent one save God." Those who have attained this state see all space and time as having existence in His knowledge and proceeding from His knowledge and perceive all existing things as manifestations of the lights of His existence. Enraptured with the spiritual pleasures, they utter with every breath that everything is from Him, and regard annihilation in the light of His existence as the price of being favored with existence.[36]

With this level of union and annihilation in the Divine existence, one sees everything in terms of His names, which leads to the love of God and His Beautiful Names. Through God's names, human beings make connections with Him. Each of these names is a key. Having such a key is a Divine gift. Gulen says:

> Experiencing and knowing the All-Beautiful Names with their own depths is a Divine favor for servants and a pleasure which will richen their spirits, and in respect of their outer and inner senses or faculties, it is an awareness of "seeing," knowing, and experiencing Him, and being seen and known by Him. Those who reach this horizon work for God's sake, begin every task for God's sake, and do whatever they do for God's sake; in the words of Bediüzzaman, they can make the seconds of their life as fruitful as the years of other people by moving and stopping "for God," "for God's sake," and "for the pleasing of God." Why should this not be possible, as the servants are His servants, the Names are His Names, it is He who is called by these Names, and the door to which the servants turn is His door?[37]

# Gulen on love

As noted above, love is a central aspect of Gulen's mystical path. As a mystic, for Gulen there is a strong emphasis on love of God, and hence love for the Prophet. In Islam, love of God requires love of the prophets of God, because the prophets are the beloved of God. The Qur'an states, "Say [O Muhammad], 'If you love God, follow me, and God will love you, and forgive you of your sins. God is the Most-Forgiving, the Most-Merciful.'" (3:31) The prophets are the ones who most perfectly reflected the Divine names and taught them to their communities. Hence, the prophets are the beloved of God. For most Muslim mystics, love for Muhammad as the Prophet of Islam has a special place in their spirituality, and Gulen is no exception. In his various supplications, Gulen expresses his love for all of the prophets, but he makes special mention of the Prophet of Islam. It is to Gulen's love for the Prophet that we will now turn.

Before delving into Gulen's love for the Prophet, it is important to examine Gulen's general understanding of love. Regarding love, Gulen says the following:

> Love is the most essential element in every being, a most radiant light and a great power that can resist and overcome every force. Love elevates every soul that absorbs it, and prepares it for the journey to eternity. Souls that have made contact with eternity through love exert themselves to implant in all other souls what they receive from eternity. They dedicate their lives to this sacred duty, for the sake of which they endure every kind of

hardship to the end. Just as they pronounce "love" with their last breath, they also breathe love while being raised on the Day of Judgment.[38]

He talks also about the Prophet's love for his community. While the companions of the Prophet loved him, he also loved them and showed great compassion for them and for his community. The Qur'an says, "Surely there has come to you a Messenger from among yourselves. Your suffering is difficult for him. He is anxious about you, and to the believers is extremely kind and merciful" (9:128). It is also narrated in a hadith that on the Day of Judgment when everyone is concerned about themselves, the Prophet would say, "my community,"[39] which shows his great love and concern for them. Similarly, his companions would have great love and respect for him. On one occasion, a companion of the Prophet came to him and asked who he had loved the most. The Prophet responded that it was his wife, 'Aisha. Then the companion said, "I mean among men." The Prophet responded, "'Aisha's father."[40] 'Aisha's father was Abu Bakr, a great friend and companion of the Prophet, who would be elected the first Caliph after the Prophet's death.

Loving the Prophet is an essential element of Sufism and Islamic spirituality. Indeed, all Muslims, theologically speaking, are expected to love the Prophet. That is why many Muslims name their male children Muhammad, or one of the Prophet's qualitative names, for example Ahmad, Mahmud, and Hamid. According to statistical data, the name Muhammad with its various transliterations has become one of the most commonly given boy's name in Britain.[41]

As another expression of this love, in many parts of the Islamic world, Muslims celebrate the birthday of the Prophet with the recitation of verses from the Qur'an and eulogy poems about the Prophet. Although Gulen finds these annual celebrations of the birth of the Prophet insufficient, he still sees them as good and acceptable expressions of love for the Prophet. While all Muslims express this love in a variety of ways, Sufis' love is much more concentrated and deeper. It is generally expressed in their mystical writings and intimate conversations with God or with the Prophet. In their conversations with God, as a result of the Divine command found in Qur'an 33:56, they ask God to send His peace and blessings to the Prophet.

For Sufis, love for the master is essential. That is because the master is seen as a representative of the esoteric function of the Prophet. Therefore, the Sufis' love for the Sufi master is by extension a love for the Prophet, and of course the love for the Prophet is an expression of the love for God. Since Fethullah Gulen does not belong to a particular Sufi order, his love for the Prophet is not based on the direction of a spiritual master. It is a direct love for the Prophet. One can see this through a close examination of his writings, particularly of his poems. Such a close examination can also show Gulen's great love for all pre-Islamic prophets. This is because of the Prophet's own love for the earlier prophets. Several hadith make this point clear. In one, the Prophet says, "I am the closest of people to Jesus, the son of Mary." His companions ask, "How O Messenger of God?" He responds, "The prophets are brothers. Their mothers are different, but their religion is the same and there is no prophet between Jesus and me."[42] Therefore, loving one prophet does not exclude, and in fact it necessitates, loving all others.

Love for the Prophet is a genre in Islamic poetical literature called *na't*, or *naat*, which literally means "an adjective" and can be translated as "description." Sometimes the genre is called *na't-i sharif*, which can be translated as "noble description," through which the poet expresses his or her love for the Prophet by describing his characteristics. Gulen's poems on love for the Prophet are important contemporary examples of this genre in Islamic mysticism.

Fethullah Gulen has many mystical predecessors who have expressed their feelings and their love for the Prophet through poetry or prose. One of the earliest mystics, Abu Talib al-Makki (d. 996), speaks of his love for the Prophet. But such a love is not a matter of assertion or lip service. This love has some signs for it. According to al-Makki, "The sign of love for God is our love for the Qur'an and the sign of love for the Qur'an is our love for the Prophet. The sign of love for the Prophet is to follow him."[43] For al-Ghazali (d. 1111), love for the Prophet is related to the spirit of the Prophet: "It is a light-giving lamp, kindled by the Divine revelation." Furthermore, al-Ghazali indicates that the love for the Prophet is the love for the Sunnah of the Prophet. He goes further by connecting love for the Prophet to the afterlife, saying, "The sign of the love of his Sunnah is the love for the afterlife."[44]

Jalal al-Din Rumi (d. 1272), perhaps the most well-known Muslim mystic in the West, expresses his love for the Prophet in an authentic quatrain. Rumi says, "I am the servant of the Qur'an as I live. I am the dust on the path of Muhammad, the chosen one." Rumi also refers to the love of the companions of the Prophet, particularly the love of Abu Bakr for the Prophet, using allegorical language. He says, "Heart and love have become friends, like Ahmad (the Prophet) and Abu Bakr who have become friends in the cave.[45] These two friends' names were different, but their spirits were one."[46] He speaks further of his love for the Prophet by saying, "When the face of Muhammad is reflected on the wall, the heart of the wall becomes alive." In another statement, Rumi once again praises the Prophet when he says, "No one like him has come to the world, and no one like him will come." While the poems show Rumi's love for the Prophet and his companions, they also show his humility.[47] Perhaps Rumi would receive such love and be inspired by other early personalities of Islamic spiritual life, such as Zayn al-Abidin, a prominent Shiite imam who indicates his love and longing for the Prophet in a well-known poem:

O morning breeze, one day if you arrive at the respected land of Haram/
Convey my greetings to the tomb in which the respected Prophet resides

The Ottoman mystic, Seyh Galib (d. 1799), a master of the Mevlevi Sufi order has a remarkable expression of love for the Prophet. In a poem entitled, "About the Eulogy of Muhammad and His Beautiful Attributes," Seyh Galib says, "Muhammad is such a Sultan that even the moon tears itself into pieces to wipe its face with Muhammad's foot [as a sign of respect for him]." In another poem, he says, "Muhammad's priceless beauty is in such a high rank that the Prophet Joseph, who is known as being peerless in beauty, can only be a servant of him." Finally, addressing his pen, Seyh Galib says, "O Pen, stop writing on the matter of the beauty of Muhammad. That is because God has written his name on the preserved tablet."[48] While some of the spirit of the originals is lost, the deep love and admiration for the Prophet is evident.

Following the Qur'anic injunction to believers to send blessings to the Prophet, "God and His angels bless the Prophet. O believers, give your blessings to him, and pray him peace" (33:56) mystics have expressed their feelings in their intimate conversations with the Prophet, through which one can witness the depth of their love, as well as their religious and spiritual experiences. Mawlana Khalid al-Baghdadi (d. 1826), a Naqshabandi master, is one of them. He expresses his feelings and love for the Prophet by describing a variety of aspects of the Prophet's spiritual life. He speaks of the Prophet's spiritual rank, the Prophet as a reflection of the Divine, as a perfect human being, and enlightenment and mercy for all of humanity. Also, the Prophet is presented as the one who opened the door of the realm of the unseen. For Mawlana Khalid, the Prophet is a shining Divine light, and through the love of the Prophet the locks on the hearts are opened.[49] It seems that Gulen's addresses to the Prophet and his descriptions of the Prophet are in line with those of Mawlana Khalid. Gulen's words, however, are meditated through the prism of the contemporary world, and as such his terminology and style speak more directly to our present situation.

All of the mystics mentioned above constitute a legacy of love for the Prophet in the tradition of Islamic spirituality. Gulen's love for the Prophet stems from this rich legacy, as well as from the Qur'an and from the sayings of the Prophet himself. It is an axiom in Islam that God loves His messenger and sends blessings to him. Furthermore, one cannot love God without loving the Prophet, and vice versa. That is because to love the beloved of God is to love God. Thus, love for the Prophet and love for God are inseparable. Gulen himself refers to a hadith Qudsi, in which God says to the Prophet, "If it were not for you, I would not have created the universe."[50] Although this hadith does not appear in the major sources of the sayings of the Prophet, its meaning is compatible with the overall teaching of the Qur'an. Emphasizing the importance of love for the Prophet and following his path, the Qur'an says, "Say [O Muhammad], 'If you love God, follow me, and God will love you'" (3:31). In a commentary on the Qur'anic verse, "Good and evil deeds are not the same" (41:34) an Iraqi commentator of the Qur'an, al-Alusi (d. 1854) says, "What is meant by 'beauty' in this Qur'anic verse is the love of the Prophet and his family, and what is meant by 'evil' in the verse is the hate for them."[51]

The Qur'an makes a strong connection between faith and love of God. In fact, verses clearly indicate that faith and love are proportionately related. As faith increases in the heart of an individual, in the same way love also increases: "Those who believe, more greatly love God" (2:165). Any love for the Prophet that is not based on the love for God is not the real love that mystics describe. For example, love for the Prophet for the sake of kinship is not the ideal love. And here we know the famous story of the Prophet's uncle, Abu Talib, who loved the Prophet and protected him. Addressing the Prophet, a Qur'anic verse says, "You cannot guide to the way of righteousness the one that you love" (28:56). For this verse, al-Alusi gives the above-mentioned example of Abu Talib. Yes, he loved the Prophet, not as a messenger of God, but as a nephew. That said, even this love is not worthless, and there will be a reward for it in the afterlife. However, such a love is not considered the love that is described in the Qur'an.

Gulen's love for the Prophet comes from his love for God and his strong faith in the prophethood of Muhammad. Analyzing Gulen's love for the Prophet, one is reminded of the famous Sufi concept, known as annihilation in the Prophet, or *fana fi al-Rasul*. One mystic described it as the melting of one's soul and flowing toward the soul of the Prophet to become united with his soul. This is a spiritual state along the mystical path through which one forgets one's personal existence and is annihilated in the existence of the Prophet. Gulen's passion and love for the Prophet should be considered under this category. Even without knowing the totality of his feelings or possessing any background information, through simply reading the poems of Gulen one is moved by the passion, depth, and religious experience manifested in his works.

It seems to me that Gulen's love for the Prophet is experiential. An analogy of cooking can be used. It is as if Gulen had a burning heart and his words were cooked in that heart, and then they came to surface to be served in the form of a poem. One can imagine that many companions of the Prophet had such a love, and in fact Gulen himself draws his love for the Prophet from the companions' love. Indicating this, Gulen says, "Prophet Muhammad's companions knew him and loved him more than they loved themselves. They were prepared to sacrifice their lives to protect him."[52] In this context, Gulen mentions the story of one of the companions of the Prophet, Khubayb bin 'Adi, who was captured by Meccan pagans to be hanged. Before hanging him, they asked him if he would like Muhammad to be in his place. Khubayb replied, "I would rather be cut into pieces than wish Muhammad were in my place. I do not want even a thorn to hurt his blessed foot in exchange for being returned to my family."[53] It is narrated that he said, "Lord, no one is here to convey my greetings of peace to the

Prophet." Momentarily the Prophet, who was with his companions, heard this statement and, responding to his greeting of peace, said, "And peace be with you too." Then he informed his companions that Khubayb was hanged at that moment.[54]

Having described Gulen's love for the Prophet in general terms, I would now like to turn my focus to his poems in order to more fully examine his love for the Prophet. Gulen addresses the Prophet in this poetry with "a burning heart" and with tremendous passion. Indeed, with this heartfelt passion, one can easily see how Gulen's poetry is a remarkable example of the *na't* genre. In the following, I will present examples from Gulen's poems and how the love of the Prophet is presented. Gulen's poems that speak of the love of the Prophet are scattered in his famous divan, known as "Broken Plectrum," or *Kirik Mizrap*. In his poem entitled, "Do Not Leave Me Alone," Gulen says,

My heart and my eyes are opened with you.
Obstacles can be overcome with you.
When your name is said, light spreads from it.
Rise upon my soul, do not burn me with the pain of separation.
For God's sake, do not leave your servant alone.
I am the servant outside your door, and you are the Sultan.
You are a refuge from God for those who have been left on the roads.
If I am a corpse, you are its soul.
Rise upon my soul, do not burn me with the pain of separation

For God's sake, do not leave your servant alone.[55]

One can see here an expression of utmost need, a need that goes beyond food and water. Gulen, through such passionate feelings, expresses his true love for the Prophet of Islam. This passion exists to such an extent that he cannot imagine his existence without the existence of the Prophet. This is what *fana fi al-Rasul* is.

In another poem, entitled, "The Rose of My Heart," Gulen says:

Any soul that loves you is majestic, O Messenger of God.
His eyes and heart are full, O Messenger of God.
I swear anyone who gets even an atom of love of your beauty
Becomes an inseparable servant at your door, O Messenger of God.
Those who have reached your realm want no other favor.
At your neighborhood, every eye is misted over.
Those who circle around your light, flying constantly,
They are a branch of your spirit, O Messenger of God.
In your climate, birds with golden wings fly.
Your climate is the path of birds, O Messenger of God.
To see you is the sweetest dream of believers
The hearts that see you are restful, O Messenger of God.

Seeing you is sweet imagination of this strange Kitmir.[56]
That imagination is the light of my heart, O Messenger of God.[57]

On another occasion, Gulen wrote a poem entitled "Moonface," the expression in poetry is indicative of the beauty of the beloved. Gulen again addresses the Prophet:

My Moonface, my open word, my soul be sacrificed to you.
My heart is amazed by you.

Your daffodil glance, how inexorable its effect.
My Sultan, I asked you for help.
Look at my heart, there is an arrow and pain in its depths.
The remedy is with you.

O one whose existence is light, whose world is happiness, whose word
    is the Qur'an,[58]
You are the remedy for all my sorrows.

I am full of fire, never leave me in separation.
My soul is mourning.

As sorrowful and miserable, and suffering with many problems
I am leaning at your door.

I don't know another ember, nor a fire. I am burned by you.
I have been awakened by you.
O light who came from the Divine throne to the world, O the full moon
    in the sky,
Your light has enlightened . . .

Eyes have not seen a charming beloved like you in the entire universe.
Your beauty is even brighter than the sun.

Open your heart through your kindness. Open so that the Kitmir is
    your servant.
Your dervish lodge is high.

Bestow upon me a drop from the ocean of your kindness.
O Sultan of my heart.

Do a favor for me, please. I do not know another door.
My sorrows are greater than the sorrows of everyone.[59]

In these poems, one can see how Gulen frequently uses terms such as "heart," "passion," and "burning," which are commonly used by almost all Muslim mystics throughout the history of Islamic spirituality. While many Sufis will experience this longing for their master in the Sufi order, and some directly for the Prophet, Gulen mainly addresses the Prophet of Islam with these passionate terms as his unique master, since he does not belong to a specific order. In a poem entitled, "You," Gulen once again speaks of hearts full of love and the allegory of honey, as many mystics do. Gulen says,

> In the mouths is candy and sherbet.
> In the hearts your name breathes.
> If one tastes your love,
> One does not care anymore about cream and honey.
> If hearts had loved you,
> If they had union with you,
> If they had entered your close circle,
> Why would they care with position and possession?[60]

Separation is a term that is frequently used by Sufis when they lament their distance from the beloved. That beloved can be the master, the Prophet, or the Divine. One can see this mystical term of separation in Gulen's writings extensively. In the following poem, Gulen once again clearly indicates his sorrow of being distant from the Prophet. He appeals to the Prophet for favors as if he is fulfilling the message of Jesus for his disciple when he says, "Ask, and it will be given to you; search, and you will find; knock, and the door will be opened for you" (Mt. 7:7). Gulen, in these poems, knocks at the door of the Prophet and asks for his favor. He also expresses his fear and his hope, the fear of loss and the hope of gain. According to Islamic theology, these too have to be balanced.

> My heart has burned with the sorrow of separation. Don't you ask me
>     how I am doing?
> Even with the edge of your tongue, don't you ask about my tedium?
> I don't know whether you have doubt about the loyalty of the friend.
> Showing kindness even once, don't you ask about my imagination?
>
> Gifts were bestowed upon friends, isn't there a favor for us too?
> My heart has become roasted, isn't there a trust in my mourning?
> I wiped my face on your track; I don't know how many days.
> I am afraid I lack the capacity to love you.[61]

Once again, in the above poem Gulen expresses his pain of separation and the pain that comes from the fear of loss. For this, he appeals to the Prophet, mentioning his friendship with him. One can see similar approaches in the writings of early mystics. For example, Khowaja Abdullah Ansari, an eleventh-century Sufi, says, "If chicory is bitter it is still from the garden. If Abdullah is a sinner, he is still one of your friends." In another poem, Ansari says,

> O God, in this world the disobedience we do makes your beloved Muhammad sad and your enemy Iblis happy. If you torment us tat [sic] the resurrection, again your beloved will be sad and your enemy happy.

O God, do not give your enemy two occasions for happiness, and your beloved two occasions for sorrow.[62]

Gulen's most known poem on his love for the Prophet is his poem entitled, "The Rose of Medina." Like many Sufis, Gulen uses the rose as a symbol for the love of the Prophet. Therefore, the Prophet of Islam in this poem is described as a rose that gives light, a rose that gives water, a rose that is beloved. In this poem, once again Gulen's annihilation in the Prophet is expressed. For Gulen, once the Prophet is mentioned, or remembered, nothing else in this world deserves to be remembered. In fact, in the Sufi parlance, this is a step that will prepare one for annihilation of the ego in God. Gulen's heart is like a dove in this poem. He wants to reach the Prophet, but needs a feather to reach him, a feather from the wings of the Prophet. Gulen asks for that feather. He is a lover in this poem, like Majnun, the famous literary character of love. He finds the face of the Prophet like the sun. If the sun sets, the Prophet's face replaces the sun. Indicating his annihilation in the Prophet, Gulen asks for rebirth. Yes, for the Sufi who embarks upon the difficult path has to "die before he dies," so that he can be spiritually resurrected. In this poem, Gulen speaks of this spiritual resurrection, which is similar to what other mystics indicate: "the Sun at Midnight rises only at the 'dark night of the soul,' or: the water of life is found in the darkest valley."[63] Let's listen to what Gulen says:

I remembered you again and everything was deleted from my memory.
Your image traveled on the hills of my heart.
Even if this is a mirage, my palpitations have ended.
I remembered you again and everything was deleted from my memory.

I wish I could sit with your love and stand up with your love constantly.
I wish I could rise like a spirit and wander in your horizon
So that I could find a way to flow into your heart.
I wish I could sit with your love and stand up with your love constantly.

I wish I knew when the order for union will come.
My heart, burning with the fire of separation, will always mourn,
Will mourn with the freshest feelings to wait always.
I wish I knew when the order for union will come.

My heart trembles like a dove because of your name.
Please give me your wing to reach you.
Give me a feather so I can fly constantly behind you.
My heart trembles like a dove because of your name.

O Rose, who turned dry deserts into Paradise,
Come and enter my heart with your swooning colors.
It is time; smile to my crying eyes.
O Rose, who turned dry deserts into Paradise,

Let me be a servant, running after you like Majnun.
Scatter an ember in me so I burn like a stove
And I escape from this painful dream that is without you.
Let me be a servant, running after you like Majnun.

My reason keeps counting the long days of separation.
It keeps spreading a foggy and smoky gloom to my spirit.
Show me your face, because the sun is beginning to set.
My reason keeps counting the long days of separation.

At least, at the last phase, let my setting become a rising.
Let my heart be filled by the freshest colors of your horizon.
Let drums be beaten everywhere, and reed flutes be heard everywhere.
At least, at the last phase, let my setting become a rising.[64]

Gulen's love for the Prophet is expressed in such a poetic style that it is a great contribution, both to the *na't* genre and to Islamic Spirituality. In particular, this helps the diffusion of the Sufi concept of love for the Prophet among people, generally through the memorization of Gulen's poems. It also attests to how the author was successful in indicating this essential element of Sufism and making it available even for laypeople. Gulen asks for a feather from the Prophet's wing to fly. Of course, this allegorical flight has something to do with the spiritual life. Gulen's use of this allegorical language echoes the writings of an early mystic, Ibn Ata Allah al-Iskandari (d. 1310), in his book *Hikam,* or what is known as *Hikam al-'Ata'iyya*, who says, "So long as the domains of the Invisible Worlds have not been revealed to him, the creature in the Cosmos is imprisoned by his surroundings and confined in the temple of his nature."[65] For Gulen, such a wing from the Prophet will help him to free himself from the cage of his body and exercise freely the Sufi's level of spirit. In another poem, Gulen again uses Sufi terminology in expressing his longing for union with the Prophet. He humbles himself by saying that even if he does not deserve such a union, he takes refuge in the kindness of the Prophet. He again uses terms "fire," "heart," "tears," "sorrow," and "remedies," as if he is in the position of utmost need of help from the Prophet. In this poem entitled, "Rise upon My Heart," Gulen says,

Open my heart and look. The fire inside is lit by hope in you.
The tears that flow from my eyes are from the color of my heart.
Even if my sorrows are without limit, the remedy is in you.
Please take my hands saying, "This is from me."

For many years I have been on the way; there is no rest anymore.
Falling and rising, made no power left for this travel.
My miserable situation, my hope for union is no longer.
Bestow your favor; what I need is only your favor.

Rise upon my heart, and resound it like a reed flute.
Make me also hear the secrets of what you have heard.
When you present roses to the Beloved, please remember this
    Kitmir too.
Despite your knowledge of his every situation not fitting your
    bright horizon.[66]

Gulen expresses his love for the Prophet in his prose as well, but here he is much more oriented toward logic, rather than toward sheer feeling. Because of this, he always speaks of indebtedness to the Prophet. For the existence of the afterlife, humanity is indebted to the Prophet. Considering the presence of the Prophet, Gulen indicates that if he were given a choice to be in the presence of the Prophet or in Paradise with all its beauty, he would prefer to be in the presence of the Prophet. Gulen says, "If Kitmir [I] were going to be in the position to make a choice between witnessing the reality of the Prophet and the swooning beauty of Paradise and its adorned hills, he [I] would prefer the Prophet."[67]

Despite all of Gulen's articulate descriptions of the Prophet, he does not forget to stick to the principle of Islam that is clearly expressed in the Qur'an, which states that the Prophet is not a deity but a human being. The Prophet is a servant of God and a messenger of God, but not a deity. Gulen quotes a narration from the time of the Prophet: "When the Prophet was eating on the ground, a woman saw him and said: 'Look at him. He eats like a slave.' The Prophet turned to her and said, 'Can you find a better slave than me? I am a slave of God.'"[68] Therefore, Gulen says, "the Prophet was a servant. On one occasion, when Gabriel was with the Prophet, they were talking about hunger. The Prophet was given a choice by God to be either a king-prophet or a servant-prophet, and the Prophet preferred to be a servant-prophet. This also explains why the Prophet is considered a perfect example for mystics."[69]

As I was finishing this chapter, Gulen delivered a speech whose message nicely closes this chapter. In this speech delivered on January 9, 2017, Gulen discussed "social spirit," the spirit that binds communities together, and the "boundless conscious," a deep consciousness that connects others and sees many areas of common ground between members of society. He suggests that there must be a chair in the heart for everyone to sit. He also suggests that the idea of revenge comes from jealousy and greed, and that one has to avoid revenge. Here, he refers to the following Qur'anic verse: "If you punish, then punish in the same manner that you were afflicted. But if you endure patiently, surely it is better for the patient" (16:126).

# PART THREE

# Practical aspects

# 8

# Prayer, asceticism,
and spirituality

The present work argues that various ways of Islamic spirituality, either within the frames of traditional Sufi orders or among individuals or non-attached Sufi groups, continue. Throughout the Islamic world and even in the West, there are numerous centers where practitioners of Islamic spirituality live a life of retreat and asceticism. In this chapter, I will give a brief account of one day in the life of the individuals in such a spiritual center. This, I feel, is central to a better understanding of the importance of spirituality's continued relevance. First, however, I will discuss the importance of asceticism for Islamic spirituality.

Asceticism or *zuhd* (in Arabic *al-zuhd*) in Islamic spirituality is similar to the Western understanding in that it has a connotation of renunciation. Many mystics have written books with this as the title. When we read these books, we see that generally they all include information on such things as moral behaviors, avoiding bad behaviors, practicing good manners, being prepared for the afterlife, etc. Generally, in In these works the lives of mystics are seen as examples and as role models. These writings often describe the Prophet and his companions' experiences of hunger, their abandonment of comforts and luxuries, and other difficulties, particularly the Prophet's experience of meditation in the cave of Hira. It is narrated that the family of the Prophet never became full, even with bread. 'Aisha, the wife of the Prophet narrates that, "Until his death, the family of Muhammad (peace and blessings upon him) never became full of barley bread on two consecutive days."[1] Abu Huraira narrates that the Prophet passed by a group of people who had roasted a lamb. The people invited the Prophet to join them, but he declined. After narrating the story Abu Huraira says, "The Prophet departed this world and did not get full of barley bread."[2]

Certainly, the Prophet's hunger could have been due to the general scarcity of food at the time, but it is clear that the Prophet could have had more food if he had wanted. Therefore, one should conclude that this anecdote is another example of the Prophet preferring to give less importance to worldly things and more importance to the Divine. Under the title "The Way of Living of the Family of Muhammad," the famous mystic Waki' bin al-Jarrah (d. 812/3) narrates that on one occasion 'Umar entered the presence of the Prophet who was on a mat made of reeds which left marks on his side. 'Umar cried and the Prophet asked why he was crying. Umar said: "O Messenger of God, I remembered Kisra [the Arabic title for Sassanid kings] and Caesar and what they are in [of wealth] of the world." And the Prophet said, "O Umar, if I wanted large mountains to walk with me as gold and silver they would."[3] It is well known that both the Prophet and his companions, such as Abu Huraira, experienced hunger, and sometimes they had nothing to eat. Under such circumstances, patience becomes very important, and therefore Islamic spirituality's literature on *zuhd* includes topics such as patience, humbleness, contemplation, avoidance of sin, loving for God's sake, and "making God beloved to people."

One important quality of people of *zuhd* is *rifq*. This is an Islamic term that implies gentleness or tenderness, and it is a quality of God. "Surely God is Tender and loves tenderness. And gives to those who are tender what He does not give those who are harsh."[4] Avoiding blemishes on the soul is also a part of asceticism in Islamic spirituality. In fact, some masters in the field have written books dedicated to avoiding blemishes on the soul. One important writer on the concept is Abd al-Rahman al-Sulami (d. 1021), who wrote a book called *'Uyub al-Nafs* (*Shortcomings of the Soul*) in which he explains at least thirty-five negative qualities of the soul, from laziness to arrogance.[5]

Since asceticism is generally associated with avoiding interactions with society and preferring seclusion, or *khalwa*, it is not surprising to see that some masters of Islamic spirituality understood asceticism to be avoiding involvement with their community, leaving people, and dedicating themselves to prayer in a private place, a room, or even a cave. This was the case for many early masters of Islam, and there are some Prophetic references that suggest this approach. For example, in one hadith, the Prophet is believed to have said, "Wisdom is divided into nine pieces, eight of which are in *uzla* [being in seclusion] and one is in silence."[6] Although the authenticity of this hadith is questionable, it is well-known among mystics.

The early personalities of Islamic spirituality who preferred this approach are Sufyan al-Thawri (d. 778), Ibrahim bin Adham (d. 778), Dawud al-Ta'i (d. c. 780), al-Fudail bin 'Iyad (d. 803), and Bishr al-Hafi (d. 850). For example, al-Fudail bin 'Iyad would say, "Anyone who gets involved with people cannot be saved from one of these two. Either [they] will immerse [themselves] into a wrong when they enter or [they] will remain silent when they see something detestable and [they] will [mostly] hear from those gathered together something that may cause them to sin."[7]

On the other hand, there are masters of Islamic spirituality who would prefer *jalwa*, or getting involved with people rather than living in isolation. Among the early masters who supported this idea are Said bin al-Musayyib

(d. 715), Shurayh al-Qadi (d. c. 699), and 'Amir al-Sha'bi (d. 721). Each of these groups has their own arguments, and perhaps it can be said that the issue of *jalwa* versus *khalwa* is related to individuals' situations and conditions. A debate in al-Bayhaki's *Al-Zuhd al-Kabir* suggests that this is similar to marriage. For some people, marriage is preferable and for some celibacy is preferable. Although there are valid reasons for living in isolation, in today's world, community involvement is more significant than isolation. To be involved with community service, good works, etc. while keeping one's spiritual life in tact is heroism, since such involvement contributes to the betterment of society, allowing one to help people by being a good example. While there are real challenges to keeping one's connection with the Divine, in our times the problems that the world faces necessitate involvement. This being said, let us now turn to a day in the life of a mystic.

# The night prayer and other voluntary prayers

Before describing the prayers, two things are important to remember. First, it should be noted that cleanliness is an essential prerequisite to any prayer. In Islam, there is a formalized process of ablution, or *wudu*, that is done before one's prayers. Basically, and at a minimum, the hands, face, head, arms to the elbows, and feet to the ankles are washed. Once it is finished, the person is considered equipped with the ritual cleansing of ablution. The details of this are found in many books of jurisprudence and there are numerous websites that show how this is done. Though ablution is required before every prayer, if one has not nullified his or her ablution through such things as deep sleep or certain bodily discharges, one does not need to repeat the ablution.

Second, the entirety of the prayer should be said in Arabic. While there are some schools of law that allow those who are not yet able to recite the prayers in Arabic to say them in their native language, for those who have the ability, Arabic should be used. Here, for simplicity, I will mainly give the English translation of the various phrases, prayers, and *dhikr*. But again, as with the ablutions, it is not difficult to find resources which have Arabic transliterations of the various elements of the prayers.[8]

Ideally one should make sure that no quarter of the day passes without prayer. Thus, the day of a mystic generally begins with the night prayer, known as *tahajjud*. This prayer will start roughly an hour before dawn breaks, though religiously speaking it can be performed any time from midnight to dawn. Regarding the merit of the night prayer, the Prophet says, "The most meritorious prayer after the prescribed prayers is the prayer in the belly of night."[9] This prayer can be done in congregation, but it is generally performed individually. Based on the availability of people, an imam or an individual would generally recite at least ten to twenty verses from the Qur'an in the first unit. The second unit would be similar, but with different verses recited. One has to remember, performing such a beautiful prayer in the early morning should give a real sense of tranquility. Especially since the Qur'an speaks of the importance of recitation in the early morning—"Perform the prayer from the declining of the sun to the darkening of the night and the recitation of the dawn. Surely the recitation of dawn is witnessed" (17:78)—such recitation of the Qur'an in prayer provides a strong attachment to the Qur'an and its spiritual message.

Occasionally, these verses will be about the connection between human beings and God. Sometimes they are reminders of the afterlife, while other times they include prayers from the Qur'an, such as, "Our Lord, we believe. Therefore forgive us, and have mercy on us, for You are the Best of the merciful" (23:109) and, "My Lord, forgive and have mercy, for You are the Best of the merciful" (23:118). One also can see that there is a focus on chapter "Al-Nur," specifically on what is known as the "Verse of Light."

> God is the light of the heavens and the earth. The similitude of His light is as a niche wherein there is a lamp and the lamp in a glass. The glass is as if it was a glittering star, kindled from a blessed tree, an olive that is neither of the east nor of the west, whose oil would shine even if it were not touched by any fire. Light upon light, God guides to His light whom He pleases. God strikes similitudes for people, and God has knowledge of everything. (24:35)

In the night prayer, many beautiful Divine names are repeated as the Qur'an is recited. One can see, for example, how the Divine names of al-Ghafur, the Most-Forgiving; al-Rahim, the Most-Merciful; al-Tawwab, the One who accepts repentance; and al-Hakim, the Most-Wise are referred to and repeated in verses that are recited in the night prayer. The night prayer generally continues until dawn, the time of the Morning Prayer.

Before delving into the details of prescribed prayers, however, it is good to give a brief summation of voluntary prayers that are performed before and after prescribed prayers. These prayers are called rawatib, and it is believed that the Prophet missed them only when traveling. We know that he did miss them on occasion, for if the Prophet had never missed one then they would have been prescribed. The first voluntary prayer is performed before the Morning Prayer. It was performed by the Prophet, and is highly recommended. This prayer has two units, and as one hadith indicates, the Prophet performed this prayer by reciting the Qur'anic verses about prophets and messengers of God, such as Abraham, Ishmael, Isaac, Jacob, Moses, and Jesus, among others. In the first unit, verse 2:136 is recited and in the second unit verse 3:52, which talks about Jesus and his disciples, is recited. Another well-known hadith suggests that in the first unit chapter 109:1-6 are is recited, and in the second unit chapter 112: is recited. This said, any verses maybe recited in this prayer and it is up to individuals to choose what they want to recite.

Like the voluntary prayer before the prescribed Morning Prayer, there are four units of voluntary prayer before the Noon Prayer. As far as performance is concerned, all voluntary prayers are similar, with the exception of how many and which verses from the Qur'an are read or recited after the recitation of the first chapter of the Qur'an. There are two units of voluntary prayer after the Noon Prayer as well. In the same way, there are four voluntary units before the Afternoon Prayer. However, these are not *rawatib* and as such, while recommended, are not as strongly recommended as the *rawatib* prayers.

There are also six units of voluntary prayer after the Sunset Prayer. Two of them are *rawatib,* and the other four units after the Sunset Prayer are called, "The Prayer of the Awwabin." This prayer is not *rawatib*, but it is more highly recommended than other non-*rawatib* ones. It takes its name from a saying of the Prophet where it is narrated that he said, "Anyone who performs six units of voluntary prayer after the sunset prayer will be registered as *awwab* [one who constantly returns to God]." *Awwab* as a spiritual quality is frequently mentioned, and it has a high place in Islamic spirituality. The term in the Qur'an is mentioned as a quality of David (38:17), Solomon (38:30), and Job (38:44). The Qur'an also describes Paradise as a place that is promised and prepared for the *awwabin* (50:31-2). Some have said that the number of the units of the *awwabin* prayer can be anywhere from two to twenty units.

There are also voluntary prayers after the evening prayer. There are two units that are *rawatib*, and there are three units of prayer known as *witr*. While schools of Islamic jurisprudence present *witr* as prescribed, the Hadith recommend them even more strongly than the *rawatib* prayers but not as prescribed. The *witr* prayer is performed like the Sunset Prayer, which is also three units, with the exception that it has a specific prayer in it called the *qunut* supplication. *Qunut* is a Qur'anic term meaning obedience, and it is ascribed to Mary (66:12). This prayer is said after bowing and before prostration. One version of the prayer goes as follows: "Our God to You we worship and pray and to You we prostrate. We hasten and move toward You. We hope for Your mercy and we fear for Your chastisement. Surely Your chastisement occurs to those who disbelieve in You." Another version of the *qunut*, which is also found in the sayings of the Prophet, goes as follows:

My God, guide me along with those You have guided. Give me health along with those to whom you have given health. Protect me along with those You have protected. Bless for me what You have given me. Protect me from all evil things. You are the Ruler. No one can rule over You. The one You honored will not be humiliated and the one You humiliate will not be honored. You are Holy and Almighty. Praise belongs to You in all things You have ruled. I ask for Your forgiveness O my Lord and repent to You.

At the end of this prayer, it is also traditional to ask peace and blessings from God for the Prophet of Islam.

One of the most important voluntary prayers is called the *duha* prayer. The *duha,* or midmorning prayer, is performed sometime between forty minutes after sunrise and noon. It consists of a minimum of two units of prayer and can have up to twelve units. It is recommended that in the first unit *Sura al-Shams*, chapter 91 of the Qur'an, is recited. This chapter describes the bounties of God. These bounties include the heavens, earth, and all creation. The chapter also talks about the rectification of the soul. In the second unit, the recommended recitation is chapter 93, or *Sura al-Duha*. This chapter of the Qur'an was revealed as a comfort to the Prophet, as it showed that God did not abandon His Prophet. It speaks of the Divine bounties and addresses the Prophet and his community, saying that they should take care of orphans and they should not repel beggars.

## The prescribed five daily prayers

The Morning Prayer, or *Fajr*, starts at dawn. It consists of two units of prayer and can be performed aloud, either in congregation or individually. However, prayer in congregation is preferable and recommended by the Prophet. Congregation is togetherness in this case. Theologically speaking, even a husband and wife praying together are considered to be praying in congregation, and thus are recipients of the spiritual benefits thereof. The first unit consists of reading or reciting the first chapter of the Qur'an and additional verses from the Qur'an. In the same way, for the second unit the worshipper reads or recites the first chapter of the Qur'an as well as some additional verses of the Qur'an. For example, chapter 55, known as *al-Rahman*, the Most-Merciful, can be recited and would be split, such that the entire chapter is recited in the prayer.[10] This chapter reminds people and *jinn* to be thankful, and it mentions the Divine bounties given to human beings and *jinn*. The exhortation, "Which of the bounties of God can you both deny?" is repeated thirty-two times in the chapter. After the prayer, as after every prayer, a form of *dhikr*, or remembrance, of God is expressed through Prophetic statements. This is called *tasbihat*. Generally, the *tasbihat* starts with these Prophetic words: "O God, you are Peace and peace comes from You. Our Lord make us live with peace." Then Qur'an 2:255, known as "*Ayat al-Kursi*," commonly called "The Throne Verse," is recited. The Prophet called this verse the greatest verse of the Qur'an.[11] The verse says,

God, there is no deity but He, the Most-Living, the Most-Sustaining. Neither slumber nor sleep can take Him. To Him belongs what is in the heavens and the earth. No one can intercede without His permission. He knows what lies in front of them and what is behind them. They cannot comprehend anything of His knowledge except what He wants. His throne [*kursi*] comprises all the heavens and earth. The preserving of them does not tire Him. He is the Most-High, the Most-Glorious.

Then the Prophetic phrases, such as "*Subhan Allah,*" which means, "God is exalted from any deficit," and, "*Alhamdulillah,*" or, "Praise be to God," are repeated thirty-three times. Then, declaring God's greatness, the worshipper will repeat the phrase, "*Allahu Akbar,*" or, "God is Greater than everything," thirty-three times. It is believed that the practice of repeating these phrases comes from the practice of the Prophet himself. The exact number, thirty-three, is significant. It is believed that the number thirty-three is similar to a key, and so repeating each phrase thirty-three times is as if one is opening the door of Divine mercy. Similarly, other oral prayers of the Prophet are said after the prescribed prayer, such as,

O God, You are my Lord. There is no deity but You. You have created me and I am Your servant. And I am keeping my promise and my covenant with you as much as I can. I take refuge in You from the evil that I have done. I return to you with your bounties upon me. I return to You with my sins. Forgive me. Surely no one forgives sins except You.

The Prophet calls this prayer the master formula for asking forgiveness from God.[12]

Another short prayer that can be said is, "In the name of God, the One nothing can harm in the presence of His name, on earth and in the heavens He is the Most-Hearing, the Most-Knowledgeable." After this prayer, Divine names may be chanted, either silently or loudly, within a formula: "You are Exalted, O Allah. You are Almighty, O Rahman. Protect us from the fire of Hell with your forgiveness, O Rahman. You are Exalted, O Rahim You are Almighty, O Karim [the Most-Generous or Most-Kind]. Protect us from the fire of Hell with your forgiveness, O Rahman." With this pattern, "You are Exalted . . . You are Almighty..." many Divine names are repeated in this *dhikr*. At the end, the last three verses of chapter 59 of the Qur'an, which contains fourteen beautiful Divine names, are recited. In fact, one can perform all of this on his or her own at home. In total, these recitations and the Morning Prayer would generally take a minimum of half an hour.

While the Morning Prayer is among the prayers that are performed aloud, the Noon Prayer, *Zuhr*, is one of the silent prayers (i.e., it is performed entirely silently) and can be performed either individually or in congregation. *Zuhr* consists of four units of prayer. For the first two units, after the recitation of the first chapter of the Qur'an, which is part of every unit of all five daily prayers, individuals can recite various verses from the Qur'an. For the last two units, only the first chapter is recited. After the prayer, the worshipper starts saying the *tasbihat*. This is similar to how after the Morning Prayer phrases of exalting, praising, and glorifying the greatness of God are repeated thirty-three times, as well as the chanting of the Divine names, though the formula would vary from the earlier one. At the end of chanting of the Divine names, there is a request to God for blessings upon the Prophet: "For the sake of all these names, O our Lord, send Your blessings and peace upon

Muhammad and his family as you have sent Your blessings and peace and mercy to Abraham and his family in the realm of creation with Your Mercy. You are the Most-Merciful of the mercifuls." Additionally, a few verses from the Qur'an are generally recited. Roughly, this prayer and the recitations would take about twenty minutes.

Like the Noon Prayer, the Afternoon Prayer, *'Asr*, is one of the silent prayers. It is four units, and after the first chapter of the Qur'an, individuals may recite any additional verses from the Qur'an. After the prayer again are the *tasbihat* and chanting of the Divine names, which are done in a similar manner as after the Morning Prayer. At the end, chapter 78, "*Al-Naba*," or "the Greatest News" is recited. This greatest news is the afterlife.

The Prophet states that the religion of Islam is based on easiness and not difficulty. Therefore, Muslim scholars of jurisprudence, following the path of the Prophet, have allowed two prayers to be combined together, if needed. Travel, weather conditions, etc. can be reasons for this combining of the prayers. As Anas bin Malik narrates, the Prophet used to say, "Make it easy [for people] and do not make it difficult [for them]. And give good tidings and do not make people hate."[13] Accordingly, prescribed daily prayers can be combined depending on the circumstance of the individual. *Zuhr* and *'Asr* can be combined either at the time of *Zuhr* or at the time of *'Asr*, depending on the person's availability. For example, if one is traveling from New York to Houston during the time of the Noon Prayer, this individual may combine the two prayers together in a way that best fits his or her travel plans. Besides these two prayers, the Sunset and Night prayers may also be combined until the time of the Morning Prayer, again depending on circumstances. Indeed, there are occasions on which the Prophet himself combined these two prayers.

Although generally morning is understood as the beginning of the day and one starts one's day with the Morning Prayer, in the Islamic calendar, like in the Hebrew calendar, days start with sunset. Hence, in Islam the day starts with the Sunset Prayer, known as *Maghrib*. For example, Monday starts on Sunday evening when the sun sets and continues until Monday's sunset. Regardless of time zones, when the sun sets it is the time of the Sunset Prayer. Like the Morning Prayer, it is also performed aloud. It has three units. The first two units are said aloud and the third is done silently. In the first two units, in addition to the first chapter, additional verses of choice are recited from the Qur'an, and in the third unit only the first chapter of the Qur'an is recited.

The Evening or *'Isha* prayer is the last of the five daily prayers in this sequence. The time of *'Isha* begins about one and a half hours after sunset and lasts until dawn, and while it can be performed anytime within this period, it is best to do it sooner. *'Isha* is four units long, and is one of the prayers said aloud. Like the other prayers, in the first two units the worshipper recites the first chapter of the Qur'an and verses of choice and in the third and fourth units silently recites only the first chapter of the Qur'an. The *tasbihat* is similar to that of the Noon Prayer, and at the end the last two verses of chapter 2 of the Qur'an are recited.

# The performance of prayer

In order to give a better picture of prayer, it is useful to provide an example of one of the daily prayers and give details of its performance. In the following, the details of a typical Sunset Prayer will be presented. First, though, a brief outline of the mystical understanding of this prayer might be useful. The wisdom in the time of sunset having a prayer is that Islamic prayer should lead us to reflect on our place in the cosmos. Said Nursi has a wonderful explanation for the times of the prayers and how they correspond to the elements of human life, the life of the planet, and the life of the universe. They are also part of the beginning of a great change and a mirror of Divine actions, and again a reflection of the encompassing Divine bounties. Therefore, people should pray at this time, because people should be thankful to God for having this day. At the time of sunset they are reminded of the bounties of God upon them.

The Sunset Prayer is composed of three units. As in all the prescribed prayer units, in each unit there are three positions: standing, bowing, and prostration. In the first, standing position, there is a silent introductory prayer, which according to some schools of Islamic jurisprudence is said before the first chapter of the Qur'an. One version taken from a Qur'anic prayer of Abraham is:

> I direct my face purely to the One who created the heavens and the earth and I am not of the disbelievers. My prayer, my sacrifice, my living, my dying, all belong to God, the Lord of the Worlds. He has no partners. With this I am commanded and I am among those who submit to the will of God.

The person performing the prayer will then read or recite the first chapter of the Qur'an.

The first unit of the prayer begins with the worshipper standing facing the Holy Shrine, the Ka'ba in Mecca, which is toward the northeast in the continental United States. In this position, the worshipper reads or recites the first chapter of the Qur'an.

> In the name of God the Most-Compassionate, the Most-Merciful.
> Praise be to God, the Lord of the worlds.
> The Most-Compassionate, the Most-Merciful.
> Owner of the Day of Judgment.
> You alone we worship, and You alone we ask for help.
> Guide us to the straight path;
> The path of those on whom You have bestowed Your grace, not the path
>   of those who received Your wrath and went astray. Amen. (1:1-7)

This short prayer is perhaps the most repeated prayer on earth, considering Muslims repeat it in every prayer, whether voluntary or prescribed. One can fruitfully compare the symbolism of this prayer for Muslims to the Christian prayer, the "Our Father."

After this prayer, still in the standing position, the worshipper recites some additional verses of the Qur'an. For reference, verses from the end of the second chapter are among the most frequently recited verses. However, many Muslims choose to recite one of the shorter chapters of the Qur'an.

The Messenger [Muhammad] believes what has been revealed to him from his Lord, and so do the faithful. They all believe in God and His angels, His scriptures, and His messengers: we do not make distinction between any of His messengers. And they said: 'we hear and obey. O Lord, grant us Your forgiveness. To You is the return.' (2:285)

Then the worshipper bows down saying, "*Allahu Akbar.*" In this position, he or she repeats silently three times, "Exalted is My Lord the Majestic." Then the worshiper stands and says, "God hears those who praise Him. Lord, to you be all praises." Following this, the worshiper prostrates. While prostrating he or she says, "Exalted is my Lord the Most-High," three times. Next, the worshipper sits on the sides of his or her feet, silently repeating, "O Lord forgive [us] and grant mercy. And You are the Most-Merciful of the mercifuls." Then the worshipper prostrates again. In the second prostration, the worshipper again silently repeats the Prophetic phrase, "Exalted is my Lord the Most-High," three times. With the second prostration, the first unit is complete.

As seen in all prayers, one unit of prayer is composed of three gestures: standing, bowing, and two prostrations. Because human beings are the supervisors of the universe, through their prayers they also represent the prayers of other creatures. Therefore, each of these positions represents not only the prayers of an individual human being, but also the prayers of creatures who are praying to God in similar positions. The standing position represents the prayer of all standing creatures, such as trees. Trees pray, but as they are unconscious, humans' prayers represent in part the prayers of the trees. Similarly, the bowing position represents the prayer of all creatures who are worshipping God in a bowing position. This would include, cows, sheep, etc., who are praying unconsciously, and so human beings represent them when they consciously pray to God. Prostration position represents the prayers of creatures worshipping God in a similar position, like turtles, snakes, and worms. This understanding opens a tremendous horizon for contemplation as well as a connection with the world around us.

After completing the first unit, the worshipper stands and begins the second unit. Again, the individual or prayer leader reads or recites the first chapter of the Qur'an as in the first unit. After finishing the first chapter, the worshipper recites or reads more verses from the Qur'an. For reference, in this prayer model, the last verse of chapter 2 has been chosen.

> God does not charge any soul except in its capacity. It is for it what it has earned [of good] and it is against it what it has earned [of evil]. [O people say] "Our Lord, do not punish us if we forget or make a mistake. Our Lord, do not put on us a burden that is difficult for us to carry as you put on the people before us. Our Lord, do not burden us with more than what we can bear. Pardon us and forgive us and have mercy upon us. You are our Master. Help us against the people of disbelief." (2:286)

After finishing the recitation, the next few steps repeat. The worshipper again bows down while saying "*Allahu Akbar.*" Then again the Prophetic phrase, "Exalted is My Lord the Majestic," is repeated three times. Following this, the worshipper stands for the short standing and says silently if alone or aloud if in congregation, "God hears those who praise Him. Lord, to You be all praises." Next, the worshipper prostrates for the third prostration and again repeats the Prophetic phrase, "Exalted is My Lord the Most-High," three times. The next position is known as the short sitting. In this position, the worshipper sits on the sides of his or her feet and silently says, "O Lord, forgive [us] and grant mercy. You are the Most-Merciful of the mercifuls." The worshipper then prostrates for the fourth prostration and three times repeats the Prophetic phrase, "Exalted is My Lord the Most-High." Then the worshipper again does the short sitting, this time while reciting the *Tashahhud*, which was taught by the Prophet and to some it recounts the Prophet's conversation with the Divine during his *Mi'raj*.[14] Whether in congregation or alone, this prayer is done silently. The prayer goes,

> All praises belong to God. All prayers, all beauties, belong to Him. [This part is said to be the words of the Prophet in his meeting with God. God responds.] "Peace be with you, O Prophet. And mercy of God and His blessings be upon you." [The Prophet then responds] "Peace be upon us and upon all Your wholesome servants." [The angel Gabriel witnessing this says] "I testify that there is no deity but God, and I testify that Muhammad is God's servant and messenger."

This prayer in this position is an enactment of the Prophet's conversation with God during the *Mi'raj*.

Following this prayer, the worshipper stands for the third unit, and again many of the steps repeat. Once again, he or she recites the first chapter of the Qur'an silently. Then again, the worshipper bows down, saying, "*Allahu Akbar,*" and then the Prophetic statement, "Exalted is My Lord the Majestic," three times. Similarly, the worshipper again stands, repeating, "Lord, to You be all praises." Following this is the fifth prostration, in which the worshipper silently repeats, "Exalted is My Lord the Most-High," three times. Then, in the sitting position, the worshipper says, "O Lord forgive [us] and grant mercy. You are the Most-Merciful of the mericifuls." Following this is the sixth prostration, in which the worshipper again silently repeats, "Exalted is My Lord the Most-High," three times. Lastly, the worshipper returns to the sitting position and recites the *Tashahhud* with the addition of, "Our Lord give Your mercy to Muhammad and his family as Your have given Your mercy to Abraham and his family. Our Lord give Your blessings to Muhammad and his family as You have given Your blessings to Abraham and his family. You are the Most-Praiseworthy and the Most-Glorious." This prayer to the Prophet, Abraham, and their offspring is repeated in the final sitting position of all prayers, whether voluntary or prescribed. As a final gesture, the worshipper turns his or her head to the right and says, "Peace be with you," and to the left and says, "Peace be with you." Even if there are no other people present, this is still said, as there are angels on both sides and thus this salutation is given to them.

# More on prayer

At this juncture, it is important to examine prayer in Islamic spirituality in a more specific way. Besides the prescribed five daily prayers and the various voluntary prayers we have examined, the present author has witnessed some mystics who dedicate additional periods of their daily lives to the supplementary readings of prayers. Although it is not a religious requirement, it can be an important element of the spiritual path. These prayers might include verses from the Qur'an and/or prayers of the prophets and saints. For example, one prayer that is frequently read is a prayer of Abd al-Qadir al-Jilani (d. 1166), known as "The Supplication of the Early Morning." It goes as follows:

> My God, the kings have closed their doors, but Your door is open to those who ask. My God, the stars have faded, eyes have slept. You are the Most-Living, the Most-Sustaining, the One who neither sleep nor slumber can overtake. My God, You are the Beloved of those who are striving in Your love and You are the Friend of those who are lonely. My God, if You reject me from Your door, in whose door can I take refuge? My God, if You cut me off from your presence in the presence of whom can I hope? My God, if You punish me surely I deserve it and if You forgive me, You deserve all generosity and kindness. My Lord, for You the gnostic have sincerely purified their souls and with Your grace the wholesome have received salvation and with Your forgiveness the negligent have returned to You. O the One whose forgiveness is beautiful, help me taste the coolness of Your forgiveness and the sweetness of knowing You. Even if I do not deserve it, surely You are the One who gives kindness and forgiveness.[15]

Despite the examples of prayers that have been given, there are still questions to be answered. For example, is prayer only verbal or can actions be considered forms of prayer as well? As the scope of this chapter allows, there will be greater elaboration on this dimension of prayer. One must confess that the English word prayer is limited in comparison to the Arabic words for prayer, such as *dua'*, *salat*, *munajat*, *tadarru'*, and *ibtihal*. In Arabic, the words that describe the nature of prayer are *salat*, which is prayer through words and performance, and *dua'*, which is prayer through words asking God to fulfill one's needs. Perhaps the reason why prayer takes such an important place in Islamic spirituality is the Qur'anic verse which states, "[O Muhammad] say: 'My Lord would not give you importance if it were not for your prayer'" (25:77).

There is no doubt that prayer is considered the most significant and mysterious connection between human beings and the Creator; it is the spirit of Islamic spirituality. As the Qur'an illustrates, all creatures pray to God, both consciously and unconsciously. In Islam, prayers of entities other than human beings result from their moving in the direction for which they were created. For a seed, then, its prayer is to grow to become a tree and to be fruitful, then to declare the beauty of the Divine names. The prayer of an apple tree is to be fruitful and provide its fruit from the Divine treasure to all who need it, be they human beings or animals. Similarly, the prayer of the bee is to make honey. In fact, what are called "natural laws," from the perspective of Islamic spirituality, are in fact Divine laws. Hence, the relationship between cause and effect bringing forth a result is a form of prayer. In other words, causes come together, and with their language of disposition they ask for the effect to happen. Causes, with their collective language, ask God for the result. For example, water, air, soil, and the sun's warmth come together through their collective prayer and ask God to bring about a result. Since the result of this collective relationship is so purposefully composed and prepared, such a result cannot be related to unconscious causes. It would be like relating a painting by Pablo Picasso to his brush and canvas and forgetting the artist.

This is the prayer of all living creatures who receive their needs and their wishes in an unexpected way at an appropriate time, with no delay or interruption. When a mystic calls upon God with a phrase such as, "O the Most-Merciful One," all these meanings are in the background of the prayer of the mystic. *Al-Rahim*, or the Most-Merciful, is one of the Ninety-Nine Names of God. Creatures are unable to provide for their needs if they are not provided for by the Most-Compassionate, the Most-Merciful. Therefore, everything—not just human beings—calls upon God to provide for them, and their prayers are accepted. One can see with the naked eye that the needs of all living things are met at the most opportune time. That means that this is a mercy from the Creator, reflected as a result of this prayer. A fish in the dark of the sea receives its sustenance; a bird receives its sustenance; newly born babies receive their sustenance. All this happens at an appropriate time and in an appropriate way. The universe is prepared and given to humans according to their needs. There is an amazing relationship between all members of creation, from a small fly to the sun in the sky.

While the rigor of the prescribed and voluntary prayers may make it seem as if prayer must be limited to these overt actions, as a matter of fact, every action if done in the way of righteousness is an act of prayer. For example, if a family member works to bring bread to the family, that work is considered an act of prayer and reward-worthy. Similarly, actions that are done for the betterment of the community are also reward-worthy and are considered forms of prayer. Buying a gift for a child and making him or her happy is an act of prayer. Therefore, in Islamic spirituality, prayer cannot be limited to the prescribed or voluntary prayers. To put it simply, one's entire lifespan is a page decorated by actions of goodness which are counted as reward-worthy.

Because of this, Muslim mystics have countless ways to gain spiritual development. One such act is fasting. It is well-known that some Muslim mystics voluntarily fast. Generally, this fasting is performed in addition to the fasting that occurs during the month of Ramadan. The Prophet himself voluntarily fasted, and according to the Hadith did so on Mondays and Thursdays. Furthermore, it is narrated that the Prophet said, "Fasting for three days each month, as well as the prescribed fasting of Ramadan, is like fasting for the entire year."[16]

In the spiritual tradition, another set of such actions are related to music. Some mystical orders such as the Mevlevi Sufi order, which is the order related to Rumi, make music a significant portion of their mystical practices. Besides their basic *dhikr*, which consists of the *Fatiha*, that is, the first chapter of the Qur'an, and saying, "*Astaghfirullah*," [I ask God for His forgiveness] 100 times, "*La ilaha illa Allah*," 100 times, "Allah," 300 times, and "*Hu*," [He] eleven times, the Mevlevi have a *Sama* performance, and are known in the West as the whirling dervishes. This Islamic art of music and chanting poems is used and practiced on various occasions, including *Mawlid al-Nabi*, the birthday of the Prophet, as well as other holy nights of the Islamic calendar, such as the commemoration of the *Mi'raj* of the Prophet. Although the Naqshabandi order likes to distance itself from music due to some concerns about the worldliness of music, the Mevlevi order focuses on the importance of music. They use music frequently, believing that it strengthens their spirituality. One has to remember that when mystics speak of music, what they refer to is music that helps with hope, inspiration, and positive feelings. Such music shows the healthiness of the spirit. Music that inspires violence, carnal desires, etc. would be rejected by all mystics.

Speaking of carnal desires, it is important to mention Islamic spirituality's perspective on the habits of daily life, such as eating, sleeping, and talking. According to the famous mystic Yahya bin Mu'adh al-Razi (d. 871), one has to make spiritual jihad against carnal desires with the sword of *riyada* [lit. religious or spiritual exercise]. This has become a principle of Islamic spirituality. Al-Ghazali, following this principle, would speak about the results of eating, sleeping, and talking less under a chapter titled "The Training of the Soul and the Rectification of the Soul," and he quotes al-Razi, saying, "From eating less comes the death of carnal inclinations. From sleeping less comes the purification of the will. And from speaking less comes safety from the dangers [of the tongue]."[17] Another seminal figure in Islamic spirituality, Abd al-Qadir al-Jilani, considers this behavior of eating less to be among the things that help in waking up for the night prayer. On the importance of eating less, he narrates the story of a group of worshippers of the Children of Israel. When the time for food would come, their spiritual master would stand up and say, "Do not eat too much. If you eat too much you will sleep too much and therefore you will pray less."[18]

When one sincerely opens his or her heart to God and fulfills these conditions of spiritual strength, such as avoiding carnal desires, there will be a Divine response in various forms of grace. Based on a Qur'anic verse, 50:16, Islamic spirituality strongly emphasizes that God is as close to human beings as they are to themselves. God knows every human being and responds to every prayer. A Qur'anic verse suggests that God is close, and He accepts the prayer of His servants: "[O Muhammad] When My servants ask you about Me, [tell them that] surely I am near. I answer the prayer of the supplicants when they cry to Me. So let them hear My call and let them trust in Me, in hope that they may be led to righteousness" (2:186). The Qur'an also emphasizes that every prayer is answered (40:60). Therefore, no one returns empty-handed from His court, because when people pray they ask the One who can meet all of their needs. When people pray to God, their mind, intelligence, and senses must be in a receptive state, so that they know surely that their prayer is heard.

While prayer times are known and some of them are determined by the individual, there are some special moments and seconds during which prayer is accepted. For example, the holy month of Ramadan and the holy days and nights of the Islamic calendar are important times for prayer. The Qur'an speaks of some of these holy days and nights. One of them is called the Night of Honor, *Laylat al-Qadr*, during which the Holy Qur'an was revealed. The Qur'an says of the Night of Honor, "The Night of Honor is better than a thousand months" (97:3), meaning that prayer during this one night is better than prayer for more than eighty years. Also, it is narrated that the Prophet said, "Anyone who keeps themselves during the Night of Honor in prayer, believing and accepting Divine reward, their past sins are forgiven."[19] Regarding the timing of the Night of Honor, it is believed to occur in the last ten days of Ramadan. Another example is Friday, which is considered to be a holy day. Believers are expected to make full use of these moments. These are the times when Divine blessings pour forth.

The Qur'an essentially says that prayers and humble supplications with sincere intentions lead to salvation in this life and also in the afterlife. Therefore, the Prophet of Islam, whose life was in total compliance with the Qur'anic ideal, is known among mystics as the Sultan of Prayer. He is the model in Islamic spirituality. He would open his hands, turn to his Lord, overflow with thanks and glorification, bow and double himself up in prayer, constantly praying to God. He did this throughout his life. He woke up every morning and did his daily prayers, both prescribed and voluntary. He would stay in God's presence at night and spend most of his night in prayer. He would continue his prayer even while eating, going to bed, traveling, returning from a campaign, confronting an enemy, experiencing earthly or heavenly disasters, witnessing miraculous events, and suffering from illnesses or troubles. For every occasion, the Prophet used to say a special prayer. 'Aisha narrates that the Prophet stood for such a long time while praying that his feet swelled. She said, "O Messenger of God, do you do this despite the fact that whatever you have [of sin] in the past and in the future has been forgiven?" And the Prophet responded, "O 'Aisha, should I not be a thankful servant?"[20]

All these practices and prayers are to be fulfilled primarily for the pleasing of God. While there are both spiritual and physical benefits, the major motivation and intention is the pleasing of God, or *rida*. Islamic spirituality understands the weaknesses of human beings; prayers are addressed to God, and one may expect to have immediate results. If there is no immediate result from the prayers they addressed to the Divine, people may feel that God does not hear them or does not answer their prayers. However, God answers all prayers, but sometimes He gives what He wants, not what the petitioner wants. But always what He gives is what is best for the petitioner. This is similar to someone who asks a doctor for medicine. The patient asks to be given medicine that tastes good, but the doctor, who knows the nature of the illness, sometimes does not give the patient what he or she wants. Instead, the doctor gives them something that will heal them, although it may not be as palatable.[21]

The Qur'an has many good examples of prayer. Since Mary is highly revered in Islamic spirituality, it is appropriate to give Mary and her mother as examples of this sort of prayer. The Qur'an narrates that Mary's mother wished for her child to be born and dedicated to the Temple, and she asked God to accept this from her. As understood from the Qur'an, she prayed to God to have a male child, but God gave her a female child. The Qur'an says,

> [Remember] when the wife of 'Imran said, "My Lord, surely I have vowed unto You that which is in my belly and consecrated it [to You]. Accept it from me. Surely You are the All-Hearing, the All-Knowing." But when she delivered she said, "My Lord, I have given birth to her, a female." And God knows better about what she had delivered. "The male is not as the female. And I have named her Mary, and I surely seek refuge in You for her and her offspring, to protect them from Satan, the cursed one." (3:35-6)

In fact, this story shows that God had accepted the prayer of Mary's mother, but in a better way. God could have given her a son, as she had prayed for and expected. Instead, he gave her Mary, who would be the mother of Jesus. This is surely better.

Similarly, there are some occasions where specific prayers are called for, just as sunset is the time for the sunset prayer. For example, in times of drought, one should pray to God for rain. Traditionally, the Prophet, when there was a drought in his time, would take people, including children and other innocents such as animals, outside of the city and ask God for rain. On many occasions, it would rain before they returned to their homes. Other natural disasters and calamities are also times for prayer. If these calamities are lifted through their prayer, this is wonderful. But if they are not lifted, people are expected to continue praying, because the time of prayer has not yet passed.

Also, there are specific prayers for lunar and solar eclipses. Even when God's cosmic work has already been astronomically predicted, one still has to pray, because lunar and solar eclipses are times of prayer. When the death of the Prophet's infant son Ibrahim coincided with a solar eclipse, people made connections between the eclipse and Ibrahim's death, suggesting the sun was eclipsed because of the death of Ibrahim. The Prophet rejected this, saying, "The sun and the moon are two signs of the Signs of God. They do not eclipse for the death or life of anyone. When you see their eclipse, hasten to *dhikr* and prayer."[22] Further, these prayers during eclipses are not for resolution to the eclipse. Rather, they are prayers to God, who has shown His majesty through such cosmic events. The details of how these prayers are to be performed are found in many manuals of Islamic jurisprudence.

# Friday

In Islamic spirituality, all days are holy and are gifts from God. Among them, however, Friday holds a special place of the days of the week. The Qur'an refers specifically to Friday, saying,

> O you who have believed, when it is called for the prayer of the Day of Jumu'ah [i.e. Friday], hasten to God's *dhikr* [here meaning prayer] and leave your trades. That is better for you if you know. Then, when the prayer is finished, disperse in the land and seek God's bounty, and remember God frequently so that you will be successful. But when they see some merchandise or amusement they go away to it and you are left standing. Say [O Muhammad]: "What is with God is better than any amusement and merchandise. And God is the Best of the providers." (62:9-11)

These verses were revealed upon the occasion of a trading caravan arriving while the Prophet was giving his Friday sermon. As usual, the drums were beating to indicate its arrival. Many people who were praying with the Prophet left the sermon and went out to trade with the caravan. Only twelve people were left in the mosque. It seems that the Prophet was upset and this is why the verse was revealed. The Prophet also made special mention of Friday.

The Prophet recommended the reading of chapter 18 of the Qur'an every Friday, and since then Muslim mystics have given more importance to this chapter, reading it in its entirety on Fridays. The chapter starts with praising God and with the story of how the "people of the cave" stood up to declare that their Lord was the Lord of the heavens and the earth, and how they would not accept any god except this Lord. Commentators suggest that these people were a group of early Christians who were forced to accept paganism, but rejected it and out of fear, took refuge in a cave. The chapter also emphasizes that one should not say anything about the future without saying "*Insha'Allah*," or "God willing." It further includes the story of two individuals, each of whom had a garden. One of them did not believe in the afterlife and thought that his garden would remain forever. His friend said to him, "How do you deny the One who created you?" Elsewhere, this chapter narrates the story of Moses and a figure called "a servant from Our servants," who is known elsewhere in the Islamic tradition as al-Khidr. Al-Khidr was and is a righteous servant of God, possessing wisdom and mystical knowledge that seems, according to some, to surpass Moses's exoteric knowledge. This story is an important one in Islamic spirituality, as it compares esoteric and exoteric knowledge. There is also the story of Dhu al-Qarnayn who may have been a prophet and protected an oppressed group from their oppressor by building a wall. The chapter ends by reinforcing the importance of the afterlife and how righteous people will receive their reward, and with a command to the Prophet: "Say: 'I am only a human being like you. It is revealed to me that your God is One God. So anyone who hopes for the encounter with their Lord, let them do wholesome deeds and let them not associate anyone in their worship with their Lord.'"

It is believed that the masters of Islamic spirituality, such as Ibn al-Arabi (d. 1240), have specific prayers which are dedicated to Friday nights, that is, the night that starts after sunset on Thursday in the solar calendar. Ibn al-Arabi's prayer goes in part:

In the name of God the Most-Compassionate, the Most-Merciful, in Him we ask for help. My God, all great fathers are Your servants and You are the Lord, unconditionally. You combined the opposites. You are the Most-Majestic. You are the Most-Beautiful. You are greater than our witnessing and more perfect than anything. You are higher than how we are describing You and more beautiful. You are exalted in Your splendor of the signs of the created things. And Your beauty is holier than to be sought by desires. I ask You with the secret by which You combined the opposites. I ask You to put together my scattered situation in a way that helps me to witness the unity of Your existence. And help me to wear

garment of Your beauty and to be crowned with a crown from Your
majesty. . . . And elevate my value in a way that all those who are arrogant
will humble before me. Guide me and make a language of truthfulness
for me among Your people and under Your command. Protect me in
Your land, in Your sea, and take me out from the city of human nature
the people of which are wrongdoers. And free me from the slavery of
worldliness and make my richness in poverty towards You of any request
that I have and make Your richness with me about anything that is asked
for. You are my Guide, my direction and You are my dignity. The return
and the end of everything is to You. You are the One who repairs the
broken and who breaks the tyrants. You are the One who protects the
fearful and makes the oppressors fear. The highest honor belongs to
You. The most encompassing reflection is to You. There is no deity but
You. You are Exalted. You are Sufficient for me and You, are the Most-
Excellent in Whom I trust. My Lord, O the Creator of the creatures, O
the Reviver of the dead, O the One who puts together what has been
scattered, O the One who gives light as a bounty to people themselves, to
You belongs the largest sovereignty. All lords are Your slaves. All kings
in Your presence are servants. All rich people in Your presence are Your
poor. You are the Rich, without needing anyone. I ask you with Your
beautiful name by which You created everything, You measured with a
great measurement and You gave to whom You want Paradise and silk
and success and great prosperity. I ask You to eliminate my greed and
to complete my deficit and You bestow upon me the clothes of Your
bounties. And You teach me of Your names by which in this world and
the afterlife I become wholesome. And fill up my inner life with mercy
and respect. You are over everything the Most-Powerful and You are the
Knower of everything and You are the Seer of everything. And peace and
blessings be upon our master Muhammad and to all of his pure family
and his honorable companions.[23]

One of the practices of Friday is to ask God to send peace and blessings to
the Prophet. Generally, asking God to send His peace and blessings to the
Prophet, which is known as *salawat* (the plural of the word *salat*), consists
of petitioning God with specific phrases. This is practiced by all Muslims,
but it has an extra importance for mystics. Although there is a short formula
which is repeated in the last sitting of the daily prayers—"Oh my Lord. Send
Your mercy to Muhammad and his family, as You have given Your mercy
to Abraham and his offspring."—mystics and saints have developed their
own ways of saying the *salawat* prayer. This is a literary genre in Islamic
spirituality, and many mystics have written very long *salawat* meditating on
the various qualities of the Prophet while asking God to bestow His mercy
on the Prophet.

It is notable that in this short formula there is also a prayer for the family
of the Prophet. While this directly relates to his immediate family, in reality

it relates to all pious believers, because in one of his statements the Prophet says, "All the pious are my family."[24] There is an authenticated hadith that the Prophet encouraged his community to pray for him through *salawat*. He says,

> On the Day of Judgement, the closest to me is the one of you who has the most *salawat* on me while he or she is in this world. Those who have *salawat* on me on the night and the day of Friday, God will fulfill one hundred of their needs seventy of these needs will be met in the afterlife and thirty will be met in this world. God appoints an angel to let me know of the people who pray the *salawat*, their names and their progeny so that I can pray for them and record their names on a white page.[25]

This detailed hadith suggests that when a person asks God to send His mercy to the Prophet, the Prophet is aware of it, and that person will be rewarded for it in both this life and in the afterlife. Also, not only is the Prophet praying for that person, he is praying for the person's offspring as well. More importantly, in Islamic spirituality, *salawat* is considered a means of spiritual connection with the Prophet. Therefore, it is highly recommended and can be said at any time. The only reason why it is given special emphasis on Friday is the greatness of the reward to be gained on Fridays. Traditionally, mystics have a daily routine of saying some prayers for the Prophet. Some might say *salawat* ten times after the Morning Prayer and fifteen times after the Afternoon Prayer, etc.

Another important aspect of Friday is to try to catch what is called the Moment of Acceptance, *sa'at al-ijaba,* which occurs sometime in the twenty-four-hour period from sunset to sunset. In this moment, God accepts all prayers. The secrecy of this moment is meant to encourage people who look for Divine grace to be more vigilant with their prayers and their spirituality on Fridays. Some have said that this moment is during the Friday Prayer itself, and some have said it is the moment that is in between two sermons before the performance of the Friday Prayer. But masters of Islamic spirituality would relate this to God and say that if one prays throughout Friday, the chances of catching that moment become greater. Such a pursuit, though, should not detract from the spirituality of the day.

The Friday Prayer has to be done in congregation, and it replaces the noon prayer on Friday. But before explaining the performance of the Friday Prayer, some explanation regarding the sermons that are said before the Friday prayer is needed. First, sermons need to be short. Second, sermons have to be spiritual and not political. The Prophet's sermons were very spiritual and focused on piety, honesty, charity, and the afterlife. The purpose of sermons at the Friday Prayer is to remind Muslims of their duties before God, fellow human beings, and their environment, as well as the importance of piety and the afterlife. This is clearly understood from the Prophet's sermons. Here I would like to give the Prophet's first Friday sermon in Medina as an example. The sermon is found in the work of the famous Muslim historian, Ibn Hisham (d. 879).

> After praising God he [the Prophet] said. "O people, prepare your soul for the afterlife. Surely you know that each of you will die and will leave no shepherd to care for your sheep. Then there will be no translator and no veil between you and God, and your Lord will tell you 'Did not my Messenger come to you and convey to you? I gave you property and bestowed upon you My bounties. What did you prepare for your soul?' Then you will look at the right and left and see nothing. Then you will look at the front and see nothing except Hell. You should protect your face from Hell by giving charity, even if it is but half a date. Those who have nothing to give let them give charity by saying beautiful words. With this, a good deed is rewarded as tenfold to 700-fold. Peace, mercy of God, and His blessings be with you."[26]

It can be argued that today's sermons in many mosques are overly political, and they need to return to the pristine spiritual message of the Prophet. This sermon should be used as an example. The Prophet's second sermon had similar connotations and was even shorter. One has to remember that the pulpit represents the Prophet, and anyone who rises to that pulpit has to be concise and fulfill the purpose of the sermon, which is spirituality and not ideology. The mosque is not the place to learn about the news of the world. Regarding this point, two things are important. First, the imam or whoever gives the sermon has to understand the spirituality of Islam, and more specifically the Qur'an, which dedicates one-third of its entire body to the concept of the afterlife. Second, unlike many imams' current practices, sermons have to be written down and read so that the spiritual message will not be sacrificed to the influence of that day's news.

As with all other prescribed payers, at the beginning of the Jumu'ah[27] Prayer there is a call to prayer. Traditionally, it is announced from the top of the minaret so that people know it is time for prayer, and more importantly so that the Oneness of God is declared to all human beings and to the world of nature. There is also a second call to prayer within the mosque. The call to prayer, *Adhan*, is performed in Arabic, usually by someone who has a good voice. The meaning of the *Adhan* is as follows:

Allahu Akbar (repeated 4 times).
I testify that there is no deity but God (repeated 2 times).
I testify that Muhammad is God's Messenger (repeated 2 times).
Come to prayer (repeated 2 times).
Come to salvation (repeated 2 times).
Allahu Akbar (repeated 2 times).
There is no deity but God.

The Jumu'ah Prayer is composed of two units of prayer and two short sermons. First, someone will give the first sermon, then after a short pause, the second sermon, after which the prayer leader leads the two units of prayer. Before the sermons and after the prayer, there are often a few voluntary prayers performed as well. For simplicity, below are the steps that are considered the essential elements of the Jumu'ah Prayer.

In the first of these steps, imam or other designated person stands up to give the first sermon. Ideally, this sermon should take less than ten minutes. The purpose of the sermon is to remind people about the important elements of religion: God, angels, afterlife, preparation for the afterlife, etc. Following the sermon, the individual sits for a moment and then stands up to give the second sermon. The first part of the first sermon is in Arabic and contains praises to God and blessings upon the Prophet of Islam and other messengers of God. The rest of the sermon can be in any language and is generally in the native language of most of the participants. The second sermon short be like the first part of the first sermon. There are also Arabic prayers petitioning God for help and grace at the end of the sermon.

In the second step, the muezzin stands up and says the *iqamah*. This is similar to the call to prayer, but it is performed immediately before the prayer itself, to line up the people for prayer. The third step is the Jumu'ah Prayer itself. It has two units. Each unit involves standing, bowing, and prostration positions, exactly like the prayers mentioned earlier. In the standing position, the prayer leader loudly recites the first chapter of the Qur'an and the people quietly follow him. After the first chapter of the Qur'an, the prayer leader recites several verses from any part of the Qur'an. While the prayer leader can choose any verse or verses from the Qur'an, one short chapter, chapter 95, is given here as an example of a typical recitation:

> By the fig and the olive, and by Mount Sinai, and this secured city. Surely we have created human beings in the most beautiful format. Then We return them to the lowest of the low except those who have believed and done wholesome deeds; theirs are rewards uninterrupted. So what then can cause you to deny the Day of Judgement? Is not God the Most-Just of the judges? (95:1-8)

The bowing and prostration, and their phrases are the same as the other prayers.

The fourth step is to perform the second unit, which is similar to the first unit. The only difference is to recite different verses after the first chapter of the Qur'an. The following is another example of what might be recited: "By the time, surely human beings are in loss except those who have believed and done wholesome deeds and advised one another with truth and with patience" (103:1-3). The other steps again repeat. Similar to other prayers, the Jumu'ah Prayer ends with the worshippers turning their heads to the right and left while saying, "peace be with you." With this greeting of peace, the prayer ends, though one can perform voluntary prayers as desired.

The Friday Prayer is expected to enrich the spirituality of believers by making them aware of themselves and the Divine bounties that have been given to them, including their own existence as well as the natural world around them. Thus, believers are taught to respect not only their fellow human beings, but all creatures of God in the realm of nature. With this in mind, the next chapter will focus on the relationship between Islamic spirituality and the natural world.

# 9

# Ecology and spirituality

To illustrate the relationship between Islamic spirituality and ecology, let me present a story, commonly told by mystics, about Yunus Emre, a famous Turkish poet and mystic (d. c. 1320), and his spiritual master, Tapduk Emre. There are several versions of this story. One is that Tapduk Emre wanted to appoint a successor from among his disciples, and so he asked each of his students to go to a field and bring back a bouquet of flowers for him. Each brought a beautiful bouquet of flowers collected from the field. Yunus Emre however, came with empty hands. The master asked why he did not bring any flowers. Yunus responded: "Master, whenever I tried to cut them, I heard them praising God. That is why I could not cut them." Tapduk then said, "Now I have found my successor."[1] Bringing flowers was a test for the disciples to see who would hear the praises of nature.

This story has not been authenticated, but based on the Qur'anic verse which says, "The seven heavens and the earth and what is in them are glorifying Him. In fact, there is nothing which does not glorify God with His praise, but you do not understand their glorification. Surely He is the Most-Gentle, the Most-Forgiving" (17:44), the story makes perfect sense, as a higher level of spirituality allows one to better hear the praises of the flowers. Yunus was at that level of spirituality and he heard the praises of nature. Similar ideas are found in Psalms 69:34 and 150:6.

Furthermore, the creation of the universe is the result of Divine love. In a hadith Qudsi, it is narrated that God says, "I was a Hidden Treasure. I loved to be known. I created the creatures so that I would be known."[2] The world of nature points to this dimension of Divine love. Anyone who looks deeply and more carefully will see this dimension. That is because for every creature there are both physical and metaphysical dimensions. In Islamic spirituality, the first is called *mulk* and the second is *malakut*. The *malakut*, or the invisible dimension, is related to Divine love. It is always pure, clean, and transparent. It reflects the transcendent love and mercy of the Divine. This dimension of nature can be seen in many Qur'anic verses.

The Qur'anic approach to nature is what can be called theocentric. One Qur'anic verse states that God "is the Creator of everything" (6:102). Without Him the heavens and the earth will collapse: "Surely, God holds earth and heaven from collapsing. If they collapse, no one can hold them other than Him, the Most-Gentle the Most-Forgving" (35:41). Being the sole Creator, God is the center of everything. In the Qur'an, all things point to Him. Sovereignty in the universe belongs only to God (6:73). Among God's creatures, human beings are the most conscious and the most precious in the sight of God. But while human beings are the most powerful and independent of God's creatures, the Qur'an explicitly states that God is humanity's Creator: "Surely We created human beings from mixed drops so that We can test them. And We made them hearing and knowing" (76:2).

Human beings are servants of God. The Prophet and other messengers of God, such as Jesus, Moses, Abraham, and Noah, are leaders of humanity in this servanthood. They are perfect servants of God. Not only prophets, but all human beings are considered vice-regents of God on earth. Yet despite this highly regarded position, human actions toward nature must fall within the limits of Divine permission. In other words, being God's vice-regents does not give human beings the authority to do whatever they want. If one uses the analogy of a factory, human beings are the managers of the factory, but cannot and should not violate the rights of the workers. This analogy applies to the reality of our universe. The workers in it are the various lower organisms, plants, and animals. The builder and owner of this factory is God. God employs the workers and entrusts the managers, that is, human beings, with ensuring the maintenance of this factory. Therefore, this supervisory role does not give human beings the right to harm nature. Harming nature is an act of disregarding the trust that God has placed on the shoulders of human beings.

In Islamic spirituality, nature is a mirror of God's beautiful names. The whole of creation is the reflection of God's name *al-Khaliq* (the Creator).[3] All of the Qur'anic verses on the subject indicate that the world was not randomly created. Instead, it was wonderfully and beautifully designed: "The One who created seven heavens one upon another, you can see no fault in His creation. Then look again. Can you see any faults?" (67:3). Concerning this wonderful design, the creation of human beings is emphasized. God has shaped humanity, nature, and all the realm of creation in the most beautiful manner. So perfectly arranged is God's creation that everything from plants to human beings is a miraculous work of art. Therefore, there is no absurdity in nature.

Elements of nature are considered Divine signs or verses, as the Qur'an states. There are two types of signs (*ayat*) of God. One is the Qur'an. Each verse is considered an *ayah,* or a statement from God. The second is nature. Each part of nature is also considered an *ayah* or a sign of God. According to the Qur'an, there are limitless signs of God: "The water which God sends down from the sky, the ordinance of the winds and clouds are signs" (2:164).

In other words, heaven and earth, night and day, land and sea, the wind, clouds, etc. are all meaningful signs of God, and "We [God] did not create the Heaven and the earth and all that is between them in vain" (38:27). Further,

> In the heavens and the earth are signs for believers and in your creation and in [the creation of] what dispersed of moving creatures that are signs for people who are certain in their faith. And there are signs for people who understand the alternation of night and day and the sustenance that God sends from Heaven and thereby revives the earth and in the directing of the winds. (45:3-5)

Like human beings, elements of nature are also servants of God. They work and fulfill their jobs not for the sake of themselves, but for the sake of their Creator. For example, the sun is a remarkable work of God's art in the house He created for human beings called the planet Earth. It is a "dazzling lamp" for humanity, and thus the sun is a sign of God's mercy towards humanity. (78:13)[4]

The main purpose of creation, according to the Qur'an, is to reflect the Divine names and to serve as a sign of God. In this regard, all members of nature serve the same purpose, shoulder to shoulder, and thus a fly is worth no less than an elephant. Furthermore, Islamic spirituality considers the world to be a place of brotherhood, since all creatures share the same Creator. Because they are connected by sharing the same Creator, they are brothers and sisters. Therefore, an atom is no less a sign of God than a mountain, because both are a reflection of God's names. In other words, microcosm and macrocosm are equally important, and they reflect the Divine names according to their capacities.

All names of God are reflected in the realm of nature. For example, life is very precious in nature. The source of life is One, and all living creatures reflect God's name *al-Hayy* (The Most-Living).[5] Mystics as a part of their spiritual exercises frequently repeat the name *al-Hayy*. Occasionally they repeat it aloud and in a group as, "*Ya Hayy*," "O the Living One," in anticipation that through this Divine name they can receive spiritual revival. Mystics are asked to recognize the Beautiful Names of God reflected in nature at the highest level, though this may differ according to their spiritual level. Some may even hear the voices of nature praising God. The Qur'an gives the foundation for this mystical aspect of the natural world: "Surely in the creation of the heavens and the earth and in the alternation of night and day there are signs of His sovereignty for people of understanding" (3:190). The Qur'an and the Prophet's message are to remind people to be aware of these inscrutable messages of nature. The Qur'an in a questioning fashion encourages human beings to look and see this dimension of the natural world around them. The Qur'an says, "Do they not look at how the camel is created? And at how the heaven is elevated? And at how the mountains are erected? And how the earth is spread out?" (88:17-20)

What are called the natural laws are also known in the Qur'an as *Sunnat Allah* (The Laws of God). The Qur'an indicates that there is consistency in nature, which reflects the unchangeable laws of God. They are encompassing principles of God with consistency and regularity. Only via miracles can the stability of natural law be interrupted. In other words, to show the truthfulness of His beloved prophets and to show that they speak on His behalf, occasionally God changes these natural laws. Abraham was thrown into fire, but fire did not burn him. Abraham was saved because, God said, "O fire, be of coolness and peace for Abraham" (21:69). Moses was able to turn his staff into a snake (7:117 and 27:10). Jesus made birds from clay, and when he breathed into them they became real birds and flew away (5:110).

Despite such miraculous events which interrupt natural law, there is a consistency of cause and effect which God has enacted. Human beings are, therefore, required to follow the laws of nature. Islamic scholars have said that not following the laws of nature leads to an immediate punishment. On the other hand, for not following the laws of the Divine scriptures, the punishment is generally received in the afterlife. For example, if the appropriate measures are not taken, disobeying the law of gravity by heedlessly throwing oneself from the top of a building or bridge can cause injury or even death. Mystics should not act as if the laws of nature are beneath them, and indeed many mystics have warned even against acts that might potentially lead to not following the laws of nature. Instead, mystics ask people to always follow the laws of nature humbly. The Divine laws are not random, and therefore there is a design to them.

Every element of creation is purposefully designed. There are several Qur'anic verses on this subject. One says, "And surely we have decorated the world's heaven with a lamp" (67:5) and another, "It is He who made for you the night that you should rest therein and the day in which you see. Surely in these there are signs for those who take heed" (10:67). While yet another verse states that the making of the night and day for human beings to rest and work is a Divine mercy and people have to be thankful for this (28:73).

The mystics' analogy of a guest house should serve well in this case. This world of nature, the planet, is a guest house. There are many guests, great and small, but human beings are the most important. The house has a remarkable Owner who is also a tremendous Artist. All human beings have been invited by this Owner. There are rules, measures, beauties, and more in the house. Guests are there to benefit from what is provided for them, and thus ought to thank the Owner and praise His art without doing any harm to the house. Human beings are to recognize that God's creation is structured for them, and they should therefore be aware of cosmic events, such as sunrise and sunset: "Be patient about what they say and glorify Your Lord with His praise before the rising of the sun and before its setting. And glorify Him some hours of the night and at the two ends of the day. Hopefully you will be pleased [with the reward you receive]" (20:130).

The relationship between human beings and nature is the relationship between a book and its readers. The world of nature is a book and human beings are the readers. As an Arab poet says, "Contemplate in the lines [of the book] of the universe/Surely each line has a message for you from on high."[6] Every element of nature is either a letter, or a word, or line, or a page from the book of the universe. Although the book is the same, readers may have different understandings of the book. This analogy reminds us that one has to remember that the Revelation's first command was also, "Read." Since this command to read is left open, a spiritual understanding of this would be read yourself, read the world, and read the book of the universe. The result of this reading is knowledge, and the highest knowledge is knowledge of God. Therefore, human beings have a great responsibility, a responsibility to look at the world of nature and to see the signs and read them. In other words, their duty is to read and understand the meaning of the verses of nature.

Accordingly, God has placed humanity at the apex of creation. Humans are to serve as the vice-regents of God, and to them nature is subjugated: "It is He who has placed you as viceroys of the earth and has elevated some of you in rank above others" (6:165). The position of human beings as vice-regents gives them great responsibility as the supervisors of nature and as the recipients of God's message. Yet because of their ability to be corrupted they can, through the use of their own free will, become lower than animals (7:179). Animals do not bear the responsibilities that humanity does, because they are not given reason and consciousness. Therefore, in Islam, just as all children before puberty are considered innocent regardless of their family or religious background, so all animals are innocents.

Perhaps for this reason, traditionally when there is drought, it is recommended that the leaders of the community take children and animals with them to the fields to pray to God and ask for rain. Since animals are innocent as well as being the artwork of God, in the circle of Islamic spirituality they are beloved. Yunus Emre once said, "We love the created ones for the sake of the Creator."[7] Yunus Emre even conversed with flowers, as in his famous poem, "I Asked the Yellow Flower." In the poem, he asks the flower why its neck is so bent and the flower responded, "Yes my neck is bent, but my essence is straight toward the Divine."[8]

The Holy Book of Islam stresses the importance of animals as a part of the natural environment, and the responsibility humanity has toward them. They are equated with humanity in terms of creation. The following Qur'anic verse forms a paradigm as far as the human relationship with animals is concerned: "There is neither an animal on the earth nor a bird flying on two wings that is not part of a community like you" (6:38). This verse indicates that the community of animals is similar to that of people, and as such humans have a heavy responsibility to care for animals and see them as creatures of the same Creator.

Several Qur'anic chapters are named after animals, such as "The Cow" (chapter 2), "The Cattle" (chapter 6), "The Bees" (chapter 16), "The Ant" (chapter 27), and "The Spider" (chapter 29). The provisions given by God are not given to human beings only; rather, they are to be shared between human beings and animals (80:32) and humans should protect the lives of animals. Animals are intended to benefit humanity, and caring for animals should be viewed as a way of receiving God's bounty. Not sharing with animals is a transgression on their rights and may be a symptom of a spiritual disease, such as greed or selfishness. One has to seek a cure for such diseases, no matter how they are manifest.

The Qur'anic story of the prophet Salih and the camel that emerged from the mountain is a remarkable testimony of how harming animals causes Divine chastisement. According to the story, the people of the prophet Salih were required to share their water with the she-camel of the prophet, which is called "the she-camel of God" [naqat Allah] in the Qur'an. Salih requests that the people share their water with her and allow her to drink. They deny this request and send a malevolent individual to kill the camel. Because they killed the animal without reason, God sent down His encompassing chastisement amongst them and they were wiped out (91:11-15).

Elsewhere in the Qur'an, the story of Salih and the camel is also mentioned. In chapter seven, people are asked to allow the camel to eat and not to harm her. Here the Qur'an says,

> We sent to Thamud their brother Salih [as a prophet]. He said, "O my people worship God, you have no god other than Him. The proof has come to you from your Lord. This she-camel of God is as a sign for you. Leave it alone to graze in the land of God and do not touch it with harm otherwise a powerful chastisement will capture you." (7:73)

A conversation between Salih and his people then takes place, after which the people of Salih "slaughtered the she-camel and they deviated from the command of their Lord, saying: 'O Salih, bring upon us what you warned us against if you really are one of the prophets.' So the earthquake seized them and they remained dead in their houses" (7:77-78).

Animals speak and have sophisticated languages and forms of communication. In one instance, an ant warned its fellow ants to take shelter in order to avoid being stepped on by the army of Solomon (27:18). According the Qur'an, certain prophets of God understood the language of animals and birds. One such prophet was Solomon who, due to a Divine bounty bestowed upon him, understood and could communicate with birds (27:16). The story also suggests that human beings can learn and gain benefits from the birds and their skills, just as Solomon did. According to the Qur'an, Solomon considered this ability to be a blessing from God and a sign of His favor.

It is also known that the Prophet of Islam knew the language of animals. There are fascinating stories of how the Prophet communicated with them. On one occasion, a camel had become wild but when the Prophet appeared, it came to him, prostrated itself as a sign of respect, and knelt beside him, so that he could put a bridle on it. Then the camel extended its neck to the Prophet as if it wanted to say something. The Prophet told those around him that the camel complained to him, saying, "They have employed me in the heaviest work, and now they want to slaughter me." The Prophet asked the camel's owner, "Is it true?" "Yes," he said. The Prophet then said to his companions, "These animals are communities, just like you. Be compassionate towards them."[9] The Prophet of Islam is also said to have rebuked a person for trying to make a camel carry too heavy a burden.

Animals also serve as the companions of and mounts for human beings. The Qur'an says, "Do they not see that We have created for them of our handiwork the cattle so that they are the owners? And we subdued for them from which are their mounts and from which they eat. And also other benefits and drinks they have within them. Will they then not give thanks?" (36:71-73) These verses illustrate that because animals are also the creation of God and they benefit humans, humans have a responsibility to care for and protect them. The purpose of animals, and that which humans are allowed to use them for, is specified in the Qur'an. Animals may be used as mounts or for food, but they are not to be abused or wasted. Islamic law, which stems from Qur'anic teachings, prohibits cruelty toward animals, such as loading animals beyond their capacity or depriving them from food and drink. Also, following the revelations of the Qur'an, the Prophet declared the holy site of Mecca to be *haram,* or protected. This can best be understood in modern terms as analogous to a national park, in which it is criminal to so much as kill an insect or uproot a plant. Some Muslim mystics have even been known to tie bells to their shoes, in order to warn small animals in their paths that might otherwise be crushed underfoot. This practice is a remarkable example of obeying the message of the Prophet.

Just as the Qur'an stresses the importance of protecting animals, it also stresses the importance of respecting other aspects of God's creation. Similar to how some Qur'anic chapters are named for animals, there are many chapters named after natural elements, such as "The Thunder" (chapter 13), "The Rock" (chapter 15), "The Light" (chapter 24), "The Dunes" (chapter 46), "The Star" (chapter 53), "The Moon" (chapter 54), "Iron" (chapter 57), and "The Sun" (chapter 91). Many natural elements are frequently referenced in the Qur'an. Among these are earth (roughly 500 times), water (more than eighty times), the sun (thirty-four times), and the moon (twenty-seven times).

Of these elements, few are as significant to life as water. Water is presented as a gift from God. It is sent by God from the sky to help plants grow and provide sustenance for human beings. "It is He who made earth as a bed for you and the sky as ceiling and by which He brought forth fruits as sustenance for you. Therefore, do not set up partners for God while you know" (2:22).[10] The Qur'an refers to water as a means of cleanliness for humanity (8:11). It is also the source of life (21:30) but has destructive qualities and can be used as punishment, as in the stories of Noah (11:40-44), Pharaoh (29:40), and Qarun (28:81). Pure water is a gift to those in Paradise, while contaminated water is a punishment for non-believers in Hell (14:16). In Qur'anic teaching, earth is a "cradle" for humanity (20:53) and is treated as a living creature, as in the verse where the Qur'an says, "And the heaven and the earth did not weep for them" (44:29). This verse, which is referencing the Pharaoh and his people drowning in the sea, treats nature as a living organism that has feelings and is even conscious, aware of what is happening, whether good or bad.

From an Islamic spiritual understanding, many examples of the bounties of God are seen in nature. Thus, thankfulness, or *shukr,* and awareness are necessary. The lack of human understanding is the result of *ghafla,* or heedlessness. The sun rises every day. Human beings see this, and they see the moon rise and the coming of the rain. In Islamic spirituality, these must be seen as Divine bounties provided for human beings and other creatures. Again and again the Holy Book wants to provoke the thoughts of human beings, to take them out of their zone of comfort: "Let human beings consider their food. How we pour water in abundance [i.e. rain]. Then tore the earth in cracks and it causes the grain to grow and grapes and animal fodder and olive-trees and palm-trees and gardens dense with foliage and fruits and grasses as provision for you and your cattle" (80:24-32).

Time and again the Qur'an reveals the things which God has created for the benefit of humanity: "And We have given you power in the earth, and appointed for you a livelihood from therein. And you are still less thankful" (7:10). A series of verses in chapter seventy-eight are dedicated to listing the things God has created as gifts for humanity. For example, earth is to serve as a cradle for humans, the mountains are to serve as protections, sleeping is to provide rest, night is to be like a covering garment, day is to be a time of work, and the sun is to be a dazzling lamp (78:6-13). Another phenomenon owing to God's mercy that the Qur'an mentions are "clouds heavy with rain:" "It is He who sends the winds as tidings heralding His mercy, until they bear a cloud heavy with rain, We lead it to a dead land, and cause water to descend upon it and thereby bring forth fruits of every kind" (7: 75). This clearly indicates that they are not meaningless.

The Qur'an speaks of nature as related to the Divine. That is to say, the Qur'an wants to open the veil of nature covering the hands of God, and thus make understood the ultimate reality of God, beyond cause and effect. Indeed, there are examples of Qur'anic verses inspiring scientists to look at the universe in different ways. One such verse is, "And heaven We constructed it with might and we made it expand" (51:47) which has been an inspiration for the investigation of the concept of entropy. Islamic Spirituality teaches people how to penetrate into this meaning of nature, and it leads them to reflect on and be thankful for all the bounties of God. This thankfulness necessitates that humanity act responsibly and protect nature, as God's vice-regents. Human beings must utilize the bounties of God carefully and without waste, pollution, or corruption, in order to express their thankfulness.

As a part of humanity's charge of being good stewards of the earth, all types of pollution are prohibited. In Islamic spirituality, the earth is a mosque and cleanliness is a requirement therein. In prayer, people must be clean and the spot on which they pray must also be clean. The Prophet said that cleanliness is half of religion, and he himself called the earth a mosque: "And the earth has been made for me a mosque and a clean place."[11] By this, the Prophet says that the earth must be clean enough to pray upon, that is, as clean as a mosque. Cleanliness is also a reflection of Divine names, particularly al-Quddus (the Most-Holy) and al-Tahir (the Clean).[12] Any corruption therefore, goes against such Divine names.

As we described earlier, Muslims are expected to perform the ritual cleansing, wudu, before each of the five daily prayers and any other voluntary salat, and mystics will generally perform this cleansing even prior to their dua' prayers. Hence, given the importance of prayer in Islamic spirituality, ritual cleansing is critical. The teaching of cleanliness in Islamic spirituality is very compatible with the modern hygienic process of preventing disease and promoting health care. As Qur'an 2:222 states, God loves those who are clean both physically and spiritually. Physical cleansing is the act of washing dirt from the body and clothes, and spiritual cleansing is the act of repentance, which is a spiritual washing of the negative impacts on the soul and other inner faculties. God loves both.

Pollution, however, is not just a failure of personal cleanliness; it is broader and includes the needless destruction of the natural world and the wasting of the bounties given by God. Here, responsibility lies on the shoulders of both individuals and the community. Everyone has to contribute to the cleanliness of their neighborhood, and by extension the planet. The Prophet emphasized the importance of cleaning in front of one's house to contribute to the entire neighborhood remaining clean. Cleanliness and thankfulness go hand in hand, and cleanliness requires respect of the Divine bounties and rejection of wastefulness.

In Islamic spirituality, Satan and the evil-commanding soul try to deceive human beings. Therefore, one has to avoid being their friends. This is why the Qur'an emphatically says: "Surely wasteful people are brothers of the devils. And Satan denies completely [the bounties of] his Lord" (17:27). Elsewhere, the Qur'an states: "God does not love the wasteful" (6:181). Wasting includes any misuse of natural resources. As such, the Qur'an teaches people to use resources economically; this lesson is so strong that a person may not waste water, even if he or she lives next to the ocean. This is not to say that one cannot use and benefit from God's bounties—far from it, for that is what they are there for. However, this must be done within the boundaries of Qur'anic principles.

In a similar vein, arrogance is a negative characteristic in human beings. One has to be humble with regard to nature. Arrogance results in considering nature an enemy or rival to be conquered, while humbleness results in considering nature a friend; not conquering, but befriending nature is essential. The Qur'an states: "Do not be arrogant in your walking on earth. God does not love the proud and arrogant. Be humble in your walking and lower your voice (31:18-19). This refers not only to the importance of cleanliness, but also of the danger of noise pollution, a phenomenon that is newly understood by science, but has been in the Qur'an for centuries. Also, the Prophet is said to have said, "Eat, drink, give charity, and have clothes as long as you do not mix it with wastefulness and arrogance."[13]

As the means of cleanliness is primarily water, it has a special significance in the Qur'an. For example, God asks Abraham and Ishmael to purify the house of God, the Ka'ba in Mecca (2:125). This verse uses the word *tahhira* to address Abraham and Ishmael, which includes the idea of, purification with water.[14] Elsewhere in the Qur'an, related words are used directly in relation to the cleansing power of water. In 25:48, the Qur'an states, "We sent down from the sky extremely purifying water." Therefore, the Qur'an indicates that the natural world is to be kept clean and not polluted, because God sends rainwater to clean the earth. It is as if the Qur'an is saying to human beings: follow the Divine plan and keep the world clean. Thus, maintaining the cleanliness of the environment is humanity's responsibility. In Islamic spirituality, just as God is the Most-Beautiful and loves beauty, God is the Clean and loves cleanliness. One has to protect the beauty of nature, since it is a reflection of the beauty of God. Similarly, God is the Pure and the Holy, and as a reflection of this, one has to maintain the purity of nature.

The Qur'anic paradigm of the environment is found in the description of Paradise, where all beauties and purities are purportedly found. Ideally, one has to make the world a Paradise-like place. The Qur'anic name for Paradise is *al-Jannah*, or the Garden. It is filled with trees, rivers of milk and honey, flowers, and fruits, as well as "palaces beneath which rivers flow." The environment of Paradise is one of water and greenery where fruits are inexhaustible and there are gardens and beautiful springs (For examples see 2:25, 3:15, 9:21, 44:52, 55:46-54, and 55:62-69). The Qur'an, by describing the beauty of Paradise, stresses the importance of the environment, which is also the reflection of the Divine name *al-Jamil*. The world, as a mirror of Paradise, should be a space where spiritual life is felt and helped.

Nature is not eternal, per se. However, through humanity's remembering God and chanting His names, it becomes eternal because the results of this remembering and chanting can be found in Paradise. This temporary world becomes eternal through the fruit of Paradise. Therefore, beautiful actions toward all elements of nature, including human beings, animals, plants, etc., will result in eternal rewards. While the world is ephemeral, the beautiful rewards of goodness are harvested in the world of eternity. Whether good or bad, nothing is lost. Everything will be seen. Even looking at nature in a contemplative way is reward-worthy, the result of which becomes eternal. This is what is meant by eternalizing the limited minutes of life into the unlimited eternal life.

Since nature is a masterpiece of Divine art, human beings are continuously in contact with nature and are expected to contemplate this art. Therefore, from the perspective of Islamic spirituality, unlike the natural sciences' approach, nature is not independent. Nature is the art of the Greatest Artist. While many natural scientists have accepted nature as independent to the extent that they consider nature to be self-governing and self-creating, other scholars have considered every aspect of nature as something dependent upon a Creator. Islamic spiritualty's approach is similar to the latter and differs greatly from the former approach. In Islamic spirituality, one name for this Creator is *al-Sani' al-Hakim*, The Most-Wise Architect. It can be argued that as a result of the former view, humanity's modern approach toward nature has often been aggressive and arrogant. Thus, a struggle between human beings and nature is inevitable. Human beings seem determined to conquer nature in order to prevail in this struggle.

While modern human beings have been trying to "conquer" mountains and other natural wonders, in Islamic spirituality, these are living beings and also pray to God. In the Qur'anic story of David, who is a model of Islamic spirituality, mountains and birds praised God with him (34:10). Also, the Prophet spoke of Uhud, a mountain north of Medina: "Uhud is a mountain that we love and it loves us."[15] Mountains are the dwelling place for many creatures. Bees are inspired by God to make their homes in mountains and make delicious honey for human beings. Honey comes as a result of remarkable cooperation and harmony between bees, mountains, and flowers. They all come together to help human beings.

Mountains are also places for contemplation. One goes to the top of the mountain and witnesses the majesty of God from such a high place on earth. It is a powerful experience for the spirit of human beings. It is interesting that the Qur'an, when rejecting arrogance, speaks with the analogy of mountains. It says: "You cannot puncture the earth [with your arrogance]. You cannot reach mountains in tallness" (17:37). Mountains are works of Divine art (27:88). It is a great loss to see the art and not recognize the Artist. Mountains are resources of the bounties of God for human beings (35:27).

More broadly, all of nature, from the perspective of Islamic spirituality, is alive and has consciousness. This is understood from the statement of the Prophet when he speaks of the merits of the call to prayer. He suggests that all things, wet and dry, ask for forgiveness for the muezzin when they hear the call to prayer.[16] Also, when the Qur'an says the heavens and the earth do not cry over the deaths of bad people (44:29) it implies that they do cry over the deaths of good people. This crying for the loss of good people suggests that the earth and heavens have real feelings and are not lifeless entities.

While the Holy Qur'an is the revealed book of God, nature is the created book of God. Both books are a means by which God reveals Himself. There are many references that elements of nature are limitless words of God. One Qur'anic verse asks the Prophet to say to human beings, "If the sea becomes ink for the words of my Lord, surely the sea would be used up before the words of my Lord are exhausted. Even if we brought more of these to help [it would not help]" (18:109). This verse indicates that the sea itself is a word of God. Thus, if the sea were doubled, it still could not provide enough ink to exhaust the words of God, because the ink in question is the word of God. One can therefore view every part of nature as a sentence or a word in the book of nature, the author of which is God. Accordingly, the study of nature is the study of the book of God.

As recitation of the Qur'an is a part of Islamic spirituality, reading the book of nature, which can be done through contemplation and studying, is also a way of remembering God. Perhaps the best description of nature then is this: a Divinely inspired chorus praising and glorifying the Perfect Artist. Believers are expected to read this book, in order to understand God, contemplate His art, and be in dialogue with Him. Human beings are endowed with the ability to think, and therefore they can see the reflection of God's beautiful names in everything of the natural world. It is narrated that after the death of Abu al-Darda, a well-known and highly praised companion of the Prophet, his wife was asked about the most meritorious prayer he had. She said, "Contemplation [taffakur] and to take lessons from everything he saw."[17]

Islamic spirituality and ecology are necessarily linked. Through contemplation of nature, human beings will inevitably realize the meanings and reflections of the beautiful names of God, and that it falls on human beings to protect them. Furthermore, as in the visible, physical world human beings are the only conscious creatures, and they are specifically required to reflect upon nature. For example, the earth with all its living creatures is a reflection of al-Hayy, the Most-Living. Similarly, all love and the capacity to love within all living creatures is the reflection of the Divine name al-Wadud, the Most-Loving. The great Sufi master Abd al-Rahman al-Jami (d. 1492) holds the idea expressed most famously by Dante Alighieri (d. 1321) at the end of the Divine Comedy, that God's love is "the love that moves the sun and other stars."[18]

Similarly, Said Nursi, speaking of the mystery of the reflections of the Divine names—in particular al-Qayyum, the Most-Sustaining—compares the movement of celestial bodies to whirling dervishes, as though each celestial body is a dervish and moves as a result of Divine love. He says,

If we want to see the greatest reflection of the Divine name al-Qayyum, we must from our imaginations make two telescopes in order to observe the whole universe. One of them will show the most distant objects, the other smallest particles. If we look through the first telescope, we see that through the reflection of the Divine name of al-Qayyum, millions of celestial bodies and stars thousands of times larger than the earth are moving without any support in the matter known as ether, which is more subtle than air, while others are made to move as a duty. Then we look through the second telescope of our imaginations in a way to see small atoms. Through the mystery of al-Qayyum, taking up orderly positions like the stars, the particles of the bodies of animate creatures on the earth are all in motion and performing their duties. Particularly the red and white blood cells in living creatures are masses made of small atoms, like the stars in the heaven, move like the whirling dervishes in an orderly movement of two motions.[19]

Other Muslim mystics and theologians called the movement of the sun a result of the delight the sun experiences in the love of God. The sustenance of all creatures is a reflection of the Divine name *al-Razzaq*, the Giver of sustenance. Similarly, the capacity to see or understand all of creation is a reflection of *al-Basir*, the One who sees everything, and the unique fashioning of all living things is a reflection of *al-Musawwir*, the Fashioner. The lofty reality of the relationship between God's names and nature can perhaps be understood as similar to the relationship between a mirror and the sun. Just as a mirror reflects the sun, every object according to its nature reflects one or more of the Divine names. The Sun is not in the mirror per se, but it is reflected in the mirror to the extent that one can perceive its light and even feel its warmth. Islamic spirituality, unlike pantheistic doctrines, does not accept nature as a part of God, but accepts it as God's art that reflects His beautiful names and attributes, which can be seen through spiritual experiences.

To reiterate, the sun's manifestation and reflection appears in all small fragments of glass, droplets of water, and other transparent objects. They reflect the sun, but they are not the sun itself. As the analogy indicates, all creatures and the natural world itself reflect God, but they are neither God nor even a part of God. In this regard, Islam and Islamic spirituality greatly differ from pantheism and other earth-centered spiritual practices which equate nature with God. From the galactic level to the atomic level, there is no randomness or chance of accidental creation in nature. Everything is created with a measure and with a purpose. This conscious measuring results in an inimitable art. Even the smallest parts of creation are artfully crafted, in painstaking detail. Qur'anic verses including, "It is He who has created then proportioned and it is He who measured then guided" (87:3) and, "Indeed We have created everything in measure" (54:49) support the idea that everything in the universe is designed, created, and guided by God.

As for the afterlife, the Divine name *al-Qadir*, the Most-Powerful, reflects fully. In the afterlife, things are created spontaneously. Thus, in Paradise, if one wants to have a peach, it is immediately available. Thus, theologically speaking, there is no need for cause and effect processes. God is fully capable of creating something from nothingness. This said, in this world, in order to get a peach one must follow the natural process. First, plant a seed in rich soil, then wait for the tree to grow, all the while making sure that the tree has sufficient water, heat, and light from the sun. Scientifically speaking, oxygen, hydrogen, nitrogen, and carbon combine in different ways to compose all plants.

It is this process through which God's will works. The very process is a cause and effect relationship. This is known as the Divine way of action in the realm of nature. In this world, God acts according to the Divine name *al-Hakim*, the Most-Wise, which requires cause and effect relationships. God is able to create without causes, but that is not the way God acts in this world. Things have causes and human beings relate those things to those causes, yet according to Islamic spirituality, one has to be aware that God is the Cause of causes. Yes, nature works like a mechanically organized machine, yet from the perspective of Islamic spirituality, Divine involvement is constant; there is no determinism or self-mechanism. Although the works of nature looks mechanical, in reality there is a constant Consciousness at work in every moment.

The relationship between cause and effect sometimes seems very strong, sometimes very subtle, and sometimes indiscernible. For example, one can calculate astronomically the time of the sunrise on a given day ten years from now, but we cannot calculate or know if there will be rain this time next year. The scientific explanation of rain cannot determine the time in which it will rain, before physical signs are present. Likewise, we may know the characteristics of life, but not what ultimately makes something live. The Qur'anic understanding, unlike that of proponents of Newtonian mechanism, indicates that, "Anything in the Heavens and the earth asks Him [for their needs]. Every moment He is bringing to existence [according to the Divine plan]" (55:29). The nature of creation, in fact, indicates that the causes that we see in our daily life are not capable of creating the remarkable results we witness. Natural causes, such as oxygen, hydrogen, nitrogen, and carbon, are basically without order, formless, blind, and unconscious. Therefore, they cannot create creatures so consciously well designed. This extraordinary purposefulness and wonderful design are the reflection of the Divine names.

The Prophet said: "If the end of time comes upon one of you, and you have a vine in your hand, plant it,"[20] and, "Any green plant that is planted and a bird comes and eats it becomes a charity for that person."[21] Therefore, greening the earth and being good stewards to the earth are a critical part of the spiritual path of all human beings. In Islamic spirituality, human beings, through the understanding of the Divine names, become connected on one side to the vast field of the universe and on the other side to the minuteness of the realm of atoms. Because these are aspects of human spiritual greatness, every human being is thus considered a universe. Therefore, in Islamic spirituality, human beings must be aware of their ecological responsibility toward the environment, since nature is a book of God and hence deserves ultimate care and respect. With this perspective, love for nature is love for the art of God, and love for the Divine art is love for God.

# Conclusion:

# Living spiritually in the twenty-first century

We have developed tremendous technology, to the extent that one can call friends on the other side of the earth and see the light in their eyes. However, in the realm of spirituality and human relationships, we still have a long way to go. By almost any measure, the last few decades have seen a tremendous quickening of the pace of life, and an increase in the amount of things that people need to do on a daily basis in order to live a "normal" life. This may have caused human beings to begin to lose connection with themselves, and hence with the Divine. A pause is needed, a comma in the long sentence that is life in the twenty-first century. A NASA scientist once told me, after witnessing the performance of whirling dervishes, "I have realized there is something more spiritual beyond materialistic life." It is this sort of pause that is needed in the world. We should still live our lives and continue to make them full and worthwhile. We cannot, nor should we retreat permanently into a cave to meditate, for by doing so we risk both alienating ourselves from the world around us and not living up to the full potential that God has empowered and entrusted us with. The practices I have described in this book I hope can help people to achieve that pause and reconnect with the Divine in the world, and with the full potential of their humanity and their spirituality. Whether one is Muslim, Jewish, Christian, Buddhist, Hindu, a follower of another religious tradition, or a follower of no religion at all, I hope that this book gives not only a glimpse into the nature of the Islamic spiritual tradition, but provides useful material from which to build one's own spiritual framework.

It is for this reason that I did not write a book on the often abstract theoretical world of Sufism. There are plenty of books on the subject which can be easily obtained. I hope that by focusing on practical issues and only the most basic necessary terminology, referencing the Qur'an and a few spiritual masters, this book has provided sufficient information on the principles involved in living life in accordance with the tradition of Islamic spirituality. Islamic spirituality is much more than an "ism." It is based in practice. Similarly, it is also more than just a collection of technical terms and intellectual debates over the meanings of abstract Arabic words, no matter their importance to many Islamic mystics. This "way of the elite" is not useful for the vast majority of people, and can even be a distraction from the real important practices of Islamic spirituality. If I can struggle to translate the terminological meaning of otherwise obscure Arabic words, what good are those specific words to anyone? As I have emphasized, what is important is giving readers a simple way of practicing Islamic spirituality. Islamic spirituality is experiential. It must be experienced at a physical level, such as the performance of prayer, reading, and speaking, to understand its real meaning. Phrases such as *"Subhan Allah"* and *"Allahu Akbar"* are powerful enough on their own.

Further, to have elaborated on institutionalized Sufism fully by focusing on various Sufi orders would have made this volume too long. My goal was to give more attention to the spiritual life, which can be practiced inside and outside of the mystical orders. I have given more space to three mystics, whose ideas fit well with this focus on the practical side of spirituality. I have also described, and in many cases translated, the prayers of early mystics so that they might be used as a guide, not just as an exercise in philology. I did not want this to be an exclusively academic book that would sit on the shelves of the local university's library and gather dust. My goal is for this book to be alive, to be read and utilized in people's spiritual quest to become closer to the Divine in their daily lives. This is why I have given so much detail on how to live a life based on the Islamic spiritual tradition.

One of the purposes of Islamic spirituality is to create awareness and consciousness. All the efforts of Muslim mystics were directed toward this. In other words, people should not only look, but should actually see what is in their hearts and in their environment. There should be awareness that even reading a short chapter from the Qur'an, such as Chapter *Ikhlas*, which is just four verses, is a spiritual pursuit. The short statements in this chapter contribute to the remembrance of God, which is *dhikr*, and as such are a critical component in Islamic spirituality. If one says, "In the name of God the Most-Compassionate, the Most-Merciful," prior to eating, as is recommended by the Prophet and practiced by all Muslim mystics, the person who is saying it remembers the practice of the Messenger of God. By remembering the Messenger of God, one remembers God, the One who sent the Message to His Prophet. Therefore, even this short statement becomes remembrance and makes the entire action reward-worthy. Such simplicity can make one's time much more productive and lead to great spiritual rewards.

As I have mentioned in several places, I have utilized the Qur'anic approach, which sees the universe as a place of contemplation. Contemplation of nature, the realm of creation, is a critical and necessary part of Islamic spirituality. This contemplation of nature, which can lead to a greater respect for all of creation and a more holistic understanding of our place in the universe, is one area where Islamic spirituality dovetails with other contemporary trends, and can help people see the great importance of living spiritually today. Generally, people are prone to look outside themselves, to politics and the social world. This work has the goal of increasing one's looking inward at himself or herself. By doing this and making one's own self the subject of study and reflection, much can be done to reduce violence, poverty, and other ills in the world. This in turn will result in social harmony, which is very much needed in our modern world.

For most of the twentieth century, life might best be characterized by a growing materiality. There seems to be a change in the twenty-first century. Almost everywhere in the world there are efforts aimed at reviving a lost element of spirituality, a spirituality which is necessary for a balanced approach to understanding human beings' place on Earth. Aided by the internet and rapid changes in our lives, we seem to be seeking something lost and missing. While the entirety of Islamic spirituality as presented in this book is certainly not for everyone, I hope that everyone seeking their lost spiritual nature can find something in this book.

Along those lines, I hope this book can be of some assistance to those, both formally and informally, in the counseling profession and those in need of counseling. I think whether one is Muslim or not, some of the practices of Islamic spirituality can be uplifting and can create a positive impact on people's lives. I have tried to highlight these throughout the book to make sure that people know that, from an Islamic perspective, it is easy to find one's spirituality and salvation. Being a good, kind, humane individual is more important than one's theoretical knowledge, or how properly one practices certain rituals. That is why the Prophet of Islam says that he was sent to complete high morals, to express the importance of morality and good behaviors as a kind of aphorism. Also, it has been said that basically religion is good behavior in your dealing with people.

This is not to say that the spiritual path is inherently easy. Praying five times a day, being kind even to those who oppress you, and so on are not easy. However, despite the difficulty in dotting all the *i*'s and crossing all the *t*'s along the path followed by Islamic mystics, God does not require this. Being sincere is what God loves in a person. To indicate the importance of good intention, the Prophet said there are two phrases that are easy on the tongue, but heavy on the scales in the afterlife: "*Subhanallahi wa bi hamdihi*" (Exalted is God with His praise), and "*Subhanallah al-Azim*," (Exalted is God the Majestic). This connects the person to the Divine. It is not the difficulty of the act, but the intention which leads to bigger and better spiritual achievements.

It is my hope that this book will contribute to the spiritual achievements of individuals, thus bringing harmony and tranquility to our modern society and in turn helping to heal the environment. All of these together will lead to inner peace, and inner peace will lead to outer peace.

# NOTES

## Introduction

1 Qur'anic verses will be cited parenthetically in the text in the form (chapter:verse).

2 Bediuzzaman Said Nursi, "Sozler," *Risale-i Nur Kulliyati* (Istanbul: Sozler Yayinevi, 1996): 178.

3 Ibn Maja, *Al-Sunan*, "Al-Zuhd," 31.

4 In the Islamic tradition, God does not have a gender, as theologically speaking this would be limiting God. However, masculine pronouns will be utilized as needed in this text for simplicity, as there is not a sufficient gender-neutral pronoun in English.

5 Nursi, "Sualar," *Risale-i Nur Kulliyati* 989. al-Qurtubi, *Al-Jami' li Ahkam al-Qur'an*, v. 2, ed. Ahmet al-Barduni, et al. (Cairo: Dar al-Kutub al-Misriyya, 1964): 172.

6 This is part of a much longer commentary from Nursi on Qur'an 9:111, on how people can use the capacities given by God to receive eternity. For the full commentary, see Bediuzzaman Said Nursi, *The Words*, trans. Sukran Vahide (Istanbul: Sozler Nesriyat, 1992): 37–40.

7 Muslim bin Hajjaj, *Al-Sahih*, Al-Tawba, 12 and 13.

8 al-Bukhari, *Al-Sahih*, "Al-Iman," 37.

9 2:83, 2:178, 2:229, 4:36, 4:62, 6:15, 9:110, 16:90, 17:23, 46:15, and twice in 55:60.

10 For more on the term *ihsan*, see Sachiko Murata and William H. Chittick, *The Vision of Islam* (St. Paul: Paragon House, 1994): 267–94.

11 Muslim, *Al-Sahih*, "Al-Birr," 32.

12 al-Bukhari, "Al-Iman," 37. Also in Muslim, *al-Sahih*, "Al-Iman," 157.

## Chapter 1

1 Grammatically, all Arabic words contain a three-letter stem onto which other letter combinations are grafted to create new words. For instance, the root k-t-b has to do with writing and books, such that *kataba* means wrote, *kutub* means books, *maktaba* (the place of books) means library, etc.

2 Nursi, "Sozler," *Risale-i Nur*, 232.

3 Ali bin Muhammad al-Sayyid al-Sharif al-Jurjani, *Al-Tarifat* (Beirut: Dar al-Kitab al-'Arabi, 1984): 112.

4 Compare this to the account in Genesis 2:7.

5 al-Qurtubi, *Al-Jami' li Ahkam al-Qur'an*, v. 15, ed. Ahmet al-Barduni, et al. (Cairo: Dar al-Kutub al-Misriyya, 1964): 299.

6  Abd al-Rahman bin Abi Bakr Jalal al-Din al-Suyuti, *Mu'jam Maqalid al-'Ulum fi al-Hudud wa al-Rusum*, ed. Muhammad Ibrahim Ubadah (Cairo: Maktaba al-Adab, 2004): 215.

7  Annemarie Schimmel, "Sufism," *Encycolpædia Britannica*, http://www.britannica.com/topic/Sufism.

8  al-Jurjani, *Al-Tarifat*, 59.

9  Abd al-Karim al-Qushayri, *Lata'if al-Isharat*, v. 1 (Cairo: al-Hay'a al-Amma li al-Kitab, n.d.): 49–51.

10  Muhammad A'la bin Ali al-Tahanawi, *Mawsu'at Kashshaf Istilahat al-Funun wa al-'Ulum*, ed. Ali Dahruj, v. 1 (Beirut: Maktabat Lubnan, 1996): 456.

11  Ibid., 457.

12  Fethullah Gulen, *Key Concepts in the Practice of Sufism*, trans. Ali Unal (Fairfax, VA: The Fountain, 1999): xiv.

13  See Qur'an, 18:28 and 18:46.

14  al-Tahanawi, *Mawsu'at Kashshaf*, 461.

15  al-Suyuti, *Mu'jam Maqalid al-'Ulum*, 214.

16  Muslim, "Al-Salat," 215.

17  The entirety of the first chapter of the Qur'an is: "In the name of God, The Most Compassionate, The Most Merciful/ All praise belongs to God alone, the Lord of all the worlds/the Most-Compassionate, the Most Merciful/ the Owner of the Day of Judgment./ To You alone we worship and unto You alone we ask for help./Guide us to the straight path/the path of those upon whom You have given Your blessings and neither of those who have been condemned [by You], nor of those who have gone astray."

18  Muslim, "Al-Salat," 38.

19  Muslim, "Al-Birr," 24, 28, 30, 32.

20  Muslim, "Al-Tawba," 12.

21  al-Bukhari, "Al-Iman," 37.

22  Ahmad bin Hanbal, *Al-Musnad*, ed. Shu'ayb al-Arnaut, et al., v. 2 (Beirut: Muassasat al-Risala, 2001): 359.

23  Nursi, "Mektubat," *Risale-i Nur*, 504.

24  al-Tabarani, *Al-Awsat*, 16:675.

25  Abu al-Hasan, Nur al-Din, al-Haythami, *Majma' al-Zawaid wa Manba' al-Fawaid*, ed. Husam al-Din al-Qudsi, v. 10 (Cairo: Maktaba Al-Qudsi, 1994): 63.

26  Abu Nu'aym al-Isfahani, *Hilyat al-Awliya wa Tabaqat al-Asfiya'* (Beirut: Dar al-Kutub al-Ilmiyya, 1989).

27  John Renard, ed., *Tales of God's Friends* (Berkeley: University of California Press, 2009).

28  Fethullah Gulen, ed., *Al-Qulub al-Daria* (Istanbul: Dar al-Nile, 2013): 21. For a list of the prayers of Abu Bakr and for his supplications, see also 22–23.

29  For the prayer and supplication of Umar, see *Al-Qulub al-Daria*, 24–27.

30  For Uthman's supplication, known as the "Supplication of the Qur'an," see *Al-Qulub al-Daria*, 27–42.

31  For Ali's supplication, weekly prayer, specific prayers for release from difficulties, and his poems of supplication, see *Al-Qulub al-Daria*, 42–59.

32  For Zayn al-Abidin's various prayers and supplications, see *Al-Qulub al-Daria*, 68–97.

33  For his supplication see *Al-Qulub al-Daria*, 122–24. See also "the Prayer against calamities and sickness" in *Al-Qulub al-Daria*, (274–75).

# Chapter 2

1  In the Islamic tradition, it is highly recommended that when one mentions the names of the prophets, one asks for peace and blessings from God for them. Since this might have a negative impact on the flow of the text, I will have it here only, and intend that subsequent mentions will have this blessing in spirit.

2  Formally, the Hadith are the words and actions of the Prophet of Islam. Distinction should also be made between Hadith with a capital "H," which refers to the entire body of the Hadith, and hadith with a lowercase "h," which refers to individual hadith. Also, hadith can be used as both a singular and a plural noun.

3  This quote can be found in Bediuzzaman Said Nursi, *Risale-i Nur Kulliyati*, "Mektubat," 443.

4  For a long contextual definition of the Qur'an, see: Nursi "Sozler," 161–62.

5  Abu Bakr bin Abi Shayba, *Al-Musannaf*, ed. Kamal Yousuf al-Hut, v. 6 (Riyadh: Makataba al-Rushd, 1409H): 118.

6  al-Bukhari, "Fada'il al-Qur'an," 34. A slightly different version is found in "al-Sawm," 58.

7  In all of these verses, there is no consensus among English translators of the Qur'an as to whether "chosen" or "purified" is the best translation. As both are meant by the Arabic words in question, for current purposes I have decided to use chosen/purified. For more information, see Louis Massingnon and M. Abd al-Razik, *Al-Tassawuf* (Beirut: Dar al-Kutub al-Lubnani, 1984): 57–58.

8  Abu Bakr al-Kalabadhi, *Al-Taarruf* (Beirut: Dar al-Kutub al-Ilimiyya, n.d.): 21.

9  Reynold Nicholson, *The Mystics of Islam* (London: Routledge, 1914): 3.

10  Linguistically speaking, the word Allah in Arabic is a combination of the definite article "*al*" and "*ilah*," the Arabic word for a god. However, the word has become elided and is used in the Qur'an as a proper name for God. In other words, Allah is the Arabic name for God. Like Muslims, Arabic-speaking Christians and Jews also use the name "Allah" for God.

11  When the Prophet says, "this is easy on tongue and heavy on the scale," he is referring to the judgment scale in the afterlife where people's good and bad deeds are weighted. If their good deeds overcome their bad deeds, they are among the people of Paradise. What is important in this measuring is not quantity but quality. The full hadith refers to several other phrases, such as, "*Subhan Allah*," (exalted is Allah), "*La ilaha 'Illa Allah*," (there is no deity but God), and "*Allahu Akbar*" (God is Greater than everything). All these phrases that are considered

by the Prophet are phrases that are simple and easy on the tongue and heavy on the scale in the Day of Judgment. This is also referred to as the remembrance of God. *Al-Bukhari, Al-Sahih*, "Al-Iman," 19. Alternative versions are in "al-Tawhid," 58 and "Al-Da'awat," 66. The version in "Al-Tawhid" also includes the phrases *"Subhan Allah al-Azim,"* or "The Almighty God is exalted" and *"Subhan Allah wa bi Hamdih"* or "God is exalted with His praise." Similar hadith are mentioned in the collection of Muslim bin al-Hajjaj. See *Al-Sahih*, "Al-Dhikr," 30.

12  al-Bukhari, "Al-Raqa'iq," 38.

13  Abdullah bin Umar al-Baydawi, *Anwar al-Tanzil wa Asrar al-Ta'wil*, ed. Muhammad Abd al-Rahman al-Mar'ashli, v. 1 (Beirut, Dar Ihya al-Turath al-Arabi, 1997): 121.

14  Ibid.

15  Abu Dawud, *Al-Sunan*, "Sunnah," 15.

16  Muslim, *Al-Sahih*, "Al-Dhikr," 3, 18, and 19.

17  Ibn Maja, *Al-Sunan*, "Al-Adab," 55.

18  Ismail Hakki Bursevi, *Ruh al-Bayan*, v. 1 (Beirut: Dar al-Fikr, n.d.) 255.

19  al-Bukhari, "Al-Tawhid," 15 and 43.

20  Muslim, *"Al-Dhikr,"* 3, 18, and 19.

21  Mahmud al-Alusi, *Ruh al-Ma'ani*, v. 1, ed. Ali Abd al Bari Atiyya (Beirut: Dar al-Kutub al-Ilmiyya): 417.

22  al-Qushayri, *Lata'if al-Isharat*, v. 1, 137.

23  al-Bukhari, "Al-Da'awat," 69.

24  Muhammad bin Ahmad Badr al-Din al-'Ayni, *Umdat al-Qari Sharh* Sahih al-Bukhari, v. 23 (Beirut: Dar Ihya al-Turath al-Arabi, n.d.): 29.

25  This formula is found in the following verses: 26:9, 68, 104, 122, 140, 159, 175, 191, and 217. It can also be found in 32:6, 35:5, 40:5, and 44:42.

26  In modern times, this supplication was brought to the Sunni tradition through Said Nursi. A version with English and parallel Arabic text is *Al-Jawshan al-Kabir*, trans. Ali Kose (Somerset, NJ: The Light, 2006).

27  This verse can be compared to Deuteronomy 6:4, "Hear O Israel: The Lord our God is one Lord."

28  Nursi, *Hizb al-Haqa'iq al-Nuriyya.* (Istanbul: Sozler Yayinevi, 1996): 121.

29  Al-Alusi, *Ruh al-Ma'ani*, v. 7, 453.

30  al-Husain bin Mahmud al-Muzhiri, *Al-Mafatih fi Sharh al-Masabih*, v. 1 (Kuwait: Dar al-Nawadir, 2012): 417. The authenticity of this hadith is not established, but there is no debate on the accuracy of its meaning.

31  Nursi has a unique way of understanding this Divine name through analogy: "a human being who does not wash his body for one month, or does not clean up his room, will find it very dirty and ugly. Therefore, this cleanliness and purity that is found in the palace of the universe always comes from a wise cleansing and a careful purifying. If there were no such cleansing and purification, all the animals who come to the Earth would drown and die in one year because of its dirtiness. Also, if there were no such cleansing, the remnants of the stars and moons would break our heads and the heads of other animals, and in fact, even

the head of the whole planet Earth by sending stones the size of mountains upon us and this would cause us to be exiled from our worldly homeland. However, there is no evidence that many stones were dropped from the skies, only few stones have come as lessons for humanity, which did not harm anyone." See "Lem'alar," 798.

32  al-Darimi, *Al-Sunan*, "Al-Wudu," 3.

33  For the types of prayers, see Zeki Saritoprak, "Prayer An Inexhaustible Treasure for the Human Spirit (A Nursi Reader)," *The Fountain Magazine*, 48 (October–December 2004), http://www.fountainmagazine.com/Issue/detail/ Prayer-An-Inexhaustible-Treasure-for-the-Human-Spirit-A-Nursi-Reader

34  Abu Nu'aym al-Isfahani, *Hilyat al-Awliya wa Tabaqat al-Asfiya*, v. 8 (Beirut: Dar al-Kutub al-Ilmiyya, 1989): 31.

35  al-Hakim al-Nisaburi, *Al-Mustadrak ala al-Sahihayn*, ed. Mustafa Abd al-Qadir Ata, v. 2 (Beirut: Dar al-Kutub al-Ilmiyya, 1990): 453.

36  Muslim, "Al-Wasiyya," 14.

37  Nursi, "Lem'alar," 580.

38  Malik bin Anas, *Al-Muwatta'*, "Al-Qur'an," 32.

39  See also 38:35.

40  This is related to Hasan al-Basri. His full statements, "One moment of contemplation is more fruitful than one night of long, voluntary prayer." Ibn Abi Shayba, *Al-Musannaf*, ed. Kamal Hathut, v. 7 (Riyadh: Maktaba al-Rushd, 1409H): 190.

# Chapter 3

1  Bediuzzaman Said Nursi, "Sozler," 102.

2  Ibid.

3  Abu abd al-Rahman bin Ali al-Nasai, *Al-Sunan*, "Qiyam al-Layl," 19.

4  Examples of *raqa'iq* include both prayers, such as prayers in the middle of the day, prayers against stress and grief, prayers for death and life, prayers for children, etc., as well as other activities. For example, the first hadith in the section on *raqa'iq* reminds people to be aware of their health and to spend their time wisely, while another discusses this worldly life in comparison to the afterlife.

5  al-Bukhari, "Al-Da'awat," 2.

6  Ibid., 3.

7  Ibid., 7.

8  Ibid.

9  Ibid.

10  Ibid., 10.

11  *Fortification of the Muslim Through Remembrance and Supplication From the Qur'an and the Sunnah*, compiled by Sa'eed bin 'Ali Wahf al-Qahtaani (NP:ND). A more complete grouping is found in Muhyi al-Din Abu Zakariyya Yahya bin Sharaf al-Nawawi, *Al-Adhkar* (Beirut: Dar Ibn Hazm, 2004).

12 Ibid., 210.

13 Ahmad bin Shu'ayb bin Ali al-Nasai', *Al-Sunam*, ed. Abd al-Fattah Abu Ghudda, "Al-Siyan" (Aleppo: Maktab al-Matbuat al-Islamiyya, 1986): 43.

14 al-Bukhari, "Al-Salat," 1.

15 See Ali bin Sultan al-Qari, *Mirqat al-Mafatih,* v. 1 (Beirut: Dar al-Fikr, 2002): 55.

# Chapter 4

1 Trans. B. R. Von Shelgell (Oneonta, NY: Mizan Press, 1990).

2 Briefly, the Islamic pyramid of creation consists of five layers. On the bottom are rocks, minerals, and other inorganic substances. These are followed by plants and then animals. Generally speaking, human beings are in the fourth layer and angels are in the highest layer. The place of human beings, however, is not static. Individual human beings can be higher than angels or lower than animals. An individual's location can even vary within his or her own lifetime.

3 Saadi Shirazi, *The Rose Garden (Gulistan)*, trans. Omar Ali-Shah (Reno: Tractus Books, 1997): 13. Contemporary mystics also use Shirazi's statement. See Fethullah Gulen, *Fatiha Uzerine Mulahazalaar* (Izmir: Nil Yayanlari, 2011): 121.

4 Abd al-Rahman bin Abi Bakr al-Suyuti, *Al-Haqa'iq fi Akhbar al-Mala'ik* (Beirut: Dar al-Kutub al-Ilmiyya, 1985): 147.

5 Abu Dawud, *Al-Sunan*, "Al-At'ima," 52.

6 Muslim, "Al-Dhikr wa al-Da'awat," 64.

7 Abu I'sa Muhammad al-Tirmidhi, *Al-Sunan,* , ed. Ahmad Muhammad Shakir, et al., "Al-Qiyama" (Cairo: Maktaba Mustafa al-Babi al-Halabi, 1975): 49.

8 al-Bukhari, "Al-Adab," 18.

9 See al-Bukhari, "Al-Da'awat," 60 and "Al-Dhikr," 70.

10 Ahmad bin Hanbal, *Al-Musnad*, ed. Ahmad Muhammad Shakir, v. 6 (Cairo: Dar al-Hadith, 1995): 539. See also Abu Yaqub Ishaq bin Ibrahim bin Rahawayh, *Al-Musnad*, ed. Abd al-Ghafur al-Balushy, v. 1 (Medina: Maktaba al-Iman, 1991): 257.

11 al-Tirmidhi, *Al-Sunan*, "Al-Da'awat," 106 (Section on the merit of repentance and asking for forgiveness).

12 al-Bukhari, "Al-Da'awat," 4.

13 Ibid., 2.

14 Ibid., 3.

15 Ibid., 4.

16 al-Bukhari, "Al-Tawhid," 50; Muslim, "Al-Tawba," 1.

17 The full text of the Hadith is as follows: "Abu Dharr narrates from the Prophet. The Prophet narrates from God, who said, 'O My servants, I have prohibited wrongdoing upon Myself and among yourselves as well. Therefore, do not wrong each other. O My servants, all of you are misled except those whom I guided. Ask Me for guidance so that I guide you. O My servants, all of you are

hungry except whom I fed. Ask Me for food so that I feed you. O My servants, all of you are naked except whom I clothe. Ask Me for clothing so that I clothe you. O My servants, all of you commit mistakes night and day and I am forgiving of all sins. Ask Me for forgiveness so that I forgive you. O My servants, you cannot harm Me or benefit Me. O My servants, if your first generations and last generations, your human beings and your jinns become as pious as the heart of the most pious person, it will not increase My power. O My servants, if your first generations and last generations, your human beings and your jinns become as evil as the heart of the most vicious person, it will not decrease My power. O My servants, if your first generations and last generations, your human beings and your jinns stand on one upland and ask Me and I give the request of each of them, this will not decrease from what I have, not even as much as the amount of water a dipped needle would take from the ocean. O My servants, it is your deeds I count for you and will respond justly back to you. Those who have found goodness, let them praise to God. Those who have found other than that should blame only their souls." Muslim, "Al-*Birr*," 55.

18  Abd al-Rahman al-Suyuti, *Sharhu Sunani Ibn Maja* (Karachi: Qadim-i Kutubkhana, n.d.): 20.

19  Muhammad Abdur-Rahman Mubarakpuri, *Tuhfa al-Ahwazi bi Sharh Jami' al-Tirmidhi*, v. 2 (Beirut: Dar al-Kutub al-Ilmiyya, n.d.): 481.

20  Nursi, "Mesnev-i Nuriye," 1329.

21  Ibid.

22  al-Alusi, *Ruh al-Ma'ani*, v. 15, 152.

23  Abu al-Hasan Ali bin Muhammad al-Mawardi, *Al-Nukat wa al-'Uyun*, v. 6 (Beirut: Dar al-Kutub al-Ilmiyya, n.d.): 772.

24  Abu Uthman Amr bin Bahr al-Jahiz, *Tahdhib al-Akhlaq* (Tanta, Egypt: Dar al-Sahaba, 1989), 15.

25  Nursi, "Isaratu'l-I'caz," 1163–64.

26  Muhammad bin Ali Abu Talib al-Makki, *Qut al-Qulub*, ed. Asim Ibrahim al-Kiyali, v. 2 (Beirut: Dar al-Kutub al-Ilmiyya, 2005): 84.

27  al-Tabari, *Jami' al-Bayan*, ed. Ahmad Muhammad Shakir, , v. 3 (Beirut: Muassasat al-Risala, 2000): 211.

28  al-Qurtubi, *Al-Jami'*, v. 2, 172.

29  Ibn Kathir, *Al-Tafsir*, v. 1 (Riyadh: Dar Tayba, 1999): 335.

30  Ibid., 336.

31  Ibid.

32  al-Alusi, *Ruh al-Ma'ani*, v. 1, 417.

33  See 62:9.

34  al-Qushayri, *Lata'if al-Isharat*, v. 1, 137–38.

35  al-Bukhari, "Al-Tawhid," 50; Muslim, "Al-Tawba," 1.

36  al-Bukhari, "Al-Iman," 39.

37  Muslim, "Al-Birr," 32.

38  Ismail Hakki Buresvi, *Ruh al-Bayan*, v. 6: 34.

39  This is linguistically related in the Jewish and Christian concept of *Shekinah*, though they not entirely equivalent.

40  For a detailed examination of the story of Qarun, see Zeki Saritoprak, "The Story of Qarun (Korah) in the Qur'an and Its Importance for Our Times," *Poverty and Wealth in Judaism, Christiantiy, and Islam*, eds. Nathan Kollar and Muhammad Shafiq (New York: Palgrave MacMillian, 2016): 23–30.

41  Ibn Abi Shayba, *Al-Musannaf*, v. 6 (Riyadh: Maktaba al-Rushd, 1409H): 25.

42  Ahmad bin Hanbal, *Al-Musnad*, ed. Shu'ayb al-Arnaut, et al., v. 24, 246.

43  Nursi, "Sozler," 160.

44  Ibid., 156. For additional details on Nursi's understanding of love, see "Sozler," 156–60 and 292–93.

45  Ibid.

46  al-Bukhari, "Al-Riqaq," 38.

47  al-Qushayri, *Lata'if al-Isharat*, v. 3, 765.

48  al-Bukhari, "Al-Da'awat," 21.

49  Ibn Kathir, *Al-Tafsir*, v. 5, 152.

50  Similar verses are 40:55 and 50:39.

51  Abu Bakr Ahmad bin al-Hasan al-Bayhaqi, *Shu'ab al-Iman*, v. 1 (Riyadh: Maktabat al-Rushd, 2003): 261.

52  Ibid., v. 7, 132.

# Chapter 5

1  al-Ghazali, *Ihya 'Ulum al-Din*, v. 2 (Beirut: Dar al-Marifa, n.d.): 35.

2  Ibid., 236.

3  al-Ghazali, *Al-Munqidh min al-Dalal*, ed. 'Abd al-Halim Mahmud (Cairo: Dar al-Kutub al-Hadith, 1965): 173–74.

4  Shams al-Din Abu Abdillah Muhammad al-Dhahabi, *Siyar A'lam al-Nubala*, v. 14 (Cairo: Dar al-Hadith, 2006): 268.

5  Ibid.

6  Muhammad bin Abdillah Abu Bakr bin al-Arabi. *Al-'Awasim min al-Qawasim*, ed. Muhib al-Din al-Khatib (Riyadh: Wazara al-Shu'un al-Islamiyya wa al-Awqaf, 1419 AH): 21.

7  al-Ghazali, *Tahafut al-Falasifa*, ed. Sulaiman Dunya (Cairo: Dar al-Ma'arif, 1961): 308.

8  al-Ghazali, *Mishkat al-Anwar*, ed. Abu al-'Ula al-Afifi (Cairo: al-Dar al-Qawmiyya, n.d.): 73–74, and al-Ghazali, *Fada'ih al-Batiniyya*, ed. Abdel Rahman Badawi (Kuwait: Muassasat Dar al-Kutub al-Thaqafiyya, n.d.): 51–109. A useful recent English translation of *Mishkat al-Anwar* is *The Niche of Lights*, trans. David Buchman (Provo: BYU Press, 1998).

9  al-Ghazali, *Al-Munqidh min al-Dalal*, 121. A good English translation with annotations is *Freedom and Fulfillment: an Annotated Translation of*

*Al-Ghazālī's al-Munqidh Min Al-Dalāl and Other Relevant Works of Al-Ghazālī*, trans. Richard J. McCarthy, SJ (Boston: Twayne, 1980).

10  Ibid., 124.

11  al-Ghazali, *Freedom and Fulfillment*, 6.

12  Ibid., 7. In the Arabic version, this quote is found on page 127.

13  Ibid., 18.

14  Ibid.

15  Ibid.

16  al-Ghazali, *The Alchemy of Happiness*, trans. Claud Field, revised and annotated Elton Daniel (London and Armonk, NY: ME Sharp, 1991): 13–14.

17  Ibid., 6–7.

18  Ibid., 12.

19  al-Ghazali, *Ihya 'Ulum al-Din*, v. 1, 319.

20  Ibid., 324.

21  Though it is beyond the scope of this chapter, al-Ghazali has important things to say on death. A good account of this is found in his *The Remembrance of Death and the Afterlife,* or *Kitab Dhikr al-Mawt wa-Maba'dahu.* Book XL of *The Revival of the Religious Sciences*, trans T. J. Winter (Cambridge: The Islamic Text Society, 1989).

22  al-Ghazali, *Ihya 'Ulum al-Din*, v. 1, 330.

23  Twice the Qur'an specifically mentions the Prophet's prayers at night. "And during a part of the night, pray an additional prayer beyond that which is prescribed for you; maybe your Lord will raise you to the position of *Maqam Mahmud* [the highest station in Paradise and the place of intersession on the Day of Judgment]" (17:79) and, "Surely your Lord knows that you and a group of those with you spend nearly two-thirds of the night, and [or] half of it, and [or] a third of it, in prayer. And God determines the night and the day. He knows that you are not able to do it, so He has turned to you. Therefore read what is easy of the Qur'an. He knows that there must be among you sick, and others who travel in the land seeking of the bounty of God, and others who fight in God's way, therefore read as much of it as is easy and establish the prayers and pay zakat and give for God a beautiful loan, and whatever of good you put on your soul, you will find it with God; that is best and greatest in reward; and ask forgiveness from God; surely God is All-Forgiving, All-Merciful" (73:20).

24  al-Ghazali, *Ihya 'Ulum al-Din*, v. 1, 346.

25  For a translation of *Ihya 'Ulum al-Din* which focuses on this issue, see: al-Ghazali, *Abstinence in Islam*, trans. Caesar E. Farah (Minneapolis: Bibliotheca Islamica, 1992).

26  al-Ghazali, *Ihya 'Ulum al-Din*, v. 3, 80.

27  Ibid., v. 3, 3.

28  Ibid., v. 4, 2.

29  Ibid.

30  Ibid., 5.

31  Ibid.

32  Ibid., 7.

33  Ibid., 51.

34  Ibid.

35  Ibid., 67.

36  Ibid., 76.

37  Ibid., 80.

38  Ibid., 83.

39  Ibid.

40  Ibid.

41  Ibid., 84.

42  Ibid., 40.

43  Ibid., 143.

44  Ibid., 145.

45  Ibid., 146.

46  Ibid., 217.

47  Ibid., 244.

48  Ibid., 247.

49  Ibid., 344.

50  Ibid., 362.

51  Ibid., 544.

52  Al-Ghazali, *Al-Maqsad al-Asna fi Sharh Asmai Allah al-Husna*, ed. Bassam Abd al-Wahhab al-Jabi (Cyprus: al-Jifan wa al-Jabi, 1987): 62.

# Chapter 6

1  Bediuzzaman Said Nursi, *The Words*, trans. Sukran Vahide (Istanbul: Sozler Nesriyat, 1992): 511. I have at points through this chapter used this translation as the basis for my own translation with modifications. Instances thus will have this reference.

2  Bediuzzaman Said Nursi, "Sozler," 141.

3  Bediuzzaman Said Nursi, "Mektubat," 503.

4  Ibid., 561.

5  Ibid., 562.

6  *The Treatise on Sincerity* can be found as the 20th and 21st Flash.

7  One version of this is published as *Hizb al-Haqa'iq al-Nuriyya*, or *Section of the Truths of the* Light, referring to Nursi's *Treatises of Light*. See: Bediuzzaman Said Nursi, *Hizb al-Haqa'iq al-Nuriyya* (Istanbul: Nesil Yayinlari, 2003).

8  Bediuzzaman Said Nursi, *The Words*, 320.

9  Ibid., 319.

10  Nursi, "Sozler," 143–44.

11  Nursi, *The Words*, 697.

12  Nursi, "Maktubat," 359.

13  Abu Muhammad al-Husayn bin Mas'ud bin Muhammad al-Baghawi, *Sharh al-Sunnah*, ed. Shu'ayb al-Arnaut and Muhammad Zuhair al-Shawish, v. 5 (Beirut: Al-Maktaba al-Islami: 1983): 36.

14  Fakhr al-Din Muhammad bin Umar al-Razi, *Mafatih al-Ghayb*, v. 1 (Beirut: Dar Ihya al-Turath al-Arabi, 1420AH): 110–11.

15  Ibid., v. 32, 229.

16  Ismail Hakki Bursevi, *Ruh al-Bayan*, v. 1: 338.

17  Bediuzzaman Said Nursi, "Lem'alar," 30.

18  Ibid.

19  al-Darami, *Al-Sunan*, "Al-Wudu," 3.

20  Nursi, "Lemalar," 579–80.

21  Ibid., 580.

22  al-Bukhari, "Al-Adhan," 155. Versions of this occur elsewhere in al-Bukhari, in Muslim, and in various other sources.

23  This and the following references can all be found in Nursi, "Mektubat," 449–51 and Bediuzzaman Said Nursi, *The Letters*, trans. Sukran Vahide (Istanbul: Sozler Nesriyat, 1992): 261–68.

24  Nursi "Lem'alar," 692. In the English version this is the twenty-fifth Flash.

25  Ibid.

26  Ibid., 695.

27  Ibid., 449.

28  Ibid.

29  Ibid., 449–50.

30  Ibid., 450.

31  Ibid.

32  Ibid.

33  Ibid.

34  Ibid., 451.

35  Ibid.

36  Nursi, "Mektubat," 536. In the English translation, this is: *The Letters,* 453.

37  Nursi, "Lem'alar," 872. The entirety of the supplication is found from 865 to 872.

38  Ibid.

39  Ibid., 655.

40  Nursi, "Sozler," 83–84.

# Chapter 7

1 Nursi, "Lem'alar," 655.

2 Fethullah Gulen, *Prizma 2* (Izmir: Nil Yayinlari, 2012): 17. In this chapter I will be utilizing both the original Turkish versions and the English translations. Generally, I will use my own translation from the Turkish, but when the English seems to be sufficient, I will use it.

3 See Zeki Saritoprak, "Fethullah Gülen: A Sufi in His Own Way," in *Turkish Islam and the Secular State: The Gulen Movement,* ed. Hakan Yavuz (Syracuse: Syracuse University Press, 2003): 156–69.

4 Fethullah Gulen, *Kirik Testi 1* (Izmir: Nil Yayinlari, 2012): 215.

5 Fethullah Gulen, *Key Concepts in the Practice of Sufism,* trans. Ali Unal (Fairfax, VA: Fountain, 1999): 23–24. Gulen's quotation for Ibrahim Haqqi's *Marife name* is important. The book itself mentions the word "heart" more than seventy times. In one of them, Haqqi says, "It has been said that the hearts of God's servants are the place where God looks at. Therefore to clean it of anything other than God is better than any worship." Ibrahim Haqqi, *Marife name* (NP: Matbaa-i Ahmad Kamil, 1914): 10.

6 Fethullah Gulen, *Bayan* (Izmir: Nil Yayinlari, 2012): 192.

7 Martin Lings, *A Sufi Saint of the Twentieth Century* (Cambridge: The Islamic Text Society, 1993): 34.

8 Nursi, "The Words," 511.

9 Gulen, *Key Concepts*, xv.

10 al-Tirmidhi, *Al-Sunan*, "Al-Birr," 55. The formal title of the work is *Al-Jami al-Sahih*, but it is known and generally published under the former title.

11 Fethullah Gulen, *Sonsuz Nur,* v. 1 (Izmir: Nil Yayinlari, 2012): 303–04.

12 On the account of Ibn Hisham of this event, see Michael A. Sells, *Early Islamic Mysticism* (New York, Mahwah: Paulist Press, 1996): 54–56.

13 Muslim, "Al-Salat," 215.

14 Sefik Can, *Fundamentals of Rumi's Thought: A Mevlevi Sufi Perspective*, ed. and trans. Zeki Saritoprak (Somerset, NJ: The Light, 2005): x.

15 Gulen, *Key Concepts*, xiv.

16 Ibid., xxv.

17 Gulen, *Kalbin Zümrüt Tepeleri,* v. 1 (Izmir: Nil Yayinlari, 1998): 14. Qur'anic verses: 24:31, 39:54, 38:44 and 50:33 are the origins of these stages, according to Gulen.

18 Gulen, *Key Concepts*, 6.

19 Ibn Abi Shayba, *Al-Musannaf*, v. 7, 96. The full version of this is: "Question yourself before being questioned and examine yourself before being examined and adorn yourself for the biggest exhibition [the afterlife]. When you are exposed, nothing of you can be hidden."

20  Abu Hamid Muhammad al-Ghazali, *The Alchemy of Happiness*, trans. Elton L. Daniel (London and New York: M. E. Sharpe Inc, 1991): 5. The section from al-Ghazali on the self is from pp. 5–15.

21  Gulen, *Key Concepts*, 7.

22  al-Bukhari, "Al-Kusuf," 2.

23  Gulen, *Kalbin Zümrüt Tepeleri*, v. 1, 24–28.

24  Gulen, *Key Concepts*, 12.

25  Fethullah Gulen, *Fasildan Fasila I* (Izmir: Nil Yayinlari, 1995): 25.

26  Muslim, "Al-Birr," 33.

27  Gulen, *Key Concepts*, 23.

28  Ibid., 153.

29  Besides his book *Sufism,* in the following books Gulen addresses the subject further: *Questions and Answers About Faith* (Fairfax, VA: The Fountain, 2000); *Prophet Muhammad: Aspects of his Life* (Fairfax, VA: The Fountain, 2000); *Criteria or the Lights of the Way* (Izmir: Kaynak Yayinlari, 1998); *Towards the Lost Paradise* (Izmir: Kaynak Yayinlari, 1998).

30  al-Bukhari, "Bad' al-Khalq," 8.

31  Jalaluddin Rumi, *The Mathnawi of Jalalu'ddin Rumi*, trans. Reynold A. Nicholson, book V (Cambridge: E. J. W. Gibb Memorial Trust, 1990): 24, verse 363.

32  See Ahmad bin Hanbal, *Al-Musnad*, v. 18, 250.

33  Fethullah Gulen, *The Emerald Hills of the Heart: Key Concepts in the Practice of Sufism*, v. 2 (Somerset, NJ: Tughra Books, 2007). The full text is available online at http://fgulen.com/en/fethullah-gulens-works/1358-key-concepts-in-the-practice-of-sufism-2/25734-ithar-altruism.

34  Ibid.

35  Ibid.

36  Ibid. and found at http://fgulen.com/en/fethullah-gulens-works/1358-key-concepts-in-the-practice-of-sufism-2/25746-fana-fillah-annihilation-in-god.

37  Fethullah Gulen, *The Emerald Hills of the Heart: Key Concepts in the Practice of Sufism*, v. 4 (Somerset, NJ: Tughra Books, 2010). The full text is available online at http://fgulen.com/en/fethullah-gulens-works/sufism/key-concepts-in-the-practice-of-sufism-4/47769-the-all-beautiful-names-of-god.

38  Gulen, *Key Concepts*, vii.

39  al-Bukhari, "Al-Tawhid," 32.

40  al-Bukhari, "Al-Fada'il," 5.

41  http://www.independent.co.uk/news/uk/home-news/most-popular-baby-names-2015-england-wales-muhammad-mohammed-mohammad-muhammed-a7222191.html. See also: https://www.thesun.co.uk/news/1720444/mohammed-not-oliver-tops-list-of-most-popular-uk-boys-names-if-you-add-up-all-the-different-spellings/

42  Muslim, "Al-Fada'il," 145.

43 al-Makki, *Qut al-Qulub*, ed. Asim Ibrahim al-Kiyali, v. 1 (Beirut: Dar al-Kutub al-Ilmiyya, 2005): 105.

44 al-Ghazali, *Ihya*, v. 3, 2426.

45 Rumi refers to the Cave of Hira, when the Prophet and his companion Abu Bakr were escaping from the persecution of the idol worshippers of Mecca on their way to Medina. Waiting in the cave, Abu Bakr was afraid, and the Prophet's famous statement was, "Do not be afraid. God is with us."

46 Sefik Can, *Fundamentals of Rumi's Thought*, 161–62. *Divan-i Kabir*, v. 2, 901.

47 William Chittick, *The Sufi Path of Love: The Spiritual Teachings of Rumi*, (Albany: SUNY Press, 1983) has a good section on love in Rumi on pages 194–231.

48 Seyh Galib, *Husn u Ask*, ed. Muhammet Nur Dogan (Istanbul: Otuken Nesriyat, 2002): 25-31.

49 Gulen, *Al-Qulub al-Dari*, 534–54.

50 Ismail bin Muhammad al-Ajluni, *Kashf al-Khafa wa Muzilu al-Ilbas*, ed. Abd al-Hamid bin Hindawi, v. 2 (Beirut: Al-Maktaba al-Asriyya, 2000): 232.

51 al-Alusi, *Ruh al-Ma'ani*, v. 18, 199.

52 Gulen, *Prophet Muhammad: Aspects of His Life*, xvi.

53 Ibid.

54 Abd al-Razzaq al-San'ani, *Al-Musannaf*, ed. Habib al-Rahman al-A'zami, v. 5 (Beirut: Al-Maktab al-Islami, 1403H): 353.

55 Fethullah Gulen, *Kirik Mizrap* (Istanbul: Nil Yayinlari, 2005), 88–89.

56 Kitmir is the name of the dog of the People of the Cave, who are better known in the Christian tradition as the Seven Sleepers. Gulen is calling himself Kitmir, which is considered an act of humbness.

57 Gulen, *Kirik Mizrap*, 90–91.

58 Gulen here is not implying that the Qur'an is the word of the Prophet, he is only indicating the closeness of the Prophet to the Word of God. Or to put it another way, the Qur'an was always on the Prophet's tongue.

59 Gulen, *Kirik Mizrap*, 92–93.

60 Ibid., 94–95.

61 Ibid., 100–01.

62 Ibn 'Ata Allah and Kwaja Abdullah Ansari, *The Book of Wisdom* and *Intimate Conversations*, trans. Victor Danner and Wheeler M. Thackston (New York: Paulist Press, 1978): 206.

63 Ibid., xv–xvi. This is from the book's preface written by Annemarie Schimmel.

64 Gulen, *Kirik Mizrap*, 337–38.

65 Ibid., 107.

66 Ibid., 340–41.

67 Gulen, *Fasildan Fasila*, v. 4, 35.

68 In a version of a similar story the Prophet says, "I eat as slaves eat. I sit as slaves sit. That is because I am a slave [of God]." Ma'mar bin Rashid al-Azdi, *Al-Jami'*, ed. Habib al-Rahman al-A'zami, v. 10 (Beirut: Al-Maktab al-Islami, 1403H): 415.

69 Gulen, *Prizma*, v. 2, 169.

# Chapter 8

1 Muslim, "Al-Zuhd," 53.

2 Ibid., 33 and al-Bukhari, "Al-At'ima," 23.

3 Waki' bin al-Jarrah, *Al-Zuhd*, ed. Abd al-Rahman al-Fariwai (Medina: Maktaba al-Dar, 1984): 338.

4 Ibid., 777. In Ahmad bin Hanbal's version of this hadith, "'Aisha says, 'I was riding a difficult camel, I used to hit him.' The Prophet said, 'Stick to tenderness. Anything where tenderness is involved would be beautiful. Whenever tenderness leaves it, it becomes ugly.'" Ahmad bin Hanbal, *Al-Musnad*, v. 41 415.

5 Abu Abd al-Rahman al-Sulami, *'Uyub al-Nafs*, ed. Majdi Fath al-Sayyid (Tanta: Maktaba al-Sahaba, n.d.).

6 al-Bayhaqi, *Kitab al-Zuhd al-Kabir*, ed. Amir Ahmad Haydar (Beirut: Muassasat al-Kutub al-Thaqafiyya, 1996): 95.

7 Ibid., 96.

8 See for instance the descriptions at http://www.islamicity.com/forum/printer_friendly_posts.asp?TID=16427 which includes both the steps of ablution and the transliteration of the Arabic components of the five daily prayers.

9 Muslim, "Al-Siyam," 38.

10 Generally, slightly more than half of the verse is recited in the first unit and the rest is recited in the second unit, as it is recommended that the first be longer than the second.

11 Muslim, "Salat al-Musafirin," 44.

12 Abu Muhammad al-Husayn al-Baghawi, *Sharh al-Sunnah*, ed. Shu'ayb al-Arnaout, et al., v. 5 (Beirut: al-Maktab al-Islami, 1983): 95.

13 Al-Bukhari, "Al-Ilm," 11.

14 Nursi has an important discussion of the *Tashahhud* in his *Rays* collection. See Bediuzzaman Said Nursi, *The Rays*, trans. Sukran Vahide (Istanbul: Sozler Publication, 1998): 110–122 and 610–14.

15 This prayer can be found in Gulen, *Al-Qulub al-Daria*, 222–23.

16 al-Bukrahi, "Al-Sawm," 60.

17 al-Ghazali, *Ihya*, v. 3, 66.

18 Abd al-Qadir al-Jilani, *Al-Ghunya li Talib al-Haqq*, ed. Abu Abd al-Rahman Salah bin Muhammad, v. 2 (Beirut: Dar al-Kutub al-Ilmiyya, 1997): 155.

19 al-Bukhari, "Al-Iman," 25.

20  Muslim, "Sifat al-Qiyama," 18.

21  For an explanation of this see the fifth point of the 23rd Word of Said Nursi.

22  Ibn al-'Athir Ali bin Muhammad al-Jazari, *'Usd al-Ghaba fi Ma'rifat al-Sahaba*, ed. Ali Muhammad Mu'awwad, v. 1 (Beirut: Dar al-Kutub al-Ilmiyya, 1994): 152.

23  Gulen, *Al-Qulub al-Daria*, 280–82.

24  Abu al-Walid Sulaiman bin Khalaf al-Baji, *Al-Muntaqa Sharh al-Muwatta*, v. 6 (Cairo: Matbaat al-Saada, 1332H): 125. The authenticity of this particular hadith is debated, but there is consensus as to the meaning.

25  al-Bayhaqi, *Fada'il al-Awqat* (Mecca: Maktaba al-Manara, 1410H): 498.

26  Abd al-Malik bin Hisham, *Al-Sira al-Nabawiyya*, ed. Mustafa al-Saqqa, et al., v. 1 (Cairo: Maktaba Mustafa al-Babi al-Halabi, 1955): 500.

27  Phonetically, based on the transliteration style I use in this book, it should be Jumu'a. However, as Jumu'ah is the most common way of referring to the Friday Prayer, I have kept the "h" here. Also, Jumma(h), is often used in English, but there is no linguistic basis for the extra "m."

# Chapter 9

1  There are many versions of this story. One can be found at https://yunusuemre.wordpress.com/2006/12/18/yunus-emre-ve-hocasi-tabduk-emre/

2  Ali bin Muhammad Nur al-Din al-Qari, *Mirqat al-Mafatih*, v. 1 (Beirut: Dar al-Fikr, 2002): 199.

3  This Divine name is found in the following Qur'anic verses: 13:16, 15:28, 35.3, 38:71, 39:62, 40:62, and 59:24.

4  Other similar verses are: 13:2, 29:61, 31:29, 35:13, and 39:5.

5  For references to *al-Hayy,* see 2:255, 3:2, 20:111, 25:58, 40:65.

6  Ibrahim bin 'Umar al-Biqa'i, *Nazm al-Durar fi Tanasub al-Ayat wa al-Suwar*, v. 17 (Cairo: Dar al-Kitab al-Islami, n.d.): 192.

7  Quoted in Ibrahim Ozdemir, "Towards an Understanding of Environmental Ethics from a Qur'anic Perspective," in *Islam and Ecology: A Bestowed Trust*, ed. Richard C. Foltz, Frederick M. Denny, and Azizan Baharuddin (Cambridge, MA: Harvard University Press, 2003): 22.

8  See Ali Duran Gulcicek, "Alevi-Bektasi Edabiyatinda Doga Sevgisi," *Turk Kulturu ve Haci Bektad Veli Arastirma Dergisi,* Issue 22 (2002): http://hbvdergisi.gazi.edu.tr/index.php/TKHBVD/article/view/513/503.

9  Ahmed bin Hanbal, *Al-Musnad*, v. 3, 281.

10  Similar verses include: 14:32, 16:65, 20:53, 22:63.

11  al-Bukhari, "Al-Tayammum," 1.

12  For the Divine name *al-Tahir,* see Abu Abdillah Muhammad al-Qurtubi, *Al-Asna fi Sharh Asmai Allahi al-Husna wa Sifatihi*, ed. Irfan bin Salim (Beirut: al-Maktaba al-'Asriyya, 2005): 221–22.

13  Ibn Maja, "Al-Libas," 23.

**14** Generally *tahhira* indicates spiritual and physical cleanliness. Many commentators use this word here to mean only cleanliness from idols, but I interpret this verse as including physical cleanliness as well.

**15** al-Bukhari, "Al-Zakat," 54.

**16** See Ibn Maja, "Al-Adhan," 5.

**17** Waki' bin al-Jarrah, *Al-Zuhd*, 474.

**18** Cited in Ian G. Barbour, *Religion in an Age of Science: The Gifford Lectures, 1989–91*, v. 1 (San Francisco: Harper, 1990): 245.

**19** Nursi, "Lem'alar," 824.

**20** Ahmad bin Hanbal, *Al-Musnad*, v. 20: 251.

**21** al-Bukhari, "Al-Muzara'a," 1.

# APPENDICES

## Appendix 1

### Qur'anic prayer samples

The following are verses from the Qur'an that start with either "My Lord" or "Our Lord." They are generally the prayers of prophets or other named figures in the Qur'an said on a specific occasion or in relation to a specific story. I have not provided the context for them, but it is clear if one looks at the surrounding verses. I have chosen to omit specific information about each individual prayer, but this information can be readily found.

"Our Lord, and make both of us *muslims* to You and from our descendants a *muslim* community to You. And show us our rites and accept our repentance. Surely, You are the Most-Accepting of repentance, the Most-Merciful." (2:128)

"Our Lord, and send among them a messenger from themselves who will recite to them Your verses and will teach them the Book and wisdom and purify them. Surely, You are the All-Mighty, the All-Wise." (2:129)

"Our Lord, give us in this world good and in the afterlife good and protect us from the chastisement of the Fire." (2:201)

"Our Lord, pour out upon us patience and firm our feet and help us against the people who are disbelievers." (2:250)

"Our Lord, do not hold us accountable if we forget or make a mistake. Our Lord, do not lay upon us a burden like You laid upon those before us. Our Lord, do not burden us with what we are unable to bear. And pardon us, and forgive us, and have mercy upon us. You are our Master, so help us against the people who are disbelievers." (2:286)

"Our Lord, do not let our hearts deviate after You have guided us and grant us mercy from Your presence. Surely, You are the Most-Giving. Our Lord, surely You are gathering the people for a day about which there is no doubt. Surely, God does not break His promise." (3:8-9)

"Our Lord, surely we have believed, so forgive for us our sins and protect us from the chastisement of the Fire." (3:16)

"Our Lord, we have believed in what You revealed and we have followed the messenger, so inscribe us among those who bear witness." (3:53; see also 5:83)

"Our Lord, forgive for us our sins and our wastefulness in our affairs and firm our feet and so help us against the people who are disbelievers." (3:147)

"Our Lord, You did not create this [the heavens and earth] aimlessly. Exalted are You. Then protect us from the chastisement of the Fire. Our Lord, surely whoever You put to the Fire, You have disgraced him, and for the wrongdoers there are no helpers. Our Lord, surely we have heard a caller calling for faith: 'Believe in your Lord,' and we have believed. Our Lord, forgive for us our sins and expiate our misdeeds and allow us to die with the righteous. Our Lord, and grant us what You promised us through Your messengers and do not disgrace us on the Day of Resurrection. Surely, You do not break Your promise." (3:191-194)

"Our Lord, we have wronged our souls, and if You do not forgive us and have mercy on us, definitely we will be among the losers." (7:23)

"Our Lord, do not make us among the people who are wrongdoers." (7:47)

"Our Lord encompasses everything in knowledge. On God we have trusted. Our Lord, judge among us and our people with truthfulness, and You are the Best of the decision makers." (7:89)

"Our Lord, pour out upon us patience and allow us to die as *muslims*." (7:126)

"Our Lord, do not make us objects of the trial for the people who are wrongdoers." (10:85)

"Our Lord, surely You know what we hide and what we disclose, and nothing hides from God either on the earth or in heaven." (14:38)

"My Lord, make me constantly fulfilling of my prayer and my offspring, too. Our Lord, and accept my prayer. Our Lord, forgive me and my parents and all believers on the day when the account is realized." (14:40-41)

"Our Lord, grant us from Your presence a mercy and better our affairs for us with guidance." (18:10)

"Our Lord, we have believed, so forgive us and have mercy upon us, and for You are the Best of the merciful those who show mercy." (23:109)

"Our Lord, avert us from the chastisement of Hell. Surely, the chastisement of it is constant." (25:65)

"Our Lord, give us from among our spouses and our offspring the apple of our eyes and make us examples for the righteous." (25:74)

"Our Lord, You have encompassed everything in mercy and knowledge. Forgive those who have repented and followed Your path and protect them from the chastisement of Hell. Our Lord, and put them in gardens of Eden, the ones You have promised them and whoever was righteous among their fathers, their spouses, and their offspring. Surely, it is You who are the Most-Honorable, the Most-Wise." (40:7-8)

"Our Lord, forgive us and our brethren who preceded us in faith and do not put in our heart jealousy for those who believe. Our Lord, Surely You are the Most-Benevolent, the Most-Merciful." (59:10)

"Our Lord, in You we trust, and to You we return, and to You is the final return. Our Lord, do not make us objects of the trial of the disbelievers and forgive us, our Lord. Surely, You are the Most-Honorable, the Most-Wise." (60:4-5)

"Our Lord, complete for us our light and forgive us. Surely, You are the Most-Powerful over everything." (66:8)

"My Lord, grant me from Your presence a pure child. Surely, You are the Most-Hearing of prayer." (3:38)

"My Lord, forgive me and my brother and enter us in to Your mercy. You are the Most-Merciful of the merciful." (7:151)

"My Lord, You have given me some sovereignty and You taught me of the interpretation of dreams. O Creator of the heavens and earth, You are my Master in this world and in the afterlife. Allow me to die a *muslim* and include me among the people who are wholesome." (12:101)

"My Lord, have mercy on them [my parents] as they raised me [with mercy] when I was small." (17:24)

"My Lord, help me to enter an entrance of righteousness and help me exit with an exit of righteousness and maker for me from Your presence a helping power." (17:80)

"My Lord, surely my bones have weakened, and my head has become white with age, and never have I been disobedient in my prayer to You, my Lord." (19:4)

"My Lord, expand for me my heart and ease for me my task and untie the knot from my tongue so that they may understand my word." (20:25-28)

"My Lord, increase me in knowledge." (20:114)

"My Lord, do not leave me childless. You are the Best of inheritors." (21:89)

"My Lord, judge with truthfulness and our Lord is the Most-Compassionate and the Helper on things which you describe." (21:112)

"My Lord, let me disembark at a blessed place and You are the Best of those who allow disembarkation." (23:29)

"My Lord, then do not place me among the people who are wrongdoers." (23:94)

"My Lord, I seek refuge in You from the incitements of the devils. And I take refuge in You, my Lord, from their presence with me." (23:97-98)

"My Lord, forgive and have mercy and You are the Best of the merciful." (23:118)

"My Lord, grant me wisdom and include me among the righteous." (26:83)

"My Lord, inspire me to thank You for Your bounties which You have bestowed upon me and upon my parents and [inspire] me to do wholesome deeds which You will be pleased with. And enter me with Your mercy among Your wholesome servants." (27:19)

"My Lord, surely I have wronged my soul, and I submit myself with Solomon to God, Lord of the worlds." (27:44)

"'My Lord, surely I have wronged my soul, so forgive me,' and He forgave him. Indeed, He is the Most-Forgiving, the Most-Merciful. He said, 'My Lord, for the bounties You bestowed upon me, I will never be a support for the criminals.'" (28:16-17)

"My Lord, surely I am poor in the things You have sent down to me of goods." (28:24)

"My Lord, support me against the people who are corrupters." (29:30)

"My Lord, inspire me to thank You for Your bounties which You have bestowed upon me and upon my parents and [inspire] me to do wholesome deeds which You will be pleased with and make wholesomeness for me in my offspring. Surely, I have repented to You and I am of the *muslims*." (46:15)

"My Lord, forgive for me and for my parents and for those who entered my house as believers and for all the believing men and the believing women and do not increase the wrongdoers except in ruin." (71:28)

# Appendix 2

## Selected prayers of the Prophet

The following are samples from the prayers said by the Prophet in the morning and in the evening.

This prayer was said in the morning and is known, in the Hadith literature, as the master statement for asking for forgiveness: "O my God! You are my Lord, there is no deity but You. You created me and I am your servant. I keep Your covenant and my promise to You as much as I can. I take refuge in You from the evil things that I have committed. I confess to You with Your bounties upon me. And I confess to You with my sins. Forgive me. Surely no one can forgive sins but You." (al-Bukhari, "Al-Da'awat," 2)

This is the prayer the Prophet said before sleeping or going to bed, and of it he said, "When you go to your bed take ritual cleansing as you do for your prayers, then lie on your right side and say" "O God, I have submitted my soul to You. I have relied on You in my matters. I have sought recourse in You to be supported by You while in yearning and awe of You. There is no recourse and no place of safety from You except in You. I believed in the Book you have revealed and in the Prophet You have sent." (al-Bukhari, "Al-Da'awat," 6)

Another narration says that the Prophet used to say the following before going to bed: "My God, You created me and You take my soul. My life is with You and my death is with You. If You revive me in the morning, protect me. If You take my soul while in sleep, forgive me. My God I surely ask You for a healthy life" (Muslim, "Al-Dhikr," 17)

When the Prophet went to bed he would say "Lord in Your name I die and in Your name I am resurrected." When he woke up, he would say, "Praise be to God the One who resurrected us after our sleep. And the return is to God." (al-Bukhari, "Al-Da'awat," 7)

This is the prayer the Prophet said before the Morning Prayer, after having awoken from a nap: "O God, bring light to my heart, light to my eyes, light to my ears, light to my right, light to my left, light above me, light under me, light before me, light after me and bring a light for me." (al-Bukhari, "Al-Da'awat," 10)

On same occasion, the Prophet also had this prayer: "O God, praise be to You! You are the Light of heavens and earth and everything in them. And praise be to You! You are the Sustainer of the heavens and the earth and what is in them. And praise be to You! You are the Truth. Your promise is true. Your word is true. Meeting with You is true. Paradise is true and Hell is true and the Hour is true. All prophets are true and Muhammad is true. O God! To You I have submitted. In You I have trusted. And in You I have believed and to You I have returned. And with Your help I have struggled. And to You I have returned for judgment. Forgive me what I have done in the past and what I will do in the future. And what I have done secretly and what I have done openly. You are the Advancer and the Delayer. There is no deity except You." (al-Bukhari, "Al-Da'awat," 10)

In times of sadness the Prophet had this prayer: "There is no deity but God, the Majestic, the Most-Gentle. There is no deity but God, the Lord of the majestic Throne. There is no deity but God, the Lord of heavens and earth and the Lord of the kind Throne." (al-Bukhari, "Al-Da'awat," 27)

In the morning and in the evening the Prophet would say this prayer: "O God! I take refuge in You from worries and sadness. And I take refuge in You from weakness and laziness. And I take refuge in You from cowardice and stinginess. I take refuge in You from the heavy burden of debts and from the coercion of wrongdoers." (al-Bukhari, "Al-Da'awat," 35)

Again in the morning, the Prophet would say this prayer: "O God! I take refuge in You from laziness and from the difficulties of aging and from debt and from sins. O God! I take refuge in You from the trial of the Fire and from the chastisement of the Fire and from the trial of the grave and from the trial of wealth and poverty. O God! I take refuge in you from the evil of the trial of the Antichrist. O God! Wash out my mistakes and faults with water of snow and hail. And clean my heart as white clothing is cleaned from dirt. And make distance between me and my sins as You made distance between sunrise and sunset." (al-Bukhari, "Al-Da'awat" 37)

Another prayer the Prophet said "when entering the morning": "O God! I ask You for health in this world and the afterlife. O God! I ask You for forgiveness and health in my religion, in my world, in my family, in my property. O God! Cover my deficits and make me safe from my fears. O God! Protect me from [the dangers] in front of me and from behind me and from right of me and left of me and from above me. And I take refuge in Your mightiness [from the danger] from below me." (Abu Dawud, "Al-Adab" 110)

On one occasion the Prophet said, "Do you want me to inform you about the most beloved phrase to God?... the most beloved phrase to God is 'Subhan Allah wa Bihamdih,' [Exalted is God with God's praise.]" (Muslim, "Al-Dhikr" 22).

One of the most frequently used phrases by the Prophet was this: "Our Lord grant us good in this world and good in the afterlife and protect us from the chastisement of Fire." (Muslim, "Al-Dhikr," 9. This is a verse from the Qur'an. See 2:201.)

In addition to "Bismillah al-Rahman al-Rahim," said before eating, the Prophet used to have special prayers said after eating. He would say, "Praise be to God who fed us and who quenched our thirst and made us among the muslims." (al-Tirmidhi, "Al-Da'awat," 55)

Another version of the prayer which the Prophet said in the morning after waking up before starting his day: "Praise be to God who revived us after He caused us to die. To Him is the return." (al-Darimi, "Al-Isti'dhan," 53)

The Prophet's prayer for his daughter Fatima and her husband Ali can be found in the Qur'anic verse: "Surely God wishes to remove uncleanness from you, O Family of the Prophet, and cleanse you with a perfect cleansing." (33:33) The Prophet called Fatima, Ali, and their two sons Hasan and Husayn, and covered them with a cloak and said, "O God! These are the people of my family and are special to me. Cleanse them from their dirt and make them thoroughly purified." (al-Tirmidhi, "Al-Manaqib," 130)

On one occasion, a man came to the Prophet and said, "I cannot learn the Qur'an. Teach me something short that suffices me." The Prophet replied, "Say, 'Subhan Allah,' 'Alhamdulillah,' 'La ilaha illa Allah,' 'Allahu Akbar,' and 'la hawla wa la quwwata illa Billah al-Aliyy al-Azim.' [There is no power and no strength except with God, the Almighty and Majestic.]" The man said, "This is all for God. What is for me?" The Prophet responded, "Say, 'O God! Bestow upon me Your mercy, give me my sustenance, give me health, and guide me to the way of righteousness.'" (Abu Dawud, "Al-Salat," 139)

Abu al-Darda, one of the Prophet's companions, narrates that the Prophet used to have what he called "The Prayer of David:" "O God!, I ask you for Your love and the love of those who love You. And I ask for the work that will lead me to Your love. O God! Make Your love more beloved to me than even myself, my family, and cold water [in the desert]." (al-Tirmidhi, "Al-Da'awat," 75)

The Prophet had a special prayer for health: "O God! I ask You for health in this world and the afterlife." (al-Tirmidhi, "Al-Da'awat," 84)

In a different statement, he says to his companions, "Ask God for forgiveness and health. Surely none of you have been given anything more important than health after certainty of faith." (al-Tirmidhi, "Al-Da'awat," 33)

This prayer was taught by the Prophet to his daughter, Fatima, and is one of the most commonly repeated prayers of the Prophet: "O the Most-Living One! O the Sustainer! With Your mercy I ask for help. Make my works wholesome. Do not make me rely on my soul, even for the twinkling of an eye." (al-Bayhaqi, Shu'ab al-Iman, v. 2, 212)

A well-known prayer of the Prophet when he returned from Ta'if, frustrated by the people of Ta'if's rejection of his request for refuge: "O God! I am complaining to You of the weakness of my power and my helplessness and my worthlessness in the eyes of people. O the Most-Merciful of the merciful! You are the Lord of the weak and You are my Lord. To whom are You entrusting me? To a faraway stranger who would be cruel to me or to an enemy by putting me in his control? If You are not angry with me I do not care about the difficulties I have faced. However, Your favor of health is more encompassing for me. I take refuge in the light of Your face that for it the darkness is enlightened and with it the matters of the world and the afterlife are settled. I take refuge in You from the sending of Your wrath against me or the occurring of Your anger to me. Everything belongs to You and there is no power and no ability except with You." (Abdul Malik bin Hisham al-Himyari, Sirah, ed. Mustafa al-Saqa, et al. v. 2 [Cairo: Mustafa al-Babi al-Halabi, 1955]: 268).

# Appendix 3

## The supplication of Uwais al-Qarani (d. 657)

In the name of God, the Most-Compassionate, the Most-Merciful. My God, You are my Lord and I am the servant. You are the Creator and I am the created. You are the Giver of sustenance and I am the receiver of sustenance. You are the Owner and I am the owned. You are the Majestic and I am the humbled. You are the Rich and I am the poor. You are the Living and I am the dead. You are the Eternal and I am the ephemeral. You are the Kind and I am the vile. You are the Beautifier and I am the uglifier. You are the Forgiver and I am the sinner. You the Great and I am the meek. You are the Powerful and I am the weak. You are the Giver and I am the beggar. You are the Trustworthy and I am the fearful. You are the Generous and I am the destitute. You are the Answerer and I am the caller. You are the Healer and I am the sick. Forgive for me my sins and absolve me with Your mercy. O the Most-Merciful of the merciful.

# Appendix 4

## The supplication of Zayn al-Abidin Ali bin al-Husayn (d. 713)

Among his many supplications, the following is what he calls the supplication of the *murids,* or the initiates.

In the name of God, the Most-Compassionate, the Most-Merciful. Exalted are You O God. How narrow are the ways of those whom You are not their Guide, and how clear is the truth in the sight of those You have guided to Your way. My God, then I ask You for the ways of reaching You, and that You make it easy for me to find the shortest way to come to You. Make for us the far one near and make easy for us what is difficult. And make us join with Your servants who are hastening towards You and who are knocking on Your door constantly and who are worshipping You at night and who are in awe of Your majesty. Those for whom You purified the fountains and You helped them to reach their goals and You made them successful in their requests and through Your bounties You provided their needs. And You filled up their hearts with Your love and You quenched their thirstiness with Your purified drink. With You they have reached to the taste of conversing with You and with You they have achieved the highest of their goals. O the One who returns to those who return to Him and with compassion toward them, return to them with bounties. And Merciful and Gentle with those who are heedless of His remembrance and by attracting them to His door, He is the Beloved and the Affectionate. I ask You to make me among those who have more shares in Your bounties and among those who have the closest station to You and among those who have the greatest of love's share from You and among those who have the best share of Your knowledge. All my efforts are toward You. My requests have turned to You. Only You and not anyone else is my wish and to You not to anything other than You are my nights and days. Meeting with You is the apple of my eye. My longing is towards You. My excitement is in Your love. Pleasing You is my request and my need. Being close to You is my request and closeness to You is all that I ask. In Your supplication is my companionship and my rest. With You is the medicine of my request and the cooling of my burning and the easing of my sorrows. Be my Friend in my wilderness. Be my Helper when I stumble. Be the Forgiver of my mistakes. Be the Accepter of my repentance. Be the Answerer of my call. Be the Master of my protection. Be the Enricher of my poverty. Do not cut my relationship with You. Do not make me away from You. O the One who is the Owner of my bounties and my paradise. O the Owner of my world and my afterlife.

# Appendix 5

## A supplication of Ibrahim bin Adham (d. 782)

Welcome with one more day and new morning. And welcome with the writing and witnessing angel. This day of ours is the day of the feast. Write for us what we say: In the name of God, the Most-Praiseworthy, the Most-Glorious, the Most-High, the Loving One, the One who is active in His creation and freely does what He wishes, I have entered in the morning as a believer in God and testifying my meeting with Him and confessing all proofs of His existence and asking for forgiveness of my sin and obeying the Lordship of God and denying all deities other than God and I am poor before God and I trust in God and I am returning to God. God is my witness and I am making His angels and His prophets and His messengers and those [angels] who are carrying His throne and all creation and the things that He is currently creating as my witness that He is God, there is no deity except Him and He is the One with no partners and that Muhammad is His servant and His messenger, peace and blessings be upon him, and that Paradise is true and that Hell is true and the Cistern of Paradise is true and intercession is true and the existence of the angels who would question people in the afterlife is true and Your promise of reward in the afterlife and promise of punishment in the afterlife are true and meeting with You is true. "And surely there is no doubt that the Hour will come and there is no doubt that God will resurrect who are in the graves." [Q 22:7] On this belief I live and on this belief I will die and on this belief I will be resurrected, God willing. O God! You are my Lord, there is no deity but You. You created me and I am your servant. I keep Your covenant and my promise to You as much as I can. I take refuge in You, O God, from any evil and from anything that has evil. O God! Surely I have wronged my soul. Forgive me for my sins. No one forgives sins except You. Guide me to a more beautiful ethic. Surely no one can guide to more a more beautiful ethic except You. Take me away from bad behaviors. No one can take away bad behaviors except You. I am obedient to You. All good things are in Your hands. I belong to You and come to You. I ask for forgiveness and I am repenting to You. O God! I have believed in all messengers that You have sent. I have believed in all scriptures that You have sent. Send Your mercy and blessing to Muhammad, the Prophet and to his family abundantly who is the end of my word and the key of my word. And send Your mercy and blessings to all Your prophets and messengers. O God, the Lord of the worlds, Amen. O God take us to the Cistern of Your Prophet and give us with his cup a drink that is healthy, easy, and removes our thirst that we will never become thirsty after that. And gather us in his group without humiliation and without breaking the promises that we gave You, without being in doubt and without trial, without receiving Your wrath upon us and without going astray. O God protect me from the trials of the world and make me successful in all things that You love and are pleased with. Make all matters that I am involved with wholesome and make me steadfast with the words that are steadfast in this world and in the afterlife. And do not allow me to go astray even if I am a wrongdoer. Exalted are You, O the Most-High, the Most-Majestic, O the Creator from nothing, the Most-Merciful, the Most-Honorable, the Omnipotent, the Most-Glorious. Exalted is the One the heavens glorify with their orbits. Exalted is the One the mountains glorify with their voices. Exalted is the One the seas glorify with their waves. Exalted is the One the fish glorify with their languages. Exalted is the One the stars of the sky glorify with their constellations. Exalted is the One the trees glorify with their roots, greenness, and fruits. Exalted is the One the seven heavens, the seven earths, what is in them and what is on them glorify. Exalted is the One everything glorifies, O the Most-Gracious. Exalted are You, there is no deity but You. You are One. You have no partner. In You we live and in You we die. And You are the Most-Living and You never die. "All good is in Your hands. You are Powerful over everything." [Q 3:26].

# SELECT BIBLIOGRAPHY

The following is a partial list of key, English language secondary sources and/or translations of primary texts for the study of Islamic spirituality. It should not be taken as a complete and authoritative list, but can be used as a guide for further study. This list should be considered in addition to the sources cited in the text.

Afifi al-Akiti, Muhammad. "The Three Properties of Prophethood in Certain Works of Avicenna and al-Ġazālī." In *Interpreting Avicenna: Science and Philosophy in Medieval Islam: Proceedings of the Second Conference of the Avicenna Study Group*. edited by John McGinnis and David C. Reisman, 189–212. Leiden: Brill, 2004.

Awn, Peter J. "Classical Sufi Approaches to Scripture." In *Mysticism and Sacred Scripture*. edited by Steven T. Katz, 138–52. Oxford: Oxford University Press, 2000.

Awn, Peter J. *Satan's Tragedy and Redemption: Iblīs in Sufi Psychology*. Leiden: Brill, 1983.

Ayoub, Mahmoud M. "The Prayer of Islam: A Presentation of Surat al-Fatiha in Muslim Exegesis." *Journal of the American Academy of Religion Thematic Studies* 47, no. 4 (D 1979): 635–47.

Barks, Coleman, trans. The Essential Rumi (New York: HarperOne, 2004)

Brinner, William M. "Prophet and Saint: The Two Exemplars of Islam." In *Saints and Virtues*. edited by John Stratton Hawley, 36–51. Berkeley: University of California Press, 1987.

Burrell, David. "Naming the Names of God: Muslims, Jews, Christians." *Theology Today* 47, no. 1 (April 1990): 22–29.

Burrell, David and Nazih Daher. *The Ninety-Nine Beautiful Names of God*. Cambridge: Islamic Texts Society, 1992.

Cornell, Vincent. The Realm of the Saint: Power and Authority in Moroccan Sufism (Austin: University of Texas Press, 1998)

Cragg, Kenneth. "'My Tears into Thy Bottle': Prophethood and God." *Muslim World* 88, nos. ¾ (July to October 1998): 238–56.

Dharmaraj, Jacob S. and Glory E. Dharamaj. "Christian-Muslim Relationship: A Theological Debate over Prophethood and Scriptures." *Asia Journal of Theology* 12, no. 2 (October 1998): 289–310.

Ernst,Carl. The Shambhala Guide to Sufism (Boston: Shambhala, 1997)

Al-Ghazālī. *Invocations & Supplications* (Kitāb al-Adhkār Wa'l-da'awāt): *Book IX of the Revival of the Religious Sciences* (Iḥyā' 'Ulūm al-Dīn). Translated by K. Nakamura. Rev. ed. Cambridge: Islamic Texts Society, 1996.

Geels, Antoon. "A Note on the Psychology of *Dhikr*: The Halveti-Jerrahi Order of Dervishes in Istanbul." *International Journal for the Psychology of Religion* 6, no. 4 (1996): 229–52.

Hagen, Gottfried. "From Haggadic Exegesis to Myth: Popular Stories of the Prophets in Islam." In *Sacred Tropes: Tanakh, New Testament, and Qur'an as Literature and Culture*, edited by Roberta Sterman Sabbath, 301–16. Leiden: Brill, 2009.

Herrera, R. A., ed. *Mystics of the Book: Themes, Topics, and Typologies.* New York: P. Lang, 1993.

Hixon, Lex. *The Heart of the Qur'an: an Introduction to Islamic Spirituality.* Wheaton: Theosophical Publishing House, 1988.

Jawad, Haifaa. "Islamic Spirituality and the Feminine Dimension." In *Women and the Divine: Touching Transcendence.* edited by Gillian Howie and J'annine Jobling, 187–204. New York: Palgrave Macmillan, 2009.

Johns, A. H. "Perspectives of Islamic Spirituality in Southeast Asia: Reflections and Encounters." *Islam & Christian-Muslim Relations* 12, no. 1 (January 2001): 5–21.

Kennedy, John G. and Hussein M. Fahim. "Dhikr Rituals and Cultural Change." In *Nubian Ceremonial Life: Studies in Islamic Syncretism and Cultural Change*, edited by John G. Kennedy, 41–60. Berkeley: University of California Press, 1978.

Khaleel, Mohammed. "The Identity of the Qur'ān's Ahl al-Dhikr." In *Coming to Terms with the Qur'an: A Volume in Honor of Professor Issa Boullata, McGill University*, edited by Khaleel Mohammed and Andrew Rippin, 33–45. North Haledon, NJ: Islamic Publications International, 2008.

Klar, Marianna. "Stories of the Prophets." In *The Blackwell Companion to the Qur'an*, edited by Andrew Rippin, 338–49. Malden, MA: Blackwell, 2006.

Kukkonen, Taneli. "Al-Ghazālī on Accidental Identity and the Attributes." *Muslim World* 101, no. 4 (October 2011): 658–79.

Kukkonen, Taneli. "Al-Ghazālī on the Signification of Names." *Vivarium* 48, nos. 1–2 (2010): 55–74.

Levenson, Michael R. and Abdul Hayy Khilwati. "Mystical Self-Annihilation: Method and Meaning." *International Journal for the Psychology of Religion* 9, no. 4 (1999): 251–60.

Lybarger, Loren D. "The Demise of Adam in the Qisas al-Anbiyā: The Symbolic Politics of Death and Re-Burial in the Islamic 'Stories of the Prophets'." *International Review for the History of Religions* 55, no. 5 (2008): 497–535.

McMichael, Steven J. "The Night Journey (al-Isra') and Ascent (al-Mi'raj) of Muhammad in Medieval Muslim and Christian Perspectives." *Islam & Christian-Muslim Relations* 22, no. 3 (July 2011): 293–309.

Mercado, Eliseo R. "Towards an Islamic Spirituality." In *Seeing the Seeker*, edited by Hein Blommestijn *et al.*, 475–82. Leuven, Belgium: Peeters, 2008.

Mir, Mustansir. "The Qur'an, the Word of God." In *Voices of Islam*, vol. 1, *Voices of Tradition*, edited by Vincent J. Cornell, 47–61. Westport, CT: Praeger, 2007.

Morris, James Winston. "Encountering the Qur'an: Contexts and Approaches." In *Voices of Islam*, vol. 1, *Voices of Tradition*, edited by Vincent J. Cornell, 65–100. Westport, CT: Praeger, 2007.

Morris, Julia. "Baay Fall Sufi Da'iras." *African Arts* 47, no. 1 (Spring 2014): 42–53.

Nasr, Seyyed Hossein, ed. *Islamic Spirituality: Foundations.* New York: Crossroad, 1987.

Nasr, Seyyed Hossein, ed. *Islamic Spirituality: Manifestations.* New York: Crossroad, 1997.

Noegel, Scott B. *Historical Dictionary of Prophets in Islam and Judaism.* Lanham, MD: Scarecrow, 2002.

Parkin, David and Stephen C. Headley, eds. *Islamic Prayer Across the Indian Ocean: Inside and Outside the Mosque.* Richmond: Curzon, 2000.

Renard, John. "*Al-Jihād al-Akbar*: Notes on a Theme in Islamic Spirituality." *The Muslim World* 78, nos. 3–4 (October 1988): 225–42.

Renard, John. *Seven Doors to Islam: Spirituality and the Religious Life of Muslims.* Berkeley: University of California Press, 1996.

Renard, John, ed. *Windows on the House of Islam.* Berkeley: University of California Press, 1998.

Schimmel, Annemarie. Mystical Dimensions of Islam (Chapel Hill: University of North Carolina Press, 1975)

Sells, Michael A., ed. and trans. *Early Islamic Mysticism: Sufi, Qur'an, Mi'Raj, Poetic and Theological Writings.* New York: Paulist Press, 1996.

Sells, Michael A., ed. and trans. "Early Muslim Spirituality and Mysticism." In *The Muslim Almanac: A Reference Work on the History, Faith, Culture, and Peoples of Islam,* edited by Azim A. Nanji, 215–21. Detroit: Gale Research, 1996.

Shannon, Jonathan H. "The Aesthetics of Spiritual Practice and the Creation of Moral and Musical Subjectivities in Aleppo, Syria." *Ethnology* 43, no. 4 (Fall 2004): 381–91.

Stade, Robert Charles. *Ninety-Nine Names of God in Islam: A Translation of the Major Portion of Al-Ghazāli's Al-Maqṣad Al-Asnā.* Ibadan, Nigeria: Daystar Press, 1970.

Takács, Axel. "Becoming the Word: Theosis in the Eucharist and Qur'ān." *Journal of Ecumenical Studies* 46, no. 1 (Winter 2011): 22–40.

Teule, Herman G. B. "An Important Concept in Muslim and Christian Mysticism: The Remembrance of God, Dhikr Allah—'Uhdōnō d-Alōhō." In *Gotteserlebnis und Gotteslehre: Christliche und Islamische Mystik im Orient,* edited by Martin Tamcke, 11–23. Wiesbaden: Harrassowitz Verlag, 2010.

Tha'labī, Aḥmad ibn Muḥammad. *'Arā'is al-Majālis fī Qiṣaṣ al-Anbiyā' or 'Lives of the Prophets' as Recounted by Abū Isḥāq Aḥmad ibn Muḥammad ibn Ibrāhīm al-Tha'labī.* Translated by William M. Brinner. Leiden: Brill, 2002.

# INDEX